PHYLLIS SECKLER
(SOROR MERAL)

THE KABBALAH, MAGICK, AND THELEMA
SELECTED WRITINGS VOL. II

Phyllis Seckler in the late 1960s

Phyllis Seckler (Soror Meral)

The Kabbalah, Magick, and Thelema
Selected Writings Vol. II

Edited by
David Shoemaker,
Gregory Peters,
& Rorac Johnson

Temple of the Silver Star
2020

First edition published in 2012 by
Temple of the Silver Star
in association with The Teitan Press

This edition published in 2020 by
Temple of the Silver Star
P.O. Box 215483
Sacramento, CA 95821

totss.org

All Rights Reserved
Printed in the United States of America

ISBN: 978-0-9976686-7-4

Design and layout by Gavin L. O'Keefe

Phyllis Seckler material © Temple of the Silver Star

Contents

Foreword	vii
"Water Closet (Caliph's Advice)" - Lon Milo DuQuette	x
Acknowledgements	xi
Introduction	xii
The Kabbalah, Magick, and Thelema	1
Selected Letters	202
A Note on Copyrights	280
About the Editors	281
Organizational Contacts	283
Index	287

Illustrations

Frontispiece: Phyllis Seckler in the late 1960s.

Photographs between pages 207 & 208

Sascha Germer, Jane Wolfe, Phyllis Seckler & Karl Germer. 1957.
Sascha and Karl Germer.
The Germer house in May, 1976.
One of the library rooms in the Germer house, May, 1976.
Another room in disarray in the Germer house, May, 1976.
Phyllis Seckler and Grady McMurtry in the early 1980s.

Foreword

Do what thou wilt shall be the whole of the Law.

I MET HER first in the fog-shrouded early morning hours of November 15, 1975 E.V. at a motel in Dublin, California. I had traveled all night by bus from Costa Mesa. It had not been a restful journey. All I could think about for every bumpy mile was the initiation I was scheduled to undergo and the curious circumstance that brought me to this moment in my life.

It had taken nearly two years of handwritten letters back and forth…letters demanding the location, date and hour of my birth, my biography, my education, my aspirations. Finally a date was set for my initiation, and my instructions were clear, simple, and utterly terrifying.

As the bus neared Dublin I was to tell the driver I wanted to be let off at a particular intersection near a certain motel. I was to walk a few blocks to the motel and check in using my own name. If there were no rooms available I was to wait in the lobby. If there was a room available I was to go there and wait to be contacted. I had no other information—no address—no phone number—I didn't even know the names of my hosts and initiators, only magical names: "Hymenaeus Alpha, 777," and "Soror Meral."

As I looked out the bus window at the cold moon rising over the abyss that is the San Joaquin Valley it occurred to me that should I fall victim of foul play—should I vanish from off the face of the earth—if my initiators were the insane remnants of some Satanic Aleister Crowley cannibal cult—should they choose to rape me, kill me, and eat me (something I was not completely convinced was not part of the program) my poor wife wouldn't even have a clue to give the police.

I didn't know it at the time, but Hymenaeus Alpha and Soror Meral were having their own doubts and fears about me, and that the reason for all the cloak and dagger dramatics was the very real concern that *I* might be a dangerous person. In the months prior to my initial inquiry some very scary things had taken place in California. The homes of several prominent people, elderly former students of Aleister Crowley had been burgled and their priceless collections of Crowley books and magical articles stolen.

The neon sign in front of the motel beamed a welcoming "Vacancy" and shortly after I awakened the poor manager and checked in I found myself stretched out comfortably on top of a not-so-hard bed. I immediately fell asleep and dreamed the most disturbing dream... of saggy-titted old women with poorly-dyed red hair, and priapic old Englishmen in goat leggings carving up my raped and murdered body and devouring my limbs with mint sauce.

"Lon!"

I heard a woman's voice distinctly and forcefully calling out my name. I woke up and jumped off the bed. "Coming!" I shouted through the door. I tidied my shirt a bit and popped a mint in my mouth and opened the door. There was no one there. I stepped out and looked in both directions... no one there.

Somewhat shaken, I returned to my room and sat down on the edge of the bed. Things were starting to get uncomfortably magical. I heard that voice as loudly and as clearly as if someone were standing right outside the door. I was hesitant to try to go back to sleep but eventually stretched out again. As soon as my head hit the pillow the phone rang—irritatingly loud. I picked up before it could wound my ears a second time.

"Hello," I answered, almost as a question.

"Lon DuQuette?" It was the voice of the woman who *wasn't* at the door. By now I wasn't surprised at anything that was happening.

"Yes."

"Have you eaten?"

"No." I confessed.

She didn't sound like a cannibal.

"Have you?"

About a half an hour later a knock on my door told me a flesh and blood Soror Meral was on the threshold. When I opened the door we both heaved a sigh of relief; I, because *she* was not a saggy-titted old woman with poorly dyed red hair; and she because *I* did not appear at the door with a butcher knife and "I'm the Anti-Christ" tattooed on my forehead.

She took me to her home, a place I can only describe as a magical gingerbread house, surrounded by beautiful gardens. The rooms were full of art and books and comfortable furniture. I was so very relieved. She was wonderful, knowledgeable, and wise. I bombarded her with questions that she answered candidly.

Our conversation naturally turned to the subject of *Liber AL vel Legis*, *The Book of the Law*. A year or so earlier I had followed the instructions (or at least I thought I was doing so) laid out in the Class A Comment on the text. I destroyed my first copy of the book after the first reading. I asked her, "Why did I have to destroy my copy of *The Book of the Law* after first reading it?"

Her answer was this: "You've got an obedience streak in you dear. You're going to have to watch that."

I had found my teacher.

Phyllis Seckler would be my formal A∴A∴ contact, and also my dear Sister in the O.T.O. which was led at the time by her then-husband Grady Louis McMurtry (Caliph Hymenaeus Alpha, 777). I would take my first two O.T.O. initiations, my Minerval and First Degree, in their home in Dublin. Shortly after my first degree initiation I wrote a little poem called "Water Closet—Caliph's Advice," which I wrote to immortalize his answer to my question, "What advice can you give to a young magician first starting out on the path?"

He answered with a cavalier lilt to his voice, "I asked Crowley the same thing the first time I met him. He simply said, 'Try to visit the water closet whenever you can. You never know when you'll get the chance again.'"

Phyllis was kind enough to publish the poem in an issue of her marvelous magazine, *In the Continuum*. I'm afraid it might not make too much sense to those unfamiliar with the Man of Earth degrees of the O.T.O. but for those who are I hope very much that you enjoy.

Love is the law, love under will.

Lon Milo DuQuette
Costa Mesa, California
January 23, 2012 E.V.

Water Closet (Caliph's Advice)

Lon Milo DuQuette (August 1976)

Bertholle tia excelsa גה – משיח ב.מ.	Adepts and Mahatmas Dance widdershins While they Devil, and Beast, and Oz it. An aspirant's day mysteriously begins With a visit to the water closet.
♃ ✵ Ida & Pingala Mucus restrictus	Forefinger on left nostril Thumb on its mate. He blows out his air and he draws it. With post nasal drip, pranayama is great, While sitting in the water closet.
Liber 333 דם	In Mass 44 Enflaméd her prays So deep that he had to gauze it. A comfort to know Repairs can be made By a visit to the water closet.
Atus xii, v. & xv Karma An Arcanum only fully appreciated by Man of Earth OTO initiates.	Hanged Man, Noah's Ark, Osiris and Seth Effect and all things which cause it. How much like birth, How very much like death Is a visit to the water closet.

Acknowledgements

The editors would like to thank the following for their invaluable assistance and support with this volume: Keith Richmond and Marilyn Rinn of The Teitan Press; Andrew Ferrell, Bill Knight, Justin Joyner, Stacy Kulyk, Ayanna Hart, and Cecile Schaefer, for document preparation and transcription; Charlotte Moore, Monika Mayer-Kielmann, Anna Tsu, Stephen Rice, and Alan Willms, for proofreading; and Lon Milo DuQuette, our Brother in the Great Work, for his support and encouragement, and for generously agreeing to contribute the Foreword to this volume.

Rorac Johnson would first like to thank his co-editors for all their work on this book, and for their incredible work in Thelema in general. It has been his great honor to again work with them on this important project. To all his family and friends new and old, his thanks go out as always for their support, patience and understanding. To the Sisters and Brothers of the Temple of the Silver Star, who are his constant inspiration, he gives thanks for their light and their dedication to the Path. Finally, he thanks and adores the Goddess for the gift of her warmth, and he offers eternal praise and gratitude unto his Angel, without whose love and guidance he would surely be nothing.

Gregory Peters would like to thank his co-editors for allowing him the honor of working with them on this very rewarding project. Thanks also go out to his two sons, who daily challenge him, though they know it not, to follow the example of his teacher and friend and also embody the Law of Thelema in his life. In the end, perhaps the best way we can honor Soror Meral and her memory is to strive, each in our own lives, to be living examples of those principles to which she devoted her life. May Light, Life, Love and Liberty be extended universally to all, under the aegis of the One Law of Thelema.

David Shoemaker would like to thank his son Andrew, and all of his family, near and far, for their unending love and support; his co-editors, for their friendship and fellowship on this project and in the Great Work; his students, for their constant inspiration, and for being the best teachers he has ever had; and Soror Meral, for her life, her words, her friendship and her wisdom.

Introduction

Do what thou wilt shall be the whole of the Law.

The present volume of Soror Meral's writings contains some of her most engaging and profound studies into Thelemic ethics, rituals, and the often colorful history of the personalities and orders which surround the subject of Thelema and Aleister Crowley. We get keen insight into her views of the Holy Guardian Angel and the practical application of this attainment in life; on the nature of Love both human and divine; on True Will, the Magick of Light, and how to embody in daily life that central maxim of which she was a radiant exemplar: The Law of Thelema.

It has been immensely rewarding for us, as editors and former students of Soror Meral, to review all of this material and recall how her wisdom informs so much of the work and legacy of her life. She had a unique ability to see through much of the mystic language of esoteric traditions, and even of Crowley's writings, and cut straight to the heart of the matter. Her students benefitted greatly from these clear insights and direct examples, and much of this penetrating and practical analysis is available in her writings as represented here.

In the recently published first volume of Phyllis Seckler's writings, *The Thoth Tarot, Astrology, & Other Selected Writings*, we presented two of her most important essays on the nature of the Thoth Tarot in relation to depth psychology and the natal horoscope.[1] These essays were originally serialized over the course of many years in *In the Continuum* (*I.T.C.*), Seckler's influential and long-running journal. Aside from essays such as these, *I.T.C.* also featured introductory letters penned by Seckler, which appeared in most issues. These letters span a vast array of topics, from practical ritual instructions to philosophical musings to critiques of the state of Thelemic culture at the time. We are proud to present the bulk of these introductory letters in this present volume, with re-drawn and corrected diagrams. These letters give a sense

---

1. Seckler, Phyllis, *The Thoth Tarot, Astrology, & Other Selected Writings*, Ed. David Shoemaker, Gregory Peters and Rorac Johnson (Sacramento: Temple of the Silver Star, 2017).

of Seckler's engagement with the embryonic Thelemic culture, and her passionate determination to help it stay true to the ideals put forth by Aleister Crowley. In reading her words, we can sense the immediacy of her task; we see the landscape of modern Thelema taking shape around her, and we feel her distress when she fears it is veering off course; but most of all, we come away with a vibrant awareness of the love she felt for the Great Work, for her students, and for the potential for Thelema to transform human life.

As in the previous volume, we have included a number of historically important or otherwise instructive letters between Seckler and various luminaries of post-Crowley Thelema, including Karl Germer, Israel Regardie, Grady McMurtry, Gerald Yorke, and Marcelo Motta. These are published here for the first time. We felt it would be useful to give a bit of context to these letters, and where appropriate, the nature of the relationship between Seckler and her correspondents. Accordingly, we have provided brief introductory comments before each set of letters, along with previously unpublished photographs of several of her correspondents.

As we have often expressed to our students, you cannot truly understand the development of post-Crowley Thelema until you have examined the life and work of Soror Meral, one of the scant handful of initiates without whom the Light of Thelema might have gone out. It is our hope that this volume will aid in the dissemination of her Light, Love, and Wisdom to all who read her words, for you are the next generation of her successors and heirs in the Great Work of Thelema.

Love is the law, love under will.

David Shoemaker
Gregory Peters
Rorac Johnson
Winter 2012 E.V.

The Kabbalah,
Magick, and Thelema
Selected Writings Vol. II

Sun of Being

Let us open our hearts and minds to the Highest
And throw off the veil of negative existence.
Come, let us tread among the stars of the blessed;
Let us control the evidence of happenstance.

Let us see the world as pure phenomena of Will,
Formed by ourselves in our going.
Let us see Adonai's hand in everything, but still
A making by ourselves, our seeds sowing.

Upon the bosom of earth our deeds are awaiting
The flowering of earth's bounty in roots and seeds,
In leaves, flowers and fruits in true trysting
With experience, a wholesome result of our deeds.

Whatever we do, there is no escape from growth,
There is no escape from nature's way.
The Law is that the soul must come forth
From delusion and terror to seek the light of day.

The sun is our nurturance, our aim, our goal.
Center of being, each one's life essence.
The sun is nature's law, of bounties untold;
The sun is in our hearts, a shield and defense.

The sun is our nature's pure being, a sensation
Reflected and absorbed in earth nature's breast.
We are that sun of being, that absorption
In the all, we are each a star in this feast.

Between sun and earth, own this grounding, this territory seen
As growth, our exploration of ourselves as a Hadit,
The point of light nestled in the bosom of phenomenon;
An outcome of our wedding with and love for Nuit.

Phyllis Seckler
1991

Selected Introductory Letters from
In the Continuum (1973-1996)

Carete Fratres et Sorores,[2]

Do what thou wilt shall be the whole of the Law.

You were asking if the publication of *The Secret Rituals of the O.T.O.* as introduced by Francis King would not destroy our Order.[3] I think not, and for these reasons:

1. Various occult orders are connected to a real Magical current which derives its power partly due to the working of those still in Life and partly due to its Founder or Founders. Some of these currents are inimical and some beneficial to the particular individual. The candidate, unfortunately, cannot know in most cases whether it is for good or for ill that he has joined up with a certain occult order. He is guided only by his past Karma and his associations with others in this and in past lives, by his intuition and by the purity of his aspiration. If some lesson is needed, even though it be extremely painful, before he can turn to the true Light, then so be it. We have noticed the Thelemic current working on our Minervals and Probationers, some of whom never make it past these elementary Grades. We have noticed others who never make it past the First Degree of the O.T.O. or Neophyte of the A∴A∴. In other words, when talking of the O.T.O., there is no doubt in our minds that the Thelemic current is working through this Order. The publication of our secret rituals is not going to change this fact.[4]

2. *The Book of the Law* lets us know again and again who might be fit to be a Thelemite. It is a matter of action sparked by an acceptance of this Book as the Law of Life. I refer you to this Book so that you can draw your own conclusions. The O.T.O. has

---

2. Originally published in: Seckler, Phyllis, *In the Continuum* 1.2 (1973): 3-6.
3. King, Francis, *The Secret Rituals of the O.T.O.* (New York, NY: Samuel Weiser, 1973).
4. In addition to the considerations discussed by Soror Meral, it should also be noted that the rituals presented in King's book are inaccurate in many ways. –Eds.

accepted the New Æon of Thelema and works with *The Book of the Law* very closely. So that, even should some take up these rituals and go through them and claim status as Thelemites under the O.T.O., it would be an empty thing, since they might not be allied with the current in its actuality. An occult order does not exist just in the imagination but has its roots in the affairs of the everyday world. Naturally, going through the ceremony with its pomp and attendant officers in actuality bears more meaning and truth than just reading about it. It is conceivable that other of the great orders of antiquity may accept *The Book of the Law*, but to date only the outer order of the O.T.O. has done so. So until such time when the Law of the New Æon shall be accepted around the world, if one feels one is Thelemic, and one wants to work in the political and social world of Thelema, it may be best to ally oneself with the O.T.O. The A∴A∴ has been devised to aid those who wish to work with the spiritual aspect of things and who do not care for the outer order. (Though there are many who work with both of these Thelemic orders).

3. No one is admitted to the Grades beyond the Third Degree in the O.T.O. except by invitation of the governing body. Since the governing body should have alliances with the A∴A∴, you can see that any spurious claims on the basis of having read the rituals would be laughable. (I mention that the governing body <u>should have</u> alliances with the A∴A∴. If these contacts are lost, the O.T.O. will suffer from the same fate as we have seen in Rosicrucianism, Freemasonry and various other major religions. That is, the true inspiration and aid from the highest sources leaves and the religion or the occult order becomes dead in its center, while still clinging to the ancient forms of worship.)

4. There is a definite set of rules and regulations and a skeleton Constitution of the O.T.O.[5] in *The Equinox*, Vol. III, No. 1 (the *"Blue Equinox"*) which can be put into effect when the Order is strong enough. No exposure of our secret rituals can destroy this structure which is meant to aid each person on the way of discovering and working their own True Will. The Master Therion did indeed build wisely.

---

5. Crowley, Aleister, "Book 194—An Intimation with Reference to the Constitution of the Order," in *The Equinox Vol. III No. 10*, Ed. Hymenaeus Beta (Boston, MA: Samuel Weiser, 1990), 173-178.

5. It may be possible to give mail order lessons on how to understand the many writings of Aleister Crowley, but nothing by mail can take the place of personal teaching by one skilled in living the Law of Thelema and in understanding various of the necessary instructions, and also in working out these instructions in personal life. The student, when writing letters often indulges in sham and lies to save his ego, even when these dodges are unknown to himself. It becomes too easy to build a dangerously unbalanced structure and on this point many a student has seen nothing but failure for his efforts. In other words, studying alone is all right up to a point, but there comes a time when an outside observer needs to steady the student or point out some bit of information heretofore neglected and which may have an application only in the one case. This cannot be done by mail. Therefore, any outfit which calls itself the O.T.O. and proceeds to initiate by mail is laughable and pitiful. Here is where the student really takes a beating at his own cost, unfortunately. Further, when learning, we need to be tested on whether that learning is complete and without error. Can you imagine taking certain sorts of exams by mail? And how about the Ordeals? They go on in spite of everything, but the student may need some help here too. And if in his letters he gives no inkling of what is going on, he may miss out on the teachings greatly. We are supposed to each of us find out the meaning of Thelema and the *Book of the Law* by our own self. But how does one start? It is very difficult to work without some preliminary guidance!

Also, in a Thelemic group, we are admonished to "Love one another with burning hearts…" (*The Book of the Law*,[6] Cap. II, v. 24). Since this is an important part of Thelema—can you imagine doing this by mail?

6. Many suggestive papers were published in *The Secret Rituals of the O.T.O.* dealing with sex magick. So now anyone at all can jump to the use of these secrets through a right application of knowledge (sometimes too shallow) and intuition. A.C. warns again and again that these practices have their own safeguards. Sex magick can be a short cut to Illumination—but it is the most

---

6. Crowley, Aleister, *Liber AL vel Legis* (York Beach, ME: Weiser, 2004), 42. [This book is also referenced in the text under the titles *The Book of the Law* or *Liber Legis*. – Eds.]

dangerous of all methods. Too many students forget that Crowley spent years training his mind, emotions and body through the practices of western magick in the Golden Dawn and of yoga from the east. He succeeded in obtaining Samadhi and a very high degree of initiation through these disciplines <u>before</u> he practiced sex magick. Do you think these brazen young people are going to do the same? Hardly likely, for they are too impatient and cannot see that the pyramid must be built with a very broad and firm foundation. You and I are going to see many occult wrecks strewn over the landscape—persons in insane asylums or nearly there, those who commit suicide or murder or who have all chances for advancement in this life or in the lives yet to come completely wrecked. There is nothing in the world that can take the place of self-discipline and a thorough knowledge of one's self. I might add here that it is really necessary for most people to go through some sort of psycho-analysis; often better if it be Jungian and/or Reichian and combine this with some sort of astrology analysis. To even begin to set foot on the path one must obey that dictum of the old and wise Greeks, "Know Thyself." You can see, I think, how the beginner may need a teacher for many aspects of this task. For instance, too many people live in a dream that they make up about themselves, and in so doing ignore the real Self.

7. Many of the needed disciplines and keys to the knowledge have been left out of *The Secret Rituals of the O.T.O.* Our Order was structured to train the student in the necessary disciplines and knowledge. Reading about these disciplines piecemeal is not going to take the place of an ordered progression through the grades under wise guidance.

8. Almost any magick is dangerous without a one-pointed will towards the Holy Guardian Angel. This is what is meant in *The Book of the Law* when Nuit admonishes, "...if the ritual be not ever unto me: then expect the direful judgments of Ra Hoor Khuit!"—also, "But ecstasy be thine and joy of earth: ever To me! To me!" (Cap. I, v. 52 & 53).[7]

As you can gather from all this, the practice of the secret rituals of the higher grades of the O.T.O. can be dangerous to the unprepared and unqualified and undisciplined student. These

---

7. Crowley, *Liber AL vel Legis*, op. cit., 33-34.

are hedged around with the necessary restrictions both from *The Book of the Law* and from the training of the O.T.O. itself; which training is engineered to aid the safety and well being of the individual. To have loosed these higher rituals upon the world in a popular book form is indeed an irresponsible act. I would shudder to generate such karma for myself.

You were asking me about another occult order which you had seriously considered. On this score, I might mention that they use the rituals of the past. *The Book of the Law* states: "Behold! The rituals of the old time are black. Let the evil ones be cast away; let the good ones be purged by the prophet! Then shall this Knowledge go aright" (Cap. II, v. 5).[8] This ought to answer your question. And maybe you should ask yourself, have you really allied yourself to Thelema? On this point, dear brother, you may need to do some soul-searching.

In matters concerning the living of the Law of Thelema, and in how to conduct your life as a Thelemite, you should be consulting *The Book of the Law*. It is very wise to obtain a good Commentary on this Book written by Crowley, as he is the Prophet and knew more on this subject due to his high Initiations and genius. In this study always remember that one must maintain a balance. Too many people have taken one or two sentences without the balance to be found in the Book and have really stumbled on their path, or lost it altogether.

If some of the passages seem to lean far in one direction, the opposite point of view can be found elsewhere in the Book. One must never give up one's own common sense in favor of fanaticism for one chapter or sentence in this Book. One works with the forces of one's own time on incarnation and with one's own karmic background of family, nation, and events caused by the true self; but always maintaining one's own balance through a developed intuition, a pure aspiration to the H.G.A., a thorough knowledge of oneself and the force of one's own karma freely willed by oneself from the beginning.

Remember that advancement in either the O.T.O. or the A∴A∴ depends on your work. It is not possible to advance in either Order without this. This must be said now as there are too many

---

8. Crowley, *Liber AL vel Legis*, op. cit., 38.

who claim high grades who have not completed the work. Their claims are laughable and they only make fools of themselves. See to it then, that you do not fall into the trap of ego-aggrandizement and boasting without solid accomplishment behind you! May your True Will become clear to you as you advance!

Love is the law, love under will.

Fraternally,
Meral

Care Frater,[9]

Do what thou wilt shall be the whole of the Law.

Let us take a look at the sentence above. It seems simple but to some its simplicity is so elusive that they are unable to live up to this injunction. There are many passages in *Liber Aleph* by Crowley which deal with this problem. Indeed, to do what thou wilt is the first task of every Thelemite.

Not only must you learn to do your own will but you must allow others to carry out their wills. Let us take as an example the simple matter of criticism of another. Among Thelemites it ought to be understood that criticism implies that the critic wishes the other person to behave according to the code of the critic. In other words, the critic is obstructing the free flowing of the will of the other. He is building a standard which is his own (the critical standard) and is applying it to another person. Does it not tell us in *Liber AL vel Legis* to "Bind nothing! Let there be no difference made among you between any one thing or any other thing; for thereby there cometh hurt" (Cap. I, v. 22).[10]

Please to understand that I am not in any way referring to what happens between the guru and the chela when the guru may have to use constructive criticism in certain very stubborn cases. This type of work—hardly criticism—is based on the knowledge the guru may have of the various factors in the nature of the chela which are obstructing the latter's way to the Knowledge and Conversation of the Holy Guardian Angel.

---

9. Originally published in: Seckler, Phyllis, *In the Continuum* 1.3 (1974): 1-7.
10. Crowley, *Liber AL vel Legis*, op. cit., 27-28.

No, I am talking about the everyday variety of criticism in which all too many would-be Thelemites might be tempted to indulge. I have seen a lot of this, and it is especially rife in orders of various types or in certain types of religious groups. Everyone formulates their own idea of the ideal and then they proceed to ask that another person should live up to this ideal. Do you see now the reason for control of the tongue? If you are going to have the freedom to do your will, then you must give this freedom to another. Let me quote from *Liber Aleph*: [see "De Eadem Re Altera Verba"].[11]

Along this line, let me remark that every person when they have but a small amount of development sees the world and others through a narrow window. This window is their own nature. As aspirants to Initiation they formulate an idea in themselves of what an Initiated person ought to be like. This idea is none other than the idea of their own higher self which has broken through into the mental and conscious life. We could also use Jungian terms and label them the Anima or Animus which Jung states is a bridge to the knowledge of the Divine. They are the ideas of all that is good or true or beautiful or of the highest that we may know. The student who has found a guru or a teacher immediately begins to project his own idea of his higher self on to the guru and begins to demand that the guru live up to this idea! If the guru is quite different from the student's ideas of him there is bound to be much disappointment. Worse, the student may be seriously hampering the guru in his function, for if the guru says not what the student expects to hear, there is much trouble. Still worse, the student is not allowing another to live in Freedom. Is not Thelema a Law of Freedom? For this reason the position of teacher or guru could be a very dangerous position for anyone not firmly set in his own will. Consider how little freedom is vouchsafed to public figures—whether he be President or Minister, Principal of a school, movie star, or any other in public life who must bear the burden of public projections. Consider the venomous letters such persons receive from poor crazed souls expert in projection who cannot see that they wish conduct from others which is fitting only for themselves.

---

11. Crowley, *Liber Aleph* (York Beach, ME: Samuel Weiser, 1991), 189.

Is it any wonder that the sage would wish to remain unknown? Unless, indeed, it is his will to teach or to bring a New Word to mankind.

Further, this habit of the projection of one's own characteristics upon another can take ominous turns. How about when the whole German nation projected their frustrations onto a man like Hitler? Or when suppressed sex is linked up with death and we have a lynching party?

The same thing happens with first loves. Indeed, some people are forever looking for their higher selves (for the Anima or Animus) in the opposite sex. For this reason they are blinded to the True Nature of the Beloved just as they could be blinded by the true nature of the guru. Of course they will never find the Anima or Animus or the higher self in the other person. This would be an impossibility against nature. Each person is a Star in and of themselves. "Every man and every woman is a star" (*Liber AL vel Legis*, Cap. I, v. 3).[12] Sometimes these people become disappointed because they cannot find the true self in the other. Sooner or later the loved one insists on being herself or himself. Such disappointments may lead to more and more marriages or the person may refuse to marry and wishes only to "play the field." Such a person has never grown to the point where he can face himself. In the case of the search for a proper guru who will combine in himself all the ideals the student wishes for himself, this may lead the student to join one occult order after another in hopes that, finding himself in another, he may then attain Initiation more quickly.

What is needed in all such situations is a more thorough understanding of one's own nature and a maturing process which leads one to know and <u>to be</u> one's own higher self. It is the path of a slave and of a coward not to realize that the ideals one projects upon another are one's own and do not necessarily belong to the other. Further, it is a serious attempt to enslave and hamper another person in their true nature to demand or even to think that he or she should live up to one's own formulated ideals. Here we see the root of the reason why the lower levels of mankind wish to pull the genius down to their own levels. The undeveloped person cannot recognize his own projections, be they of the higher

---

12. Crowley, *Liber AL vel Legis*, 25.

or lower variety, and so when he learns of others who live above the laws of his herd mind, he becomes afraid of such freedom and desires to pull the genius to his own level of thinking. This is one reason why the *Book of the Law* states, "Ye are against the people, O my chosen!" (Cap. II, v. 25).[13] For ramifications of this problem it might be very profitable for you to study Nietzsche and especially his *Thus Spake Zarathustra*.[14]

By the way, it is a mark of a slave religion if everyone is expected to come up to the ideals of the founder of that religion. Christianity is a good example of this. Or perhaps I could say Churchianity?

Sometimes I think that Crowley deliberately acted to break some projection or other that his students were thinking up. Therefore, we hear strange stories about his behavior to others. Should we not consider that this might have been one of his motives for action? Let us refer to *Liber Aleph* again: [see "De Mysterio Mali"[15] and "De Virtute Tolerantia"[16]].

Of course you have observed how each person will seek out and befriend those who come closest to his own ideals and type of thinking. Also, you know from everyday experience how those who deviate from their own mental capacities are criticized and avoided. By this means, we also enslave ourselves as we build a fence of misunderstanding around ourselves. We refuse to learn from a large segment of mankind because they are not like us.

Actually, each contact one has with one's fellow beings may become a lesson of smaller or greater magnitude. Each contact has been freely willed by the soul to begin with, even as it has willed the circumstances of birth and death. Life is a school—it is a living out of the will. This can scarcely be better expressed than it is in *Liber Aleph*: [see "De Harmonia Voluntatis Et Parcarum"].[17]

Because this matter of projection is so common and so little understood by most people, I would suggest that you make a record of the times when you expected others to act as you think and feel. Why do someone's actions make you angry? You would

---

13. Crowley, *Liber AL vel Legis*, 42.
14. Nietzsche, Friedrich, *Thus Spoke Zarathustra* (New York, NY: Penguin Books, 1988).
15. Crowley, *Liber Aleph*, 145.
16. Crowley, *Liber Aleph*, 146.
17. Crowley, *Liber Aleph*, 142.

not be angry if you did not have the tendency in yourself, for we do not recognize that which we have never had as a part of ourselves. All events which cause a strong emotional or mental reaction can be analyzed as showing yourself to yourself. Take the responsibility for your reactions, for this is your mirror to nature and life. The key to your being lies here. If projections are not controlled and understood, if the aspirant to initiation does not know the nature of his own Being, then he is indeed in a dangerous position when his own demons come home to roost.

There is great danger that the person obsessed by the contents of his own unconscious may project the demonic nature of his own self upon other people or even upon disembodied entities. He may sink under the horror of the repressed areas of the unconscious. He may become maddened. All humans are made up of positive and negative factors, of the demon and the angel, of the beast and the man. The first task, then, of He who Goes, is to Understand Yourself.

Indeed, until you understand yourself, you are not fit to teach others, for you would then have a tendency to fasten your own projections, good or bad, on the students. I think you can deduce from all this explanation how very dangerous certain "occult" teachers may become to the unwary student. This is a blade with two edges, of a certainty. For this reason, Crowley said that no one was fit to teach unless he be a 5°=6▫ (or in other words, had attained to the Knowledge and Conversation of the Holy Guardian Angel).

This Way to the K. and C. of the H.G.A. is so personal that any informed teacher would shudder to dictate any part of the path. Each person must grow on his own. Each person, even though his going seems a stumbling, must somehow bring himself to this attainment.

However, the God would find it difficult to indwell a temple poorly prepared. "Wisdom says: be strong! Then canst thou bear more joy" (*Liber AL vel Legis*, Cap. II, v. 70).[18]

Towards this aim, you can strengthen yourself. You can analyze the projections, the emotions, the thoughts, so that you can understand the self and begin to know the will and to carry it out. Sometimes a teacher can be helpful in these first steps, pointing out the weaknesses which may become major stumbling blocks,

---

18. Crowley, *Liber AL vel Legis*, 49.

or prescribing the exercises both mental and physical which will enable the body and mind to withstand the rapture of Union with the H.G.A. without going under.

But remember that the teacher is only a bystander to the inner growth, a helping hand, a person who puts up signposts for a path through the forest. Remember that the teacher is not your own higher self; even though the type of teacher that you choose is close to your idea of the higher self! Also, remember that the work to be done is of your own choosing, as was the choosing of the teacher. Both events will give you insights into the self.

In summation, in order to know ourselves, we must take the responsibility for our own thoughts and actions and for the events that happen to us. You have made your life to a startling degree. I think it is one of the marks of an initiate that he or she knows this, and knowing it begins to create events under will.

In the great complexity of our being, we need to single out a few salient ideas and work on them for a time so that they do not again catch us so unawares and so vulnerable to our own unconscious depths, repressions which warp our thinking and projections both terrible and idealistic. For the present, let us work on the latter since it can be so great a block to Initiation.

May you find success in this work!

> Love is the law, love under will,
>
> Soror Meral

Care Frater,[19]

> Do what thou wilt shall be the whole of the Law.

You were asking some questions about your horoscope and I agree that interpretation is very difficult when you are just beginning. To make matters worse, the books on the market from which to study are much too numerous. Some are too simple and some are too complicated and just where does one start?

To further entangle the thinking, there is no book which can give the interpretations for three or more planets closely aspected to each other. Every horoscope is different from every other and the planetary pattern is not repeated again in something over 2,300 years.

---

19. Originally published in: Seckler, Phyllis, *In the Continuum* 1.4 (1974): 8-16.

Some Astrological Correspondences

Hebrew Letter	Symbol	Meaning	Tarot Card Correspondence
Aleph	△	Air	0. The Fool
Beth	☿	Mercury	1. The Magus
Gimel	☽	Luna	2. The Priestess
Daleth	♀	Venus	3. The Empress
Hé	♒	Aquarius	17. The Star
Vau	♉	Taurus	5. The Hierophant
Zain	♊	Gemini	6. The Lovers
Cheth	♋	Cancer	7. The Chariot
Teth	♌	Leo	11. Lust
Yod	♍	Virgo	9. The Hermit
Kaph	♃	Jupiter	10. Fortune
Lamed	♎	Libra	8. Adjustment
Mem	▽	Water	12. The Hanged Man
Nun	♏	Scorpio	13. Death
Samekh	♐	Sagittarius	14. Art
A'ain	♑	Capricorn	15. The Devil
Pé	♂	Mars	16. The Tower (War)
Tzaddi	♈	Aries	4. The Emperor
Qoph	♓	Pisces	18. The Moon
Resh	☉	Sun	19. The Sun
Shin	△	Fire	20. The Aeon
	✴	Spirit	
Tau	♄	Saturn	21. The Universe
	⏚	Earth	

Table A.

Well, let us tackle the matter so that at least you have a grounding in interpretation and can read the books with a little more insight. For your convenience, there is a chart at the end of this letter [see Table A] with the various astrological symbols and their meanings worded briefly. You must familiarize yourself with these symbols. They will also figure later in the qabalistic correspondences, and we shall tie our astrology into a study of the qabalah and the Tarot cards. Very few authors have done this, but you will see that Crowley made a start. There is another author who wrote a book on astrological interpretations for the placement of the Sun in reference to the Tarot, but her book is now out of print and difficult to get. If you can have it searched and somehow obtain it, I would recommend that you do so. It is *Pursuit of Destiny* by Muriel Bruce Hasbrouck.[20]

Let us first look at the overall planetary pattern. Are most of the planets on one side of the chart? Or are they spread around? We must look at the horizon to gain an idea of the planetary placements. The horizon is defined by the rising degree — whether that degree is in Gemini, Leo, Sagittarius, or what have you. From the rising degree we draw a line to the exact opposite degree on the other side of the chart. This is the horizon. For convenience sake I have included a diagram [see Diagram A].

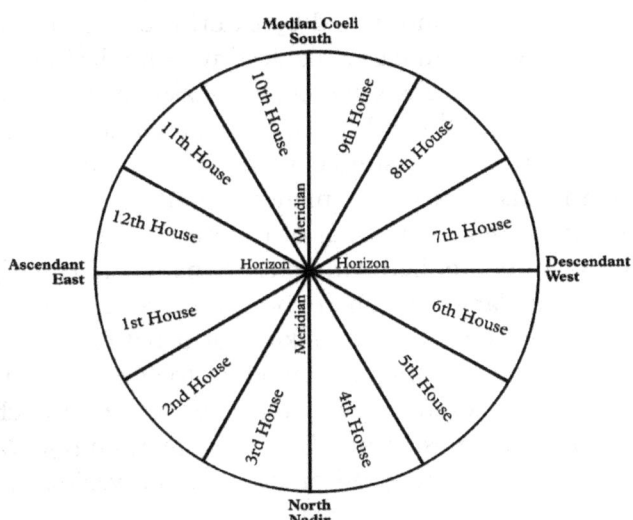

Diagram A. Mundane Houses

---

20. Hasbrouck, Muriel Bruce, *Tarot and Astrology: The Pursuit of Destiny* (Rochester, VT: Destiny Books, 1986).

If all planets are below the horizon, that is, in the houses 1 through 6, the native lives in more subjective realms. He lives an interior life, is aware of the interior self and of those things below the threshold of consciousness. He has internal reactions to events and is an introverted and intuitive type. For this reason, this type will carve out his own destiny. He has a great deal of freedom to do things as he likes without too much reference to outer events or other people.

If all planets are above the horizon, that is, in the houses 7 through 12, the native is affected by the visible exterior world and everything that can be perceived by the senses. He is affected by others and events outside himself. He is a collective type and his inner consciousness is formed by external events. Here we find a tendency to extroversion and an objective, often materialistic viewpoint.

If all planets are east of the meridian the native is able to make his own choice in whatever issue comes up and even to create issues at will. His destiny is entirely in his own hands and we see here a tendency to a healthy self-realization. The elements of life are held in control. Thinking is accented as an element of free will (Houses 10 through 3).

If all the planets are west of the meridian the native is managed by other people or agencies and must accept what happens to him. Life is more conditioned by exterior events and there is not the same freedom to carve his destiny as he desires as in the above paragraph. There is a feeling emphasis in this half of the houses (4th through 9th) and much external conditioning.

Few horoscopes are so simple as the above paragraphs might suggest. If the majority of the planets lie either east or west of the Meridian, or north or south of the horizon, then the above descriptions can be applied with exceptions to the rule signified by the planet or planets which are not in the general pattern.

Next we must consider what kind of a pattern the planets make; for instance, are they all bunched together, are many of them in opposition, or are they scattered all around the chart?

Marc Edmund Jones in his *The Guide to Horoscope Interpretation*[21] has given a very good analysis of the various types of

---

21. Jones, Marc Edmund, *The Guide to Horoscope Interpretation* (Wheaton, IL: Quest Books, 1981).

planetary patterning. I shall use his terms and try to describe briefly how these patterns form the individuality.

If the planets are distributed fairly evenly around the zodiac, this is called the Splash type. There is here a gift for universal orientation. We find people who spread things, who carry ideas, who expand experience. They have many interests and lack inhibition. At their best they can bring order out of confusion and at their worst they can waste things and experience bitter failure because there are too many interests. They can lead others astray through a dispersion and wasting of energy and have the ability to disintegrate experience. If the energies are used positively, these people can bring the Universe to a center through their wide interests and broad approach and can be capable of an impersonal organization. Sometimes they exhibit great prodigality.

The Bundle type has all of the planets within the trine aspect or at least the majority of planets within a trine segment of the zodiac. Here is a bunching of interests within very narrow limits and these people can show a great deal of inhibition. They are least responsive to universal stimulus (world events, the news, other people, etc.). At their best they have a great capacity for making much out of little and of building small and insignificant beginnings into great and often final results. Their energies are so concentrated that you often find trailblazers among people of this type. They consider things in terms of immediate and personal usefulness and their engine of will can prove to be formidable. At their worst they can be very selfish and much too concerned with themselves and their own world.

The Locomotive type has planets through most of the zodiac except an empty trine. One third of the chart is empty and the other two thirds contains the planets. This is an eccentric balance and the native has a strong sense of a lack or need or of a problem to be solved. He goes about it like a locomotive, running over anything in his path. Here we have a self-driving individuality with lots of power. He is dynamic and exceptionally practical, efficient and persistent. He is moved more by external events rather than by aspects of his own character. The way he applies his powerful drive is shown by the leading planet. This is the one which makes its aspect across the empty trine clockwise on the wheel. The house this planet is in will be very important. Also if this empty trine is thrown across the ascendant there will be a personal form of pioneering. If it is across the midlevel he will be a prophet in his age. At his best he can be a dynamic executive and at this worst he can be a ruthless, roughshod type of self-seeker. He is more concerned over the "how" than the "what" of his activity.

In the Bowl type, the planets lie to one side of the zodiac and divide the circle in halves. A hemisphere emphasis can be seen in some of this patterning—as described earlier. If the rim of the bowl is even, marked by the opposition of two planets, it will make an individual who has a sense of mission. The Bowl configuration shows self-containment, a person who has something to bear or some special reason for existence—just as a bowl has a reason to hold things. This type feels set off against the part of the world signified by the empty hemisphere and he can place the elements of his character with consideration of larger matters. The occupied hemisphere reveals the type of activity and self organization and the empty hemisphere shows the part of the world that the native feels he cannot hold but which engages his attention at the same time. This person will be found advocating some cause or he will have a mission in life. He has an introspective concern over the purpose of experience and always has something to give to others. The leading planet is quite important in this pattern, and is more so if it makes an opposition aspect. This planet can show where and how the native tries to justify his existence or to carry out his mission. Attention should be paid to which sign and house it is in. The leading planet would not be as strong if it has no opposition aspect or if there is a hemisphere emphasis.

The Bucket type has all planets but one in a bowl or bundle formation. This is like a handle on the bowl. This singleton planet set in a different half of the zodiac from the other planets is very important. All the development of the individual will be thrown into an expression which is signified by the planet; which sign and house it is in. The person has a singular capacity or a gift for action according to the single planet. Sometimes the handle is formed from two planets in conjunction. If the position of the handle is upright or perpendicular to the bowl, the special direction of the energies is intensified. If it lies slightly to the left, life tends towards caution and self-conscious preparedness. If it is towards the right, life is more impulsive and the native is inclined to respond towards immediate challenges rather than to future promise. With this type there will be an underlying interest in a cause but not too much concern over the end results. There is usually no basic desire to conserve the self or the resources. At its best this person can be the instructor and inspirer of others and at its worst this can show the agitator and malcontent. In all cases the native is one who dips deeply into life and pours forth the results of experience with a great deal of zeal.

The Seesaw type shows a symmetrical clustering of two groups of planets opposing each other in the horoscope. It can be two opposed to eight, or three to seven, or four to six, or five to five. The two opposite segments ought to have at least a square aspect span each, but this rarely happens. However, the two unoccupied sections must always be present in opposition. Neither section should be less than a sextile. This is similar to the bucket personality but is less sharp and more refined. The native moves to achieve a balance and this action is like a see-saw effect. He acts through a consideration of opposing views and is sensitive to contrasting and antagonistic ideas. He lives in a world of conflict. At his best he can develop through unsuspected relations of ideas and actions and at his worst he may waste energies through a bad alignment in various situations. The life tends to be more significant on the side of the zodiac where there are most of the planets.

The Splay type has a strong and irregular grouping of planets at irregular points. No single planet shows up as the focal point and the planets seem to lie at random in the signs and houses. The native will show a good deal of certainty in the approach he makes to the problems of life. It is difficult to place this person into any neat pattern of ideas as he is quite individual and impersonal in his action and thinking and interests. He can be quite an opportunist and have widely diversified talents and activities. At his worst he can show a great deal of stubborn self interest.

These are the main general types. Some horoscopes do not lend themselves easily to such typing. The analyst must use his own best judgment in such mixed-up cases.

Now let us look at the triplicities and the quadruplicates. The triplicities involve three signs of the zodiac and are divided into our familiar fire, earth, air and water.

Fire signs are sanguine and show <u>inspiration</u>. They are energy, force, the power of doing, courage and self-reliance, enthusiasm, zeal, daring, the ability to command the love of activity.

Cardinal fire is Aries as this sign is in the cardinal position of the fire signs. Fixed fire is Leo and mutable fire is Sagittarius.

Earth signs are melancholic or bilious and show <u>practicality</u>. These show fixation and express ideas concretely and always with a practical slant. People of these signs apply patience to the affairs of life and all that they contact is turned to some material use. They rely upon reason and the report of the senses. They are toilers with the affairs of earth.

Cardinal earth is Capricorn, fixed earth is Taurus, and mutable earth is Virgo.

Air signs are choleric and show <u>aspiration</u>. Natives of these signs do a lot of thinking; they are mentally alert and nervous, volatile, changeable and socially inclined. They live on the mental plane and desire refinement and intellectual pursuits.

Cardinal air is Libra, fixed air is Aquarius and mutable air is Gemini.

Water signs are lymphatic and show <u>emotion</u>. These natives live in the emotions, are centered in the affections, are sympathetic, dreamy, timid, submissive, receptive and mediumistic and are influenced by their surroundings.

Cardinal water is Cancer, fixed water is Scorpio, and mutable water is Pisces.

The quadruplicates involve four signs of the zodiac and arrange themselves as a cross. These are: rajas or cardinal, tamas or fixed, and sattva or mutable or common. The *Bhagavad-Gita* has a very good explanation of rajas, tamas and sattva, or the three gunas. I recommend that you read about them.

Rajas or cardinal is action and doing. Many planets in cardinal signs make the doers of the world; they are pioneers and are very energetic. On the positive side they have ambition and are enterprising and enthusiastic and like to be at the head of things to be happy. They love change and activity. On the negative side they are self-assertive, capricious, uncertain and aggressive. These people break trails for others to follow and start actions for others to finish. Often they don't care to finish for themselves.

Tamas or fixed are the perfectors, the builders of the world. People with many planets in fixed signs have a great resistance to pressure of all kinds and are difficult to alter in any way, either as to character or environment. On the positive side they are strong, dependable, steadfast and reliable. They are patient and have a great deal of pride and dignity. They have self-reliance and independence and a considerable amount of firmness and perseverance. On the negative side they are inert and stubborn, firm, rigid, immobile and dogmatic. In short, very stubborn with a sort of drowsy inertia. They are not enthusiastic originators nor do they develop matters very much; but when development does occur, they help to work out improvements.

Sattva or mutable is adaptable and versatile. People with many planets in mutable or common signs seldom originate action but they do develop it. They are sympathetic, sensitive, and fond of intellectual pursuits. They have much understanding and are flexible and have the ability to tune in on events and other people when being positive. When behaving negatively, they are indecisive and often not sufficiently firm and determined and they need to cultivate thoroughness. They are often inconstant and have a feeling of want and of discontent with the self. They exhibit restlessness and uncertainty and in order to be happy they need to cultivate a firm self-reliance.

There are many and various combinations of the three gunas (rajas, tamas and sattva) and of the four elements (fire, earth, air and water) in the individual horoscope. The ideal combinations would be fairly evenly balanced but few horoscopes are ideal. If one of the gunas or one of the elements is missing, then we can expect a gap or weakness in character signified by that guna or element. Sometimes there is a very heavy emphasis on one guna or element. If this is the case, then we can expect that the person will function according to the emphasis.

Next, let us look at the aspects which the planets make. If all planets are in close aspect to each other; that is, if the aspects are not wider than 2 or 3 degrees for the planets, and about 5 degrees for the lights, then we can expect a near genius, or one who is capable of accomplishing much, provided the planets do not say the reverse due to overwhelmingly bad aspects or poor placements in signs. Further, even though the energies of the planets are dissonant, we could still expect that the person will be able to pull all the elements of his life together and achieve what Jung calls "integration."

The horoscope which shows too many easy and good aspects and which also has some planets not in aspect with others at all is a weak horoscope and the native will be tempted to drift with the tides of life, not achieving very much, nor leaving much of a mark on the world.

Now it is time to look at the placement of the Sun. This is where our *Book of Thoth*[22] can be put to very good use. Observe which Court Card rules the section of the zodiac wherein the Sun is placed. This will be an overall description of the person involved. There will be other fine modifications of the character and for these; one can refer to any good astrology book. I append a list of some that I have found useful and accurate.

The Ascendant degree can also be referred to a Court Card in the Thoth Tarot if you remember that the Ascendant will rule the outer face that the native shows to the world—it is the personality. The Sun represents the deeper forces of the Individuality and this is the part that we do not change. "Yea! Deem not of change: ye shall be as ye are, & not other" (*Liber Legis*, Cap. II, v. 58).[23] Aspects can be modified in their effect and the emotions represented by the Moon can be controlled, but we do not change our deepest Individuality, we merely try to live up to its best potential.

Now I think you can see how important it is that you understand your own best way of action. It is like gaining a road map where there was none before. The Joy mentioned in *Liber Legis* comes from living up to one's own best potential and fulfilling the will that is foreshadowed in the horoscope.

I have merely given you a toehold on astrology in these pages, and I think you can now turn to the various books and figure out a few things for yourself.

You asked why a certain person was not suited to the College of Thelema or to the Ordo Templi Orientis. Please, let us be very clear on this point. You have been chosen with the greatest of care, as Thelema needs successes, not failures. Since the movement is small at present, it is judged in the eyes of the world by its members. Should we allow the drifter, the drug abuser, the selfish and careless, the criminal types, the weak, within our ranks, we would not long hold together as an order or a college. The weak would drag down the strong, as they have always done since the dawn of history.

---

22. *i.e.*, the Tarot.

23. Crowley, *Liber AL vel Legis*, 47.

Not for one instance did Crowley condone the inept, the egomaniac, the confused or the lazy. Thelema is for the strong. You might refer to *Liber AL vel Legis* for more on this theme.

Now a further caution in your conduct in the world. *Liber Legis* states in Cap. III, v. 42, "argue not; convert not; talk not overmuch!" [24] We are not out to convert the world like the Christians and the Mohammedans tried to do.

Crowley, from the first to the last of his work with the O.T.O., hoped to find within its ranks the finest of the human beings that were possible. A great many of the ordeals were structured on the hope that he had Kings and not slaves as members. "If he be a King, thou canst not hurt him" (*Liber Legis*, Cap. II v. 59).[25] So then, dear fellow, raise your head high that you are among the chosen, and may you accomplish the discovery of your True Will and shine as a star among us.

Love is the law, love under will,

Meral

Care Frater,[26]

Do what thou wilt shall be the whole of the Law.

The question has come up about astral entities and whether they can be inimical to man; whether a man can be influenced to do that which he would not normally do, and whether he can be harmed by these entities from other planes.

There is enough material in occultism in general which would make it pointless for us to argue whether astral beings exist or not. Surely such phenomena have been talked and written about endlessly. What is not very clear is whether the individual concerned with astral manifestation is responsible for the event which startles and appalls him, and which may even obsess his imagination to such a degree that he is sure the astral happening is real beyond any doubt.

It is also pointless to argue whether the astral entities are

---

24. Crowley, *Liber AL vel Legis*, 61.
25. Crowley, *Liber AL vel Legis*, 47.
26. Originally published in: Seckler, Phyllis, *In the Continuum* 1.5 (1975): 1-8.

outside of ourselves, or are inside and are a manifestation of unconscious powers of which we are for the most part in woeful ignorance. Perhaps both things are true, perhaps not. Perhaps it is the adept who can settle this question satisfactorily for himself. But this does not mean that we should not try also to settle it. Each of us must struggle towards the Light. As Thelemites, we must ever be conscious that we are working by the method of science and that our aim is a religious one, the knowledge of the true Center of our own Being. As workers in the scientific method, we ought not to become emotionally involved regarding the existence of astral entities inside or outside of ourselves. We should take a detached, scientific view of "astral happenings" and, most important of all, of ourselves. Indeed, this latter matter, that of ourselves, becomes the most important element in our consideration.

We each see the world only through our own eyes, our own senses, our own emotional, physical and mental patterning. In one sense, everything any other star sees or feels is very unreal to us.

It is a known psychological fact that the unconscious mind will produce phenomena according to the pictures offered to it by conscious thought and emotions. It won't produce events by intellect or reasoning in particular, but according to the strength of emotional pictures. Thought pictures of positive emotions and feeling and aspirations will produce positive results. Thus, in the Banishing Ritual, you are presenting the unconscious with a series of pictures and symbols which, if done carefully, with full attention to the picturing and imagining of the Cross of Light, the pentagrams in blue fire, the thought forms and imaginings of the Gods, the Presence of the Archangels and how they look, and so forth, can never fail to impress the unconscious mind with what you want. Likewise, *Liber 7* and *Liber 65* are full of pictures which impress the unconscious and this is why memorizing these books will prove an invaluable aid to you.

Consider, on the other side of the coin, how fear manages to produce in the life happenings of just that thing which is feared. Fear is so powerful an emotion it easily impresses itself upon the astral light. What do you think a person could produce on the emotional or astral plane through fear? Anything he believes in must be the answer to this.

In *The Magical and Philosophical Commentaries on the Book of the Law* we might quote from p. 214: "'Dost thou fail? Art thou sorry? Is fear in thine heart?' — This verse brings out what is a fact in psychology, the necessary connection between fear, sorrow and failure. To will and to dare are closely linked Powers of the Sphinx, and they are based on — to know. If one have a right apprehension of the universe, if he know himself free, immortal, boundless, infinite force and fire, then may he will and dare. Fear, sorrow and failure are but phantoms."[27]

Also, this is probably why *The Book of the Law* is so vehement that we must "Fear not at all; fear neither men nor Fates, nor gods, nor anything. Money fear not, nor laughter of the folk folly, nor any other power in heaven or upon the earth or under the earth" (Cap. III, v. 17).[28]

There is also the question whether obsession by astral beings or their manifestation to the mind of the beholder could have a physical basis. Undoubtedly, in some cases, it does. We are all aware of how the unmated adolescent can produce poltergeist phenomena. This would be based upon the non-satisfaction of the sex urge. This is one of the most powerful emotions known to us and the drive to sex can build up emotional states which are so powerful they can produce phenomena very much out of the ordinary.

The alcoholic in advanced stages also produces things on the astral plane. The same is true of those who partake of drugs in an uncontrolled fashion. Think of the astral plane as rather like an unseen Light which is extremely plastic and which can be formed at the will of the operator into that which he desires. Then we will have the usual occult phenomena which abound in novels, accounts of mystics and religious persons, those who see ghosts, spiritualists, and hundreds of other types. In this extremely plastic light everyone goes on creating, whether he knows of it or not. Sometimes his creations have such a force of emotionality that they stay alive for a long time. These are the "dead shells" of the Qlippoth or of the lower astral realms. Often psychics invite

---

27. Crowley, *Magical and Philosophical Commentaries on the Book of the Law*. Eds. J. Symonds and K. Grant (Montreal, Quebec: 93 Publishing, 1974), 214. See also: Crowley, Aleister, *The Law is for All*, Ed. Louis Wilkinson and Hymenaeus Beta (Scottsdale, AZ: Falcon Press 1996), 127.
28. Crowley, *Liber AL vel Legis*, 54.

these dead shells into their auras deliberately and, since the shells have no vestige of the soul who created them, the psychic can be dreadfully harmed.

Then there are astral manifestations which might occur to sick persons. Some persons can also produce this type of event by deliberately sleeping too much. Dreams and astral occurrences can be the result if the body is prevented from carrying out its will towards action and movement. Certain persons, in oversleeping too much, slow down the action of the heart and this affects the blood surge to the brain. This in turn will produce phantasms which the person has in his unconscious mind, frightening or not, and which he himself has put there.

Today hyper-insulinism due to a surfeit of sugar and starches, alcohol, depleted white flours, food additives and other poisons can lead to very deleterious effects. It is now known, for instance, that schizophrenia can be cured by taking the person affected off all of the above items and feeding him a natural diet fortified with certain large doses of vitamins and minerals. How many other mental illnesses could be treated in this way is anyone's guess. And how many astral influences could be circumvented by such a regimen as given to the schizophrenic should perhaps also be our study. We should ask ourselves if our temporary aberration from our true star light was caused by some physical condition.

How much then, of any person's "astral visions" or encounters with astral entities depends on bodily conditions and how much of these events would depend on emotional or mental set?

The person who spends his time hating, should conditions warrant an astral experience, will meet his hate face to face. He has, after all, created it. The person who spends a great deal of time with science fiction, should he also delve into subconscious or astral realms, will meet there just what he has programmed into it, which is astral experiences which sound like science fiction when he comes to retell the event.

We all know that the person who religiously inclines to the Jesus theory will see that person on the astral if they enflame the emotions and mind sufficiently to do this. The religious experience is known to exactly fit the aspirant's thoughts, emotions and mental pictures which he has presented to the unconscious.

I hope that by now you have read William James' *The Varieties* of *Religious Experience*[29] and Dr. Bucke's *Cosmic Consciousness*.[30] Both of these books will give you quite an insight into the workings of the human mind. Though they do not give much information on astral entities, still such apparitions are affected by our own minds. This is an extremely important point and we need very much to study the mind in order to understand and even to control what we term astral events. In short, haunting can occur very easily because of our ignorance of natural Laws. Let us, then, try our best to discover what these laws are.

I shall quote again from the Commentary on *Liber Legis*: "Ye are against the people, O my chosen!"[31] — "Still deeper, there is a meaning in this verse applicable to the process of personal initiation. By 'the people' we may understand the many-headed and mutable mob which swarms in the slums of our own minds. Most men are almost entirely at the mercy of a mass of loud and violent emotions, without discipline or even organization. They sway with the mood of the moment. They lack purpose, foresight and intelligence. They are moved by ignorant and irrational instincts, many of which affront the law of self-preservation itself, with suicidal stupidity. The moral Idea which we call 'the people' is the natural enemy of good government. He who is 'chosen' by Hadit to Kingship must consequently be 'against the people' if he is to pursue any consistent policy. The amassed maggots of 'love' devoured Mark Anthony as they did Abelard. For this reason the first task of the aspirant is to disarm all his thoughts, to make himself impregnably above the influence of any one of them; This he may accomplish by the methods given in "Liber Aleph," "Liber Jugorum," "Thien Tao" and elsewhere. Secondly, he must impose absolute silence upon them, as may be done by the 'yoga' practices taught in "Book 4 (Part I)," "Liber XVI," etc. He is then ready to analyze them, to organize them, to drill them, and so to take advantage of the properties peculiar to each one by employing its energies in the service of his imperial purpose."[32]

With all this laboring then, let me just state that we are all

---

29. James, William, *The Varieties of Religious Experience* (New York, NY: Random House, 1999).
30. Bucke, Richard M., *Cosmic Consciousness* (New York, NY: Arkana Books, 1991).
31. Crowley, *Liber AL vel Legis*, 25 [*Liber Legis*, Cap. II v. 25 – Eds.].
32. Crowley, *The Law is for All*, 115-116.

responsible for events in our own lives, whether astral or physical, to a startling degree. One of the differences between an initiate and an uninitiate is that the former knows this and takes on the responsibility for his creations. He becomes as Nemo and tends his garden. He prunes some tendencies and emotions, cuts out some altogether and encourages others, all according to the dictates of his True Will.

The uninitiate, on the other hand, is likely to blame any other source than himself for what happens. It seems to him easier this way if he becomes the pawn of Fate. He does not have to take on the responsibility for what happens. He can say the whole event was due to conditions beyond his control. Unfortunately, this attitude can lead to insanity if the astral event was horrendous enough. It harms no one to admit that his own mind may have been responsible for the astral incident. If one had a hand in it then what can one do to dispel the effects? This way, you have given yourself a path out of any difficulty. You have begun to think in terms of the warrior, ready to do battle against your own debilitating tendencies, whether physical, emotional or mental. As Thelemites, we ought not to forget that we are fighters and that part of our fight (nay, a good deal of it) is against those parts of ourselves which interfere with the True Will. This is probably why the third chapter of *Liber Legis* is so full of the sound of battle. As humans, we are the 'child,' the product of the play of Hadit with Nuit.

In the Commentary to *Liber Legis* we read in Cap. II, v. 19, "Is a God to live in a dog? No! but the highest are of us. They shall rejoice, our chosen: who sorroweth is not of us."[33]

"A god living in a dog would be one who was prevented from fulfilling his function properly. The highest are those who have mastered and transcended accidental environment. They rejoice, because they do their Will; and if any man sorrow, it is clear evidence of something wrong with him. When machinery creaks and growls, the engineer knows that it is not fulfilling its function, doing its Will, with ease and joy."[34]

And in *Liber Aleph*, there is this wisdom: [see "De Hoc Modo Dissolutio"].[35]

---

33. Crowley, *Liber AL vel Legis*, 40.
34. Crowley, *The Law is for All*, 101.
35. Crowley, *Liber Aleph*, 196.

Here then, is a path out of difficulties with astral entities. One must first clean up one's own house and attend to the work of the various tendencies. Then one must seek to know and accomplish the True Will. Set your feet on this path and no astral creature of force can interfere with you. Is it not said in *Liber Legis*, Cap. I, v. 42-43, "Let it be that state of manyhood bound and loathing. So with thy all; thou hast no right but to do thy will. Do that, and no other shall say nay."[36]

Now, then, if these quotes have not settled your problem, may I suggest that they could be memorized and imagined about and pictures made of them, which you then present to your unconscious? Do this often enough and it won't be long before the unconscious will respond by presenting you with the series of events which you will need as a way out of your difficulties.

Further, along this line. What to do in case of attack? There are many paths. I have found the Middle Pillar Ritual in combination with the Banishing Ritual to be the most efficacious. You might refer to Regardie's book, *The Middle Pillar*.[37] Then I think I have clearly given enough quotes for you to know that you must aim to the Highest within you, whatever that may be for the present. We can call it the True Will, or the Knowledge and Conversation of the Holy Guardian Angel, depending on which stage of development you are in. You must ruthlessly weed out the unworthy parts of yourself which interfere with this high aim, and you ought willingly to work out the details of your karma, which you yourself have ordained. Thelema has the most lofty ideals, but these must be worked out by each individual to fit his own case with the guidance of *The Book of the Law*.

Further along this line let me quote again from *Liber Aleph*: [see "De Via Per Empyraeum"].[38]

And following this: [see "De Cultu"].[39]

Further, when accosted by hostile spirits or forces, you should try the spirits. If you would but trace a pentagram or a cross if it seems more natural to you and demand the spirit's name, you will find this a great help. Usually inimical spirits will dissolve before a pentagram and purity of aspiration on your part. All

---

36. Crowley, *Liber AL vel Legis*, 19.
37. Regardie, Israel, *The Middle Pillar* (Woodbury, MN: Llewellyn, 2002).
38. Crowley, *Liber Aleph*, 15.
39. Crowley, *Liber Aleph*, 16.

spirits <u>have</u> to obey since you are complete and they are not. All spirits whatever, no matter how frightening, are partial beings. Man is both God and animal and all in between. Man is a perfect star in his true nature. You literally can't be haunted, influenced or harmed by astral beings unless you yourself have cut yourself off from your true star nature or godhead. Remember always that you are a God and that you can command and create as does a God. If you have cut yourself off from the true self, then you can also restore the link since you are Hadit in your inmost Self and have this power.

So now, dear brother, you have your work cut out for you. Do not shirk this work, for it would but hamper you on your path to the realization of your own starry nature. May you win your Battle.

Love is the law, love under will.

Fraternally,
Meral

Care Frater,[40]

Do what thou wilt shall be the whole of the Law.

It is time we gave more attention to the glyph of the Tree of Life. On this diagram we can place all ideas in the Universe. Therefore, it must be very flexible and that is why you see so many versions of the use of the Tree in the illustrations which follow. These diagrams were also meant to elucidate more clearly the point made in Crowley's article "Qabalistic Dogma."[41] We must become very familiar with the method of referring all ideas to the Tree of Life, for that Tree is the Self [see Diagrams B-F].

Man is a lesser picture (the Microcosm) of the Whole of Life forces or of the Universe (the Macrocosm). At any rate, all that he can know exists within himself. As the point of light (Hadit) he seeks ever to unite himself to Experience which exists in the starry Space of Nuit. As this process proceeds, he is ever uniting with Nuit. For this reason I have shown how the Tree of Life

---

40. Originally published in: Seckler, Phyllis, *In the Continuum* 1.6 (1975): 2-6.
41. Published as an appendix to Crowley, *The Collected Works*, Vol. 1. (Foyers, S.P.R.T., 1905), 265-269.

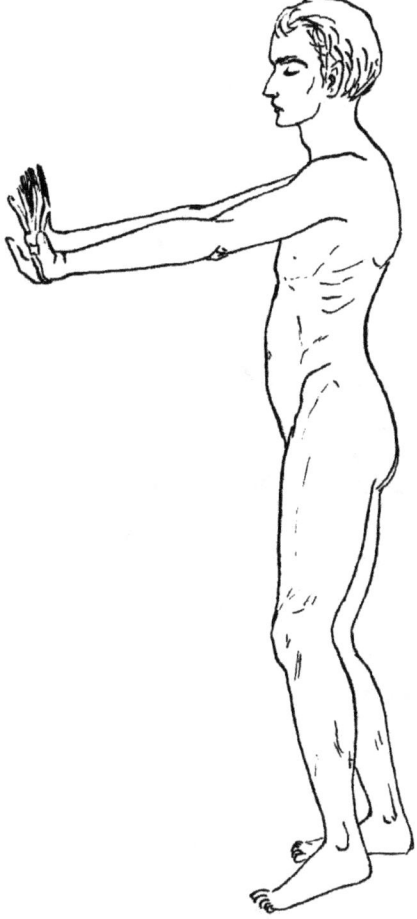
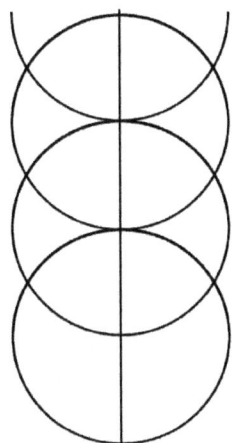

Man has 3½ curves in the spine, hence there are 3½ generating circles in constructing the Tree of Life.

He has a left side (the Pillar of Mercy—Jachin) and a right side (the Pillar of Severity—Boaz) and a central spine (the Pillar of Mildness). When you look at a Tree of Life Diagram on paper you are seeing a mirror image. To picture the tree as yourself, imagine that you back in to the diagram.

In the Yogic system the spine has 3 columns which are termed Ida, Pingala and Sushumna for the middle column.

Further, you can count 10 orifices in the human body (7 of these are in the face). There are 10 fingers and 10 toes, etc.

AS ABOVE SO BELOW was an Hermetic axiom.

Diagram B.

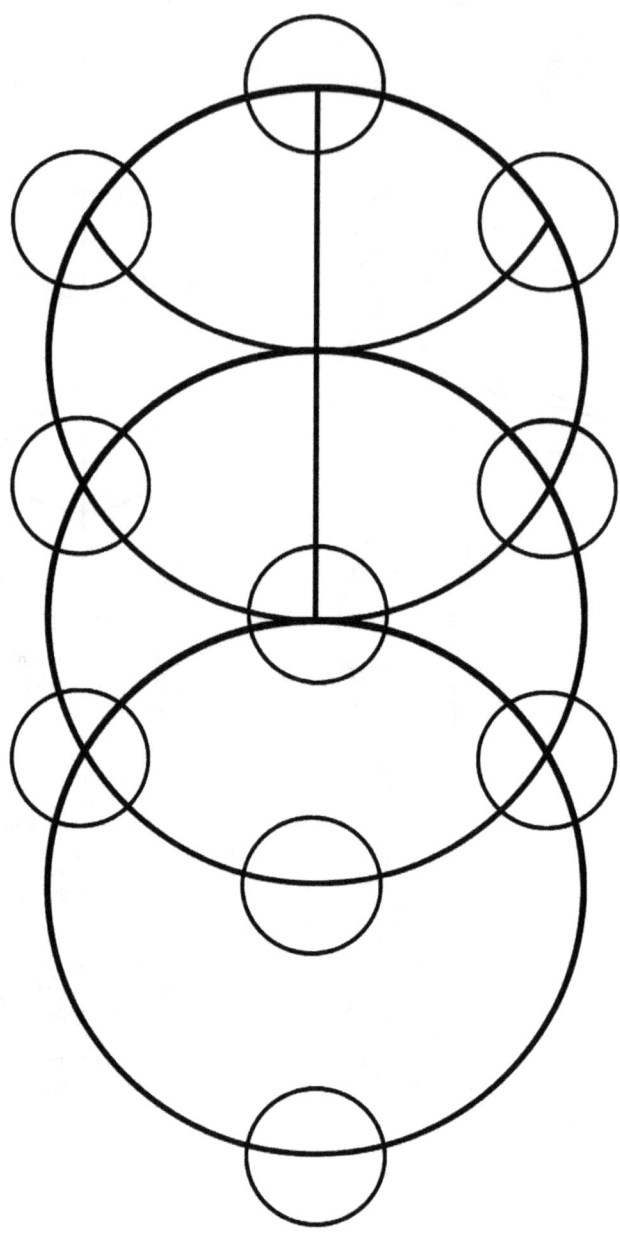

Diagram C.

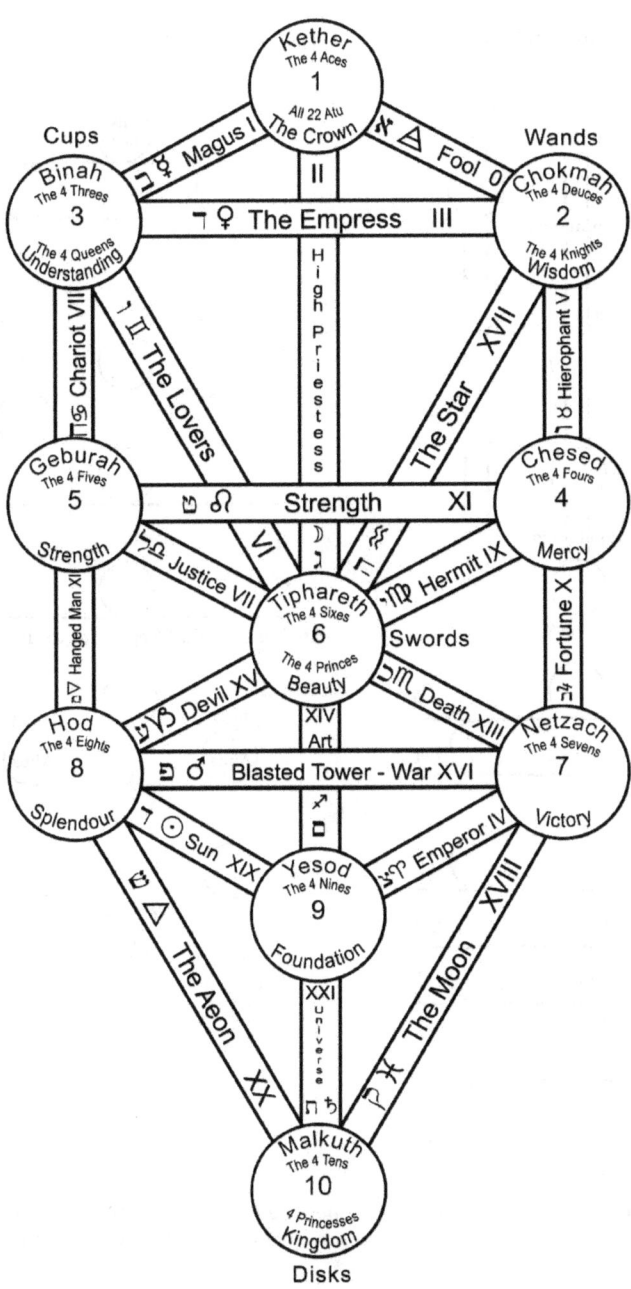

Diagram D.

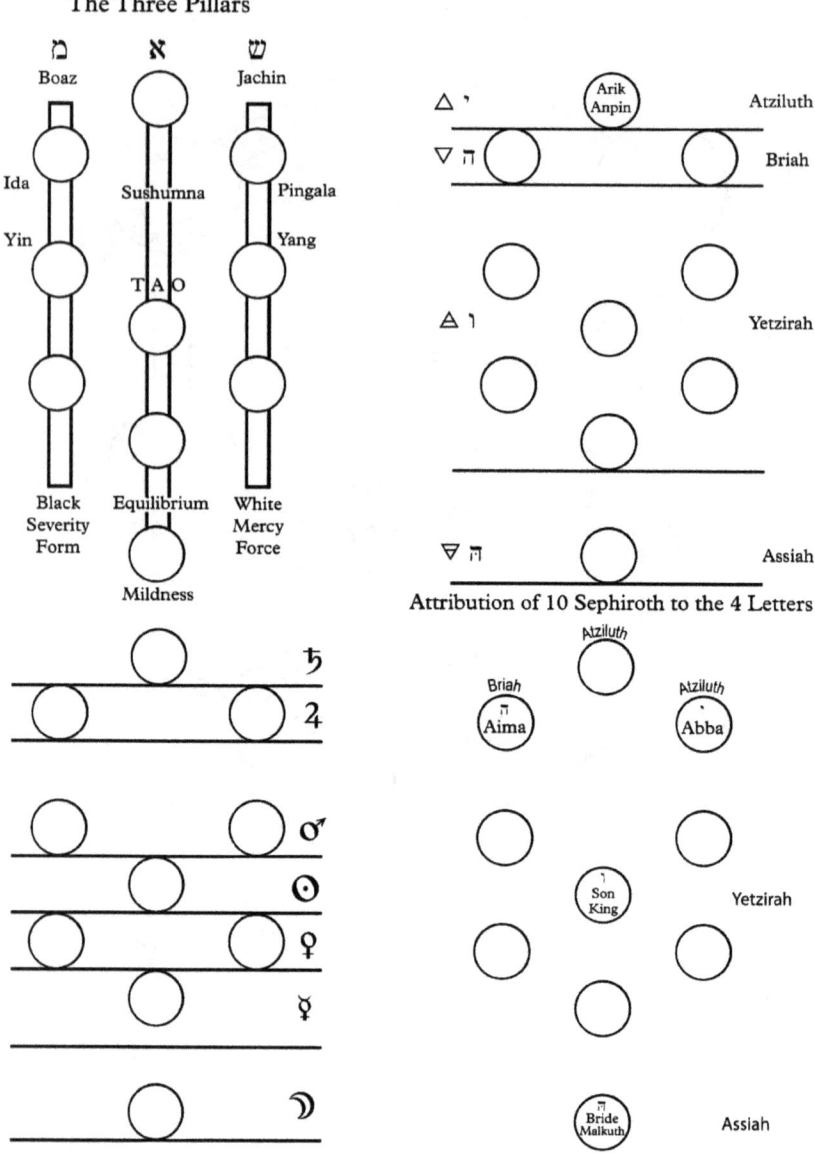

Diagram E.

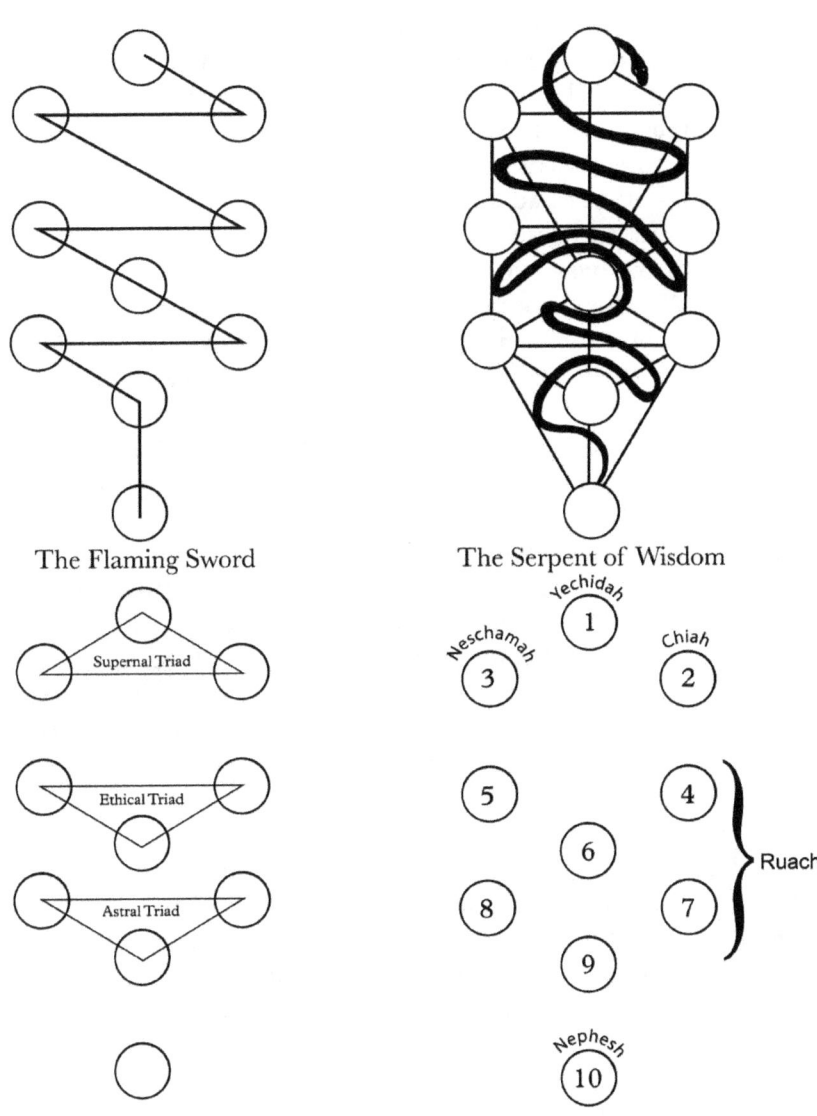

Diagram F.

is constructed on man's spinal cord and bones. As an aside, I might mention that Saturn rules the formation of bones and the structure of the character, just as bones are the structure of the human figure. Saturn is ascribed to Binah, the sphere where the idea of form is first formulated. And this sphere belongs to the Supernals—that is, across the Abyss.

There are 32 "paths" in the Tree of Life. When we speak of "paths" in this way, we are also including the 10 spheres along with the 22 Atus or paths which connect the spheres. In the human backbone there are 33 vertebrae. However, if we add the sphere of Daath to our original number of 32, we come up with the number 33.

You will notice that there are three pillars which make up the Tree and that these pillars correspond to the three channels of force described by Hindu thought: the Ida, Pingala and Sushumna of the serpent Kundalini.

Some students get a bit mixed up about which side of the Tree of Life refers to their right side and which refers to the left side of the body. Imagine yourself backing up into the Tree. On the page you are seeing but a mirror image of what it really is. Therefore, the right side has the spheres of Binah, Geburah and Hod to represent it and the left side has the spheres of Chokmah, Chesed and Netzach. Here again there might be puzzlement—why is the right side the feminine side and also why should the feminine side be called the Pillar of Severity. You perhaps thought that the feminine in nature was soft and yielding. We are all prisoners of some false conceptions. Also, one must take a great deal more into consideration about this negative, yielding nature of the feminine. How about the fierceness of the mother animal if you threaten her young ones? How about the new discoveries in scientific investigation that shows the female can withstand pain better than the male and can perform as well on the athletic field as long as she doesn't give in to misconceptions about herself and soften her muscles with long periods of inactivity? How about the known occult fact that females have a great deal of energy which may be tapped for useful purposes by the trained occultist? Why do you think that certain Hindu sects stress Maithuna with a young and vigorous female? And why not refer to *The Book of the Law* in Chapter One and discover for yourself some more facts about the so-called negative side of nature—the female side.

I might mention a quote from this chapter, verse 61: "Ye shall gather goods and store of women and spices." Why should it mention women in with goods and spices, and that they shall be gathered? Dion Fortune states that women are the energy source for an occult group and seem to work harder at getting things done than do the men. We have only to look at some primitive tribes to see this type of action in full force. It is not really because women have been oppressed by the male—though that has happened too—that we see the women doing the work of agriculture, raising the children, and being very responsible for the welfare of the family; in short, doing the bulk of the work that needs to be done. It is because women somehow tap the universal energy sources in a much more efficient manner than men.

Enough of this digression. The Tree of Life really represents both male and female bodies. Also, remember that there is no progress in nature or in the occult life unless there is a balance. So we see the soft and yielding with some of its other virtues represented as a balance on the side of Severity. If you will remember, I warned in one of my other letters to you that you must always seek a balance in *The Book of the Law*. If one chapter or verse is too severe, it must be balanced out against a verse or chapter that is not severe at all. This way I should hope that you will avoid the dangerous unbalance which only too often strikes those who are students of the occult. The results of unbalance are only too sad and they become very much more aggravated when one first becomes a Minerval or a Neophyte. Let me quote from *Book 4*, Part II, Chapter VI, by Crowley:

Of the methods of destroying various deep-rooted ideas there are many.

The best is perhaps the method of equilibrium. **Get the mind into the habit of calling up the opposite to every thought that may arise.** In conversation always disagree. See the other man's arguments; but, however much your judgment approves them, find the answer.

Let this be done dispassionately; the more convinced you are that a certain point of view is right, the more determined you should be to find proofs that it is wrong.

If you have done this thoroughly, these points of views

will cease to trouble you; you can then assert your own point of view with the calm of a master, which is more convincing than the enthusiasm of a learner.

You will cease to be interested in controversies; politics, ethics, religion will seem so many toys, and your Magical Will will be free from these inhibitions.[42]

As the Tree of Life is balanced within each path and within each Sphere, so must you be balanced too. Here are some relevant passages from *Liber Aleph*: [see "De Auro Rubeo," "De Sapientia In Re Sexuali"].[43]

As you keep your magical diary it might be wise to write therein in what manner you have become unbalanced. Do you experience an excess of emotion? Seek its antidote in activity, in study, or the like. Do you have too much of materiality? Then try to offset it with spirituality and growth in the Law of Thelema. Are you active without thought and without understanding? Then you should certainly try to think about the results of action. Are you prey to the phantoms of the mind? Surely you can find the opposite thoughts to cancel those out which so unbalance you?

If you desire to succeed in the mastery of yourself, it is incumbent upon you to root out the unbalance which is there; to become a more perfect Tree in yourself and thus to mirror the perfection of the Universe. Balance is to be found, then, by relating everything to the True Will and discovering if what is happening is a hindrance or a help to that will.

Sometimes the neophyte will say he doesn't know his True Will. There is more about this matter in *Liber Aleph* and it would well repay you to study this book well. However, for now we can say that every human is bound to evolve and ever travel upwards on the Tree of Life, as does the Serpent that touches all the paths. In the Center of the Tree we see Tiphareth. This represents the Knowledge and Conversation of the Holy Guardian Angel in a very exalted form. Surely you can keep this ideal in your mind as you seek to find if you are achieving a balance. Do your pet ideas of emotions or thoughts or actions aid or hinder you in your evolution?

---

42. Crowley, *Magick Liber ABA: Book Four Parts I-IV*, Ed. Hymenaeus Beta (York Beach, ME: Samuel Weiser, 1997), 70-71.
43. Crowley, *Liber Aleph*, 43-44.

Thus if you have become a prey to one of your own obsessions about the nature of love, about the nature of various processes—whatever seems to be your worst struggle—you should be able to find the balance to the idea and thus you can draw the sting of involvement which seems so to upset and unbalance you. Nature herself gives us a clue. If something we are doing or feeling or thinking makes us dreadfully unhappy, then we are on the wrong path. The H.G.A. will come more readily to a nature calm and balanced and unruffled by the circumstances and accidents of life.

Love is the law, love under will.

Meral

Care Frater,[44]

Do what thou wilt shall be the whole of the Law.

In the complexities of learning to live the Law of Thelema we often can get royally confused. You were asking if you should help X. of our Order, and you give as your reason your love of him. Further, you cite the injunction of the First Degree of the O.T.O....[45]

The reply to your question must necessarily be complicated by many considerations. The problem of aid and of the freedom of the individual are inextricably combined, so it will be best if we consider both.

For instance, if, in your type of assistance, you encourage X to develop and to hang on to his weaknesses to the detriment of the rest of us, would you call this true assistance? Those very weaknesses may be the same ones which will trip him up inexorably later on his path; whereas, if he faced them now and suffered somewhat in so doing, they might the more easily be overcome. If certain weaknesses are allowed to grow and develop when a person is on the path to Initiation, the fall that can result may be fatal and may last through several lives while the seeker tries to straighten out his karma. Whereas, if they are tackled now, while

---

44. Originally published in: Phyllis Seckler, *In the Continuum* 1.8, (1976): 7-13.
45. Redacted. The passage in question relates to providing assistance to brethren. – Eds.

they are recognizable and small, and even though the person involved suffers, the final results might not be so awful. Nature is cruel and favors the strong. Does not *Liber AL vel Legis* exhort us to be strong and then specifically say in Cap. II, v. 48, "Pity not the fallen! I never knew them. I am not for them. I console not: I hate the consoled & the consoler?"[46] Can you tell if the person you are concerned about is one of the "fallen?" For it would indeed be poor policy to rob nature of her just effects, and a fellow of his lawful karma.

You object that Crowley was supported and helped by others in his later years. It is a bit of a failing, it is true, among many of our members to point to Crowley and claim a like license to do as he did. If Crowley did it, the reasoning goes, then it is alright for me. (This is called being obsessed by the Demon Crowley.) But such a weak one forgets that his own path is very different from Crowley's path. Let us look at the record:

Crowley squandered his fortune in printing his literary works. These writings will benefit mankind for centuries. He almost always took a loss when pricing the books for sale but this didn't stop him from having them done on the finest paper possible so that they would last.

Crowley also worked unceasingly to write and instruct the rest of us and did so without remuneration of any kind. His accomplishments, abilities and Initiations benefited others.

Karl Germer recognized the quality of Crowley's work and had the vision to see that Crowley needed aid to finish his Work in his later years. He and his wife Sascha sent him $200 a month or more, and sometimes even larger sums of money, just so that the writing and publishing could continue.

These three sacrificed themselves on the altar of mankind's need. Crowley could accept Germer's help in honesty and gratitude in the spirit in which it was given. All knew that without the freedom of the individual, life would not be worth living.

In another sphere of life, it is also true that Vincent Van Gogh's brother supported him. We have only to look at the quality and quantity of Vincent's work to realize that this was necessary—again for the sake of mankind—so that men might realize and see the particular kind of beauty that Vincent saw.

---

46. Crowley, *Liber AL vel Legis*, 45.

There are similar cases like this wherein a person deserves the support or aid of another, and it is the will of the other to lend his assistance. A person may need a modicum of aid or assistance to discover his True Will. Or he may need some aid in accomplishing a will already established and your will might be in consonance with his—both of you perhaps having the general weal of all in the order in mind. Each case must be judged on its own peculiar merit. You should ask yourself, what is the quality and quantity of the work already produced by this person which would justify you in aiding him? Does the person know his finite will (at least) and is he striving without cease to accomplish it? If so, is he able to convey his purpose to you clearly enough so that you can readily comply in freedom to assist him?

However, there are many causes in my experience and knowledge which do not at all justify any kind of assistance.

What then if the brother in poverty should hold his state over your head, saying that you are bound to support him because of your mutual interests? Would this not then be a great mischief? Again, this is not encouraged in the O.T.O. I refer you to the "Duties and Privileges" in *Liber CI*, in the "Blue Equinox."[47]

Then too, an indulgent woman may aid or mother or financially support a grown man in the name of "love." But she may only be encouraging him to continue in a habit of alcoholism or in a habit of serious and severe personal selfishness. She may actually manifest a Kundry type as delineated in the opera Parsifal by Richard Wagner by aiding or abetting, allowing or condoning the serious weaknesses of the man she supposedly loves. She thus prevents him from accomplishing his True Will or even from finding it through his serious battle with the circumstances of life. Is this freedom or Liberty for either one? Such a so-called "love" only weakens her man further. Have you not noticed this in your experience?

Indeed, when money considerations enter into love then the partner who must foot the bill must face the fact that he or she may be "buying" sex. *Liber Legis* mentions love but does not use the word sex. And love must be "under will." Also, in Cap. I, v. 41, it says, "There is no bond that can unite the divided but love:

---

47. Crowley, *The Equinox Vol. III, No. I* (York Beach, ME: Samuel Weiser, 1995), 211-224.

all else is a curse. Accursed! Accursed be it to the æons! Hell."[48]

The first thing anyone who tries to accomplish his will must do is to eat and then to put a roof over his head. Should we condone the parasite who cannot do this? I am not here talking of pregnant women, children, or of the aged and ill who have earned their way already by a productive and useful life for the benefit of the rest of us in our Order.

In aiding another you may be interfering with his will to die as he will, or to suffer so that he can learn. Lessons which, often, carry much suffering and trouble are sent by the Holy Guardian Angel. It is an incontrovertible fact that people won't learn unless they suffer. A life of ease and happiness only produces the mediocrity. So then, would you be standing between the Angel and the individual by such aid? Worse still, you may be jeopardizing your own freedom. If a person is old and someone of the order offers to take care of him, how much better it is for his independence if he can say, "Thank you, but I have already provided for my old age and though I know you offer this boon in what you think is love, still it is a karmic bond that would interfere with my personal Liberty and I would rather avoid it."

There are so many nuances in this thorny question of whether you can offer aid to another in a discreet fashion, of course, or whether by so doing you are interfering with his Liberty. We really ought not to encourage the parasite in our Society, no matter what his grade. For if this is to be an order of free men and women we could not be free if even one of us is a slave or exploited by another, or by the order as a whole.

Then, too, is your desire to lend assistance tainted in any way by the martyr complex? This can be pretty subtle and deep within the unconscious mind. But mostly it works out like this: the person suffering from this complex has a set of fine ideals to help his fellow man. Then he puts these ideals into practice and he sees that his fellow man takes the assistance—becomes a real low-down taker—and gives nothing in return. The martyr becomes incensed when he realizes that his protégé does not return the compliment and is not about to help anyone else at all. Even worse, he is not grateful enough to the martyr's ideals and

---

48. Crowley, *Liber AL vel Legis*, 31.

high principles. The martyr then suffers a revulsion of feeling and his reactions may include resentment, hate, incrimination and a whole welter of terrible emotions. He may become self-righteous and proud and boast about his generosity and will criticize others. In fact, we could have a hell's broth. On this attitude, let me quote from *Liber Aleph*: [see "De Stultis Malignis"].[49]

I think that we must each face the fact that we are bound by our tendencies. We are especially vulnerable in that part of our nature which "loves" or is emotionally dependent on another. We face a quagmire of contradictions and frustrations until and unless each one of us works out his own Way in freedom to express his love, neither enslaving another by assistance (so-called), nor withholding assistance truly deserved. Does a person love because he is in need of flattery, or emotional support, or of mothering, or of financial support, or any of a thousand other extraneous reasons which really have nothing to do essentially with love? This is not pure love, then, is it? And if it is not, how can any assistance be rendered at all? The more such unhealthy dependence on others manifests, the more will that person be a slave to his own peculiar psychology of action and feeling and thinking. Ask yourself if anyone can be truly a Thelemite if he or she is a slave to his own worst tendencies and dependent on others to satisfy his hunger for satisfaction of these tendencies and is so dishonest as to name it "love?" Is he not a slave to his own lower nature and does he not enslave others in asking them to satisfy this lower nature?

As an example we are only too familiar with the woman who uses the fact of a child as issue between the two of them as a bludgeon to limit the freedom of her mate.

And *Liber Legis* warns us about the man who will not let his wife work outside the home or in other ways find her own will beyond childbearing and housekeeping: "The word of Sin is Restriction. O man! refuse not thy wife, if she will! O lover, if thou wilt, depart!"[50]

In marriage or the love relationship or the Brotherhood relationship of Thelema various kinds of tyrannies can be too easily displayed and worked to the detriment of the beloved or of the

---

49. Crowley, *Liber Aleph*, 148.
50. Crowley, *Liber AL vel Legis*, 31. [Cap. I, v. 41. – Eds.]

friend or of the order. This tyranny is all the more powerful when sex enters into the relationship since sex and fear are the two most potent forces to create images and entities on the Astral plane and these effects can literally obsess the person who created them to the point of insanity. If love is not controlled and transcended, and placed "under will" and dedicated to Nuit rather than to any one person; if fear is not mastered by facing that which is feared, then we do not have free men or women. We are instead laboring some monster in our midst, who not only destroys himself but also manages to destroy others around him, who are not protected from such effects. This is why Nuit says in Cap. I, v. 52, "If this be not aright; if ye confound the space-marks, saying: They are one; or saying, They are many; if the ritual be not ever unto me: then expect the direful judgments of Ra Hoor Khuit!"[51]

The verse on fear is also explicit. See Cap. III, v. 17: "Fear not at all; fear neither men nor Fates, nor gods, nor anything. Money fear not, nor laughter of the folk folly, nor any other power in heaven or upon the earth or under the earth. Nu is your refuge as Hadit your light; and I am the strength, force, vigor, of your arms."[52]

Contemplating that verse, can you truly say that your desire to assist another was not born of fear or public opinion if you did not?

All too often we see the weak person going down under the "love" tyranny or perhaps he goes down under fear. Is the person you desire to help in either of these conditions? Would it not be wiser to let him face his dependence on another person or his fear by himself?

Each person needs to enquire carefully if it be his will to be enslaved by the need of another. Would he hinder his own or the protégé's growth? Psychologically, what cowardice is lurking in the person who even needs assistance? And are you going to feed that cowardice by supplying your assistance in the name of love? Are you enabling this person to shrink from the battle of Life and thus of true Liberty?

Many and subtle are the attempts to breach the bastions of

---

51. Crowley, *Liber AL vel Legis*, 33.
52. Crowley, *Liber AL vel Legis*, 54.

freedom for each individual. Many and subtle are the attempts to enslave another even in the name of assistance needed or given. Are we as free men and women to allow this in an order dedicated to the freedom of each individual? If your true love enslaves you, or your brother likewise, can you cast him or her out? Can you strike your own blows in your own intimate life to gain your own freedom?

Also, there is this point: hasty and ill-considered help could precipitate a crisis in yours and another person's life. This too has its uses for growth but perhaps you should be prepared for unforeseen results. The true Magician controls as many variables as he can.

In the article by Crowley, "The Revival of Magick,"[53] we see some comments at the end about "perfect love, perfect faith, perfect trust." This attitude is probably behind the injunction from the First Degree which you cited, but it can be worked by an advanced Magician. The rest of us do not have controlled emotions, and are likely to react when the "taker" among us takes all and then turns and spits in our face. If the emotions that will be caused by such an event would be too much for you, then perhaps you should be more prudent. As a note for students, the old woman mentioned was Crowley's mother-in-law, and when the events were happening, he didn't exactly react as described. He threw her out of the house at one point. She encouraged Rose, his wife, in her dipsomania and even supplied her with drink. It was only later on that he could win to such detachment as is described in the article. Some people would hold the resentment for life!

Think carefully, then, how can you accomplish either your own finite or infinite will if you are hobbled by the needs of another? Are you going to be truly free? Would some aid not lead to more aid later? If you do not have the courage to turn your back on a crippling dependence of someone else on you, then perhaps you are only drifting, a prey to your own emotions and tendencies and weaknesses and blind to the Light of Liberty. Also, perhaps you cannot really apply the scourge of Love, which is sometimes as necessary as the softness and ease of Love.

---

53. Crowley, *The Revival of Magick and Other Essays*, Eds. Hymenaeus Beta and R. Kaczynski (Las Vegas, NV: New Falcon. 1998), 13-39.

Plunge deeply then, into your own unconscious and dig up all your motives! Dear Brother, may you settle your problem in the Light of Thelema, which is a Law of Liberty and Love.

    Love is the law, love under will.

Fraternally,
Meral

Carete Fratres et Sorores,[54]

    Do what thou wilt shall be the whole of the Law.

The three gunas are the three qualities of nature, or of Prakriti. In Sanskrit guna means "thread" or "quality." In our astrology we divided up the twelve signs into these gunas — Thus: rajas is a quality of Aries, Cancer, Libra and Capricorn; tamas is a quality of Taurus, Leo, Scorpio, and Aquarius; and sattva is a quality of Gemini, Virgo, Sagittarius, and Pisces.

However, the *Bhagavad-Gita* states that the gunas are in everything but that at any one time one or the other predominates. The gunas are shown very well in Atu X of the Tarot as the figures that revolve on the outer rim of the wheel.

Since their description is very clear in the *Bhagavad-Gita*, let me quote from that work.[55]

I suggest that you review your horoscope and analyze which of the three gunas is most prominent in your nature. Rajas = cardinal signs, tamas = fixed signs, sattwa = common signs. Some people have these gunas quite evenly balanced and so may at any one time, behave according to one or the other of the gunas. Others will have a heavy balance towards one or the others of

---

54. Originally published in: Phyllis Seckler, *In the Continuum* 1.9 (1977): 7-19.
55. In the original essay, Seckler quoted three chapters of the *Bhagavad-Gita* at great length, but we have chosen not to reproduce them here. The relevant doctrines are discussed in chapters XIV ("The Book of Religion by Separation of the Qualities"), XVII ("The Book of Religion by the Threefold Kinds of Faith"), and XVIII ("The Book of Religion by Deliverance and Renunciation"). Seckler relied on the Swami Prabhavananda and Christopher Isherwood translation: *Bhagavad-Gita: The Song of God* (Hollywood, CA: Marcel Rodd, 1944), but there are, of course, also a number of good more recent translations.– Eds.

the gunas and in that case, the majority of their actions will lean towards the guna which is accented in the horoscope.

Another note is added in the *Gita*, that the person who is heavily tamas, may try to become a little more of the rajas personality in his striving, and the rajas may help himself by incorporating more of the sattwa. The latter seems to lead more closely to the highest aims of the soul.

This matter is also foreshadowed in the alchemical process by the representation of sulphur as rajas, of salt as tamas, and of mercury as sattwa. More on this can be studied in *The Book of Thoth* under the Xth Atu.

When the *Bhagavad-Gita* talks in such terms as non-attachment, we as Thelemites must remember that the same thing is asked of us by Nuit in Chapter I of *Liber Legis*, v. 44, "For pure will, unassuaged of purpose, delivered from the lust of result, is every way perfect."[56]

There are many other parallels. To obey the scriptures would mean in our particular language to obey the injunctions in *Liber Legis*.

Further, you must realize that these gunas are on the rim of the wheel and in our cycles of life and death, we experience a surfeit of each of them until we can learn to arrive at the center of the wheel.

And if you read all this correctly, you will discover that there is a positive and negative side to each guna. At first glance there seems to be no hope for the action of the tamas type. But think a little further, and you will see that the world must have those who farm and who supply the commodities. What would we do without the modern business leader as suggested by the rajas guna to get the products of labor to us? We can't all be a priest or prophet. But the qualities best expressed by sattwa can be worked at and a definite effort made to incorporate them into the life. Then the positive side of the particular guna can be used instead of the negative. This is true also of each astrological sign. There is no sense in manifesting the most negative side of the gunas or of the signs as then you heap bad karma on your head and perhaps trip yourself up from true attainment. What is will

---

56. Crowley, *Liber AL vel Legis*, 31.

all about? You have a finite will which indicates what kind of work you do in the world so that you can eat and have a roof over your head. Once this duty to yourself is taken care of, then you can concentrate on the infinite will, which is the same for everyone. At this point in our progress it is called the Knowledge and Conversation of the Holy Guardian Angel and we are only concerned with one step at a time.

As in *Liber LXV*, Cap. 5, v. 49, "Let not the dwellers in Thebai and the temples thereof prate ever of the Pillars of Hercules and the Ocean of the West. Is not the Nile a beautiful water?"[57]

Life is a school, and we are here to learn. If we don't learn then we can expect the same lesson again and again. That is the way karma works. It is also the way that the transit of Saturn in the horoscope works, which is the working out of karma in a single lifetime.

The study of the gunas should then be a help to discover the finite will and a clue as to the lessons we must learn.

You know, Crowley had six planets in tamas or fixed signs. When he claimed he was the laziest man in the world in his autobiography, he was telling the truth about it. Also, with so much tamas, what happened to him in his youth had an indelible impression. He never really got over it, and his hatred for Christianity showed up again and again in his writings, and in spite of his Libran nature, which seeks to balance things, the hatred often got the better of him because of the heavy emphasis on tamas. It is very hard to change a tamas type individual as they have too much inertia. What is learned early lasts for the rest of the incarnation.

However, Crowley also had the genius to realize some of the things that were wrong with his character expression in this particular lifetime and to work on them. He worked hard at magick and yoga and if he can attain with so much hampering him, then perhaps you and I can take hope. The key is to work hard and to Know Thyself, so that your map for your progress through life is clearly understood. There would be no sense in working against who you are!

As it says in *Liber Legis*, Cap. II, v. 58: "Yea! deem not of

---

57. Crowley, *The Holy Books of Thelema* (York Beach, ME: Samuel Weiser, 1988), 81.

change: ye shall be as ye are, & not other."[58] But we can be the positive and constructive sides of ourselves and we need not give in to the negative states which work against the *will*.

By now you should know that Thelema does not mean to do as you please. This ought to be obvious to those who have joined us but I must report that it is not always the case. This is one reason why some beginners fail in the first year and then are dropped from the order.

To do what you will means the most strict and most severe self-discipline. It is not imposed from without but at the same time it must be imposed by yourself from within. Naturally, there are plenty of would-be occult students who do not wish to do this. How then, can we call them Thelemites, no matter what they say about their feelings on the outside?

Let us face it, the people who do not wish to impose the discipline of the accomplishment of their wills (whether finite or infinite) will remain slaves. Those who can work hard and who have the one-pointed will arrive at the Joy as promised in *Liber AL vel Legis*.

This has been a long letter but I hope it is helpful to you in your Going and in your Understanding of yourself.

Love is the law, love under will.

Fraternally,
Meral

Carete Fratres et Sorores,[59]

Do what thou wilt shall be the whole of the Law.

Where does one draw the line between the freedom of the individual and the recognition of authority in a Thelemic occult order? The final answer to this must be a result of the work of each individual, but I might point out a few ideas.

The first thing you may need to ask yourself is why did you join? All motives for joining are valid except that you ought not to fool yourself as to your true motive and believe in a false motive

---

58. Crowley, *Liber AL vel Legis*, 47.
59. Originally published in: Phyllis Seckler, *In the Continuum* 2.1 (1978): 1-6.

as an ego- or face-saving attempt. Be honest with yourself or else the map you are making for your path towards the peak of the accomplishment of your True Will will not work well enough.

You may have wished the society of others who think along some of the same lines that you do, or you may hope to rise in your chosen occult society and become a leader of men; you may want Power. You might have the ambition to place initials after your name such as those who have obtained an M.A. or a Ph.D. You may be imbued with other enthusiasms, and be thinking in terms of evolution and the use of your talents for the betterment of humanity. You may have in mind that you have to reincarnate again, and that you would wish to incarnate in a more perfect society, and that the work you do now will bear fruit in the future lives. You may wish to bring more freedom to humanity and of course to yourself. Or you may mistake license for freedom, and may have joined because you think that you can then do as you like under the sanction of an occult order. Or perhaps you are looking for a guru or teacher and an occult order seems a good place to find one. You may think that the order you have joined will aid you in achieving the Knowledge and Conversation of the Holy Guardian Angel.

Some of these reasons for joining an occult order will be aided and some will be hindered by that order itself.

Let us suppose that you are looking for a guru and have thought that a high ranking member of the order should be your teacher because of his grade. Not necessarily—as some are good at steering a ship of state who are unable to teach. However, if it is a guru you wish, does he come up to some of the standards Crowley wrote of in many places? Let me quote a little from Letter 61 in *Magick Without Tears*, where he discusses the A∴A∴ and by inference something about the O.T.O.

> In our own case, though Our authority is at least as absolute as that of the Pope and the Church of Rome, it does not confer upon me any power transferable to others by any act of Our will. Our own authority came to Us because it was earned, and when We confer grades upon other people Our gift is entirely nugatory unless the beneficiary has won his spurs.

> To put it in a slightly different form of words: Any given degree is, as it were, a seal upon a precise attainment; and although it may please Us to explain: the secret or secrets of any given degree or degrees to any particular person or persons, it is not of the slightest effect unless he prove in his own person the ability to perform those functions which all We have done is to give him the right to perform and the knowledge how to perform.[60]

To the bewilderment of many, Crowley may have given degrees in emergency situations which have become nugatory with the passage of time because of the behavior of the candidate. Does such a person fit your idea of a guru or teacher? Has he won his spurs or done the work? Have you tested him by asking questions and finding then if he knows what he is talking about? Does he display Initiated Wisdom? Has he answered your questions and given you a little more enlightenment? Has he helped you? Has he displayed brotherly love towards you?

It is so necessary that you yourself apply the acid test as too many in this time of great confusion pretend to degrees which they do not qualify for in either the A∴A∴ or the O.T.O. We have many such examples around us, and we are likely to wallow in even greater darkness until the ideas of the Master Therion and *The Book of the Law* can be put into effect.

If you are socially minded and belong to a Thelemic occult order just for the company of others, the Law is for all. Thus it is incumbent upon all of us to learn how to live by the precepts of *Liber Legis*. You should supply yourself with one of the better commentaries of this Book and study it carefully.

Please notice that I said a Thelemic occult order. Let us gain a little perspective. The O.T.O. is only one of the great orders of antiquity to accept the Law of Thelema. There will be others. There will even be new Thelemic orders which might be moved to apply those things written about the O.T.O. in *The Blue Equinox* to their own work. The A∴A∴ is more truly Crowley's own order and does not suffer from the ills of sociability and politics as does

---

60. Crowley, *Magick Without Tears* (Tempe, AZ: New Falcon Publications, 1991), 374.

the O.T.O. You should make a very careful comparison of the two as you are working on your map for your own guidance.

Because we live in a time of emergency and confusion, too many people have been able to abuse privileges and their behavior may curtail the real expression of freedom of others in the order. Too many may have been elevated to high grades who have not deserved the honor. Both orders are full of beginners and very short on adepts. Crowley was adamant that beginners should not work with each other or even know each other, as you can see from reading in *Magick Without Tears*. It is too much like the blind leading the blind.

When a student is not too highly developed, he or she is apt to look to others for leadership. This is the way of all humanity. Further, a great deal of harm is worked in any occult order by expectations people have for others. They fail to see that the expectation should be applied only to themselves. So when you get no inspiration from those who are supposed to lead, and no real leadership and no model for you to base your own behavior on, you are only too ready to quit.

Can it be that you have been behaving as a slave? In more modern terms, we have called such people sheep. It may be that there will be many difficult times over leadership — this is bound to be, because we are pioneers. However, remember this: It is a mark of cowardice and weakness to blame others for what happens to you. Each of us is the cause of the effects which we enjoy or hate. The causes of our karmic effects are facets of our own original nature and this includes the way you behave towards others and the way you think of them. Your own causes or modus operandi bring reactions from the Universe, which is defined as all that you can be conscious of. If you are unhappy with your own events of life and the effects of your own causes then your behavior needs to be modified. You need to work on the causes you set in motion to produce the effects that you dislike or that make you sad. You can't modify others, either by force or by criticism, not even those whom you object to, for they have a right to be what they are, whether you think it is for their own good or ill, or whether for the good or ill of your favored Thelemic occult order.

If your True Will is being hampered by other persons in an occult order or in outside life, you have the option of moving off and away, or you can fight, or you can modify yourself if your thoughts and actions do not truly express your own True Will.

Please note further that for every action there is a price to pay. "Everything must be paid for to the uttermost farthing," as Crowley states in *Magick in Theory and Practice*.[61] You need to calculate what the cost of your action is going to be or is, after you have acted, and whether you want to pay this price? The price may bring happiness and joy to you, or it may bring dissatisfaction, sorrow and unhappiness. If you are experiencing a good many of the negative emotions, the cause is yourself; you have lost your way, and that this is a signal for you to do something about it, a signal to change. As *Liber Legis* states: "We are not for the poor and sad: the lords of the earth are our kinsfolk" in Cap. II, v. 18.[62] Many similar verses tell you that this is the way you should look at it.

When you are unhappy, dissatisfied with life and yourself, disgruntled, fault finding of others, and so on, you have lost the golden thread which leads to the K. and C. of your H.G.A., for He expresses Himself as Joy. Simply then, if the price—the effects of your action—bring joy and happiness as by-products, then you are on the right track.

There are some actions or causes which do not bring joy immediately. Think of the disciplines the artist or the expert on yoga must go through. Think how the recluse must pay the price of loneliness, or the overly sociable person may lose all contact with his Inner Self. A selfish person may lose his loved ones; a hot temper may carry a price of injury to yourself or others. The list goes on. Wisdom consists in using your own character traits "under will" to further your own purpose. If one or several difficult traits are rampant they can destroy you or the Expression of your True Will. If you baulk at a difficult price or task to accomplish this True Will, you do not wish to expend the energy, you may bring about a split between the expression of energy as opposed to the true purpose of your existence. This blocks the Will and the end result will be failure. Thelema is not for the failures in life, Thelema means a great deal of self-discipline and work. Not someone else's — whoever he may be or whatever Grade he may have in either Thelemic order — but your own.

---

61. Crowley, *Magick Liber ABA*, 245.
62. Crowley, *Liber AL vel Legis*, 40.

Lazy people not willing to harness their own powers become slaves to their lower selves. They could scarcely realize the promise and the emancipation which is Thelema. They do not know what freedom is. They confuse what is real authority and power, and what is spurious.

I bring these various points to your mind so that you may realize finally that the leadership you desire is your own higher self. There is actually no other leader, guru, or teacher who can give you all of the help you may need. When someone you look up to has seemed to fail you it might be that you have been playing that old game of projection again. For a simple explanation of this please read again the article in *In the Continuum*, Vol. I, No. 3.[63] No leader or teacher can be perfect and no leader can carry the projections of everyone.

Further, it may be that a teacher can set up signboards or give good advice, but he cannot do the work for you. He can only guide the beginner a little way. The true teacher is the H.G.A. and when you have learned to listen to His voice, you will need no other. You will scarcely need anyone in a position of authority in an occult order unless it is your will to work with that order in some fashion. Remember that your will is single, it is not a mass of unrelated and conflicting impulses.

Now then, if a leader of the occult order of your choice does not represent the ideals of the order as a whole, those ideals which have been written down and which have inspired you to join, what are you going to do about it? Do you acquiesce in his leadership, shutting your eyes to actions which harm the image of the order to which you choose to belong, and thereby harming you, if you would but think of it? How do you prevent yourself from being tarred by the same brush as any leader may tar himself with? If a leader or teacher fails the order which he or she represents, how do you set things right when you cannot interfere with this person according to Thelemic law?

Since no person in authority is perfect, you must look to yourself and realize that the Holy Guardian Angel represents perfection for yourself. If you are not far enough advanced to gain even a part of this realization then you will need to recognize that

---

63. Reprinted on pages 8-13 in the present volume – Eds.

Aleister Crowley and what he wrote is your leader and your guru. Not Crowley the man, the only too fallible human; not Crowley who represents the projections that you have performed of your own traits and ideals, but Crowley the avatar of the Æon; the adept who has shown humanity the next step, who has worked out the practices to be done to achieve this next step, who has taken down by dictation *The Book of the Law* which you have willed to make the Law of your own life.

The more truly integrated humans and adepts or those who are approaching these states that we have among us in either of the present Thelemic orders, the more chance that order will have of growing and enlarging its scope.

Well, maybe I have been laboring a point, but the point I am driving at is this: Your will includes affiliation with a Thelemic occult order? You deplore certain aspects of this order? Its leadership is not what you could hope for? You think because of this you may not have the freedom to accomplish your will? The answers to these questions lie within yourself. The most potent answer is: perfect yourself, work and earn your degrees. If you are truly interested in this occult order, you are its representative. What if you should become one of the leaders or teachers in the future should this be your will? If so, will you be able to put into practice all that you have perfected; can you become something better than what is now manifesting? Can you bring to fruition on this earth those ideals which you have tried to demand or ask of others? Can you become a living example of the ideals and thought of Thelema? This will be up to you!

Through your own work then, the freedom you generate will be your own; the authority you recognize will be in accordance with your own will. Neither freedom nor the demand for the recognition of authority can be given to you nor foisted upon you unless you will it.

Love is the law, love under will.

Soror Meral

Carete Fratres et Sorores,[64]

Do what thou wilt shall be the whole of the Law.

Here is the story that was promised to you about the rescue of Crowley's literary remains from the hands of the State of California. This is a story that has been told in fragments to many of you, but somehow it always seemed to lose some of its interesting details in the telling as it is long and involved. Complete records have been kept of every event so that you need not wonder how much of this tale has been embroidered upon and twisted out of its truth. You may rest assured that this account is as accurate as it is possible for one person to make it — one blessed with a very good memory as well as being the keeper of copious records.

First let me say that since the death of Crowley, I became very interested in preserving his works. It seemed to me that if many copies of his writings were spread around the world, that some of them would survive when and if a dark age came upon us. At this stage in history it was very difficult to get Crowley published as he was mostly unknown. It was due to the efforts of Karl Germer and Israel Regardie and a few others that now his genius is being recognized.

At the time of Crowley's death there were still many important manuscripts that had had few or no copies made, and had not been published at all.

Crowley died on December 1, 1947. Agape Lodge was the only working Lodge of the O.T.O. at that time, so far as is known. We had been working with Crowley for many years, sending money for his publishing and other needs. Since it was the depression years, many of us could hardly earn enough to keep a roof over our heads and food in our mouths. But it was Karl Germer who raised over $25,000 for publications and for Crowley's support. For many years he had sent at least $200 monthly to Crowley. There was no one more devoted.

For quite a few years Karl had been Grand Treasurer of the Ordo Templi Orientis and was so named in Crowley's will. Karl later exclaimed that after Crowley's death, there were three tons of materials sent to him from England. He moved these

---

64. Originally published in: Phyllis Seckler, *In the Continuum* 2.2 (1978): 5-24.

literary materials to a house in Hampton, New Jersey, and there began the work of filing and record keeping. Before the materials had been sent to the United States a copy had been made of everything in manuscript form. Afterwards, Karl and Gerald Yorke collaborated on sending each other a copy of anything that Crowley had written which the other did not have. There was also a third person in England who obtained many copies of various of Crowley's writings. Mr. Yorke later sent much of his collection to the Warburg in London where it remains in the library there to this day.

But I did not know of all this, and many of my actions and concern were based on the belief that there was only one copy of the unpublished writings of Crowley.

Then Karl proclaimed himself as the Outer Head of the Order (O.H.O.). I can remember the disappointment of many IXth degree members that they had not been allowed to vote for the O.H.O., as seemingly instructions existed that this was to be done a year and a day after Crowley's death.

When Karl was in Hampton, New Jersey, I wrote about my concern that some of the unpublished works of Crowley might be lost to the world unless some copies were made. He agreed about my concern and the upshot of this correspondence was that I began to type copies. The first summer I typed part of the *Confessions*. The second summer, in 1952, I typed *The Vision and the Voice* with all its complicated notes in the text. I was glad of my knowledge of the qabalah, for it aided me in spotting typist errors in the manuscripts. The third summer I typed *Magick Without Tears*. The two later typings were done on multilith plates which were sent to Karl in Hampton, and there he had the assistance of two devoted members of the Order to make reproductions.

Since I was also going to College during those years and raising a family of three single-handed, you can imagine what a project this must have been for me. But I had the summers free to carry on this work and even though the children milled about me with their noise and childish concerns, I was still able to complete a book within the summer vacation time. Karl was deeply grateful for my labor and efforts, and gifted me with Crowley publications from time to time. Since I had also had a chance to type everything carefully, and to learn from it in that way, I was more than rewarded.

Jane Wolfe, my teacher for many years, helped me to correct any errors. In fact, Jane was used to driving out to my small house every week to do this work, or to visit in years and times when I wasn't so engaged. But this is another long story and I hope that someday I can tell it also.

Soon after *Magick Without Tears* was printed Karl came to California. He had been about seven years in Hampton, and in California he at first did not have a regular base of operations. After about two years or a little more he found a house in West Point, about six miles out from the town.

He then set up the library again, which had been packed away, and engaged himself in sending Crowley's writings to various publishers and had several things done in a professional way. As I look back on these events, I suspect it was he who was mentioned in *Liber LXV*, Cap. V, v. 20, "Thou shalt dwell among the people as a precious diamond among cloudy diamonds, and crystals, and pieces of glass. Only the eye of the just merchant shall behold thee, and plunging in his hand shall single thee out and glorify thee before men."[65]

Karl had been a merchant of machinery during most of his working life and had traveled a good deal in this vocation.

Karl died in late October of 1962, and I was almost the first one to be informed by Sascha of his death. This was because Karl and I had always remained on good terms. I did what I could to help Sascha with the various business matters that came up after Karl's death, but incurred her wrath because of what I said about him in a letter to Marcelo Motta. She had given me this correspondence to take care of but when I criticized Karl for being unbalanced on the subject of magical attacks, she was furious. But then, Crowley and Jane had offered the same sort of criticism on this subject as well, as I was to find out later. I had the policy of showing everything to her, perhaps naively expecting that she could appreciate extreme openness and honesty, and also hoping that she would not display the usual suspicious attitudes which had been rife in hers and Karl's behavior. I was wrong, of course, and she showed me the door and carried an enmity towards me to her grave.

---

65. Crowley, *The Holy Books of Thelema*, 78.

Karl did not expect to die; he was very certain that he was going to live another eleven years. This attitude shows up in his correspondence up to the very end. Therefore, the will he made to dispose of Crowley's literary remains remained unchanged. This will provided that all of the Crowley materials should go to the Heads of the Ordo Templi Orientis and that Sascha Germer and Frederick Mellinger between them should act as executors of the will. All personal property was to be left to Sascha.

At the time of Karl's death no one knew where Mellinger was. After a good deal of difficulty Sascha discovered his whereabouts in his home in Germany through the help of the Swiss Ordo Templi Orientis, headed by Herr Metzger and which had been operating under a valid charter from Karl for quite some time.

A correspondence was begun between Sascha and Frederick, but the latter was deeply suspicious of the value of coming to California to help with the disposal of the Crowley material, as he had been unjustly and suspiciously treated by both Karl and Sascha in the past. Soon after this, Mellinger died and Sascha was left with the task of discovering what to do about the A.C. and Germer library, correspondence and other materials. She disliked me so would no longer have me about, and probably I had done the wrong thing to tell her that on the evening of the news of Karl's death, I had asked for help from other planes and had been told clearly to care for the Crowley-Germer library. Since this was an inner prompting, Sascha had her doubts about that kind of instruction, as well she might.

The upshot of Mellinger's defection from such a duty was that Sascha was left quite helpless and was not really suited for such a task. Consequently, even though she considered several alternatives, everything was left as it was at Karl's death.

One of my instructions, which I passed on to Sascha, was that she was not to let anyone in Southern California hear of Karl's death. Intuitionally, I was alarmed that all the materials should be guarded only by one helpless widow and I felt that something was terribly wrong in Southern California. I was to be proven right about this later. Also, Sascha was suspicious of almost everyone, especially if they belonged to the former Agape Lodge. She even repelled an offer of help from Dr. [Gabriel] Montenegro [Vargas], who had been a member of the Lodge and a good friend of Karl's.

Five years later the news of Karl's death had trickled to Southern California, and the upshot of this was that a group of people came to Sascha's door over the Labor Day weekend of 1967 and announced that they were the O.T.O. Sascha fell for the trick and opened the door. Immediately they blew some kind of gas in her face and overpowered her, an easy thing to do, and administered some sort of shot which put her out completely, and then took their time to ransack the library on the second floor. Before she was completely overpowered, she had a glimpse of the woman's hands, but not of her face as the woman of the group seems to have worn a hat which overshadowed the face.

This group took all of the O.T.O. rituals and other secret instructions. They took many first editions, *The Book of Thoth* being one of them, and they took Crowley's magical robes and his book of sigils which presumably still had much power in them. At this time none of the O.T.O. rituals or other secret instructions had been published. Now, everything of this sort is published. They had previously cut Sascha's telephone wire before the attack so it was a little time after she recovered before she was able to contact the Sheriff. The local Constable arrived and Sascha poured out her tale. They could see the way the library looked—much was still remaining—and as Sascha talked more and more, they put her story down to the wanderings of the demented mind of a lady who had been alone too long. They did not take fingerprints but took some snapshots of the state of the library.

Then Sascha immediately got on the phone after it had been repaired and wired to me that [one of Soror Meral's family members] had done this deed. Here is the text from her telegram:

"I request that all stolen goods, stolen books papers are returned without delay. I accuse you of long time conspiracy toward me getting entrance to my person under false pretension Sept. 3; attacking me personally harming me impairing my eye sight enduring; robbing with help of three other men the library completely; destroying willfully all library furniture; breaking open wooden strong boxes cleaning out their contents; being held against my will by one man under sedatives against my will during the whole time bound of hands and feet. Mrs. Germer."

You can imagine my extreme shock when this was read to me over the telephone. When I recovered, I wired back that she was mistaken and that not one person of my family would touch one hair of her head. This telegram got to her, but when I wrote a letter to follow it up with complete details that [the family member] had been in church at the time of the robbery and that we had witnesses to prove it, she sent the letter back unopened.

Naturally, I was alarmed that [the family member], an innocent person if there ever was one, and completely uninterested in Crowley literary remains, would be harmed by these insane accusations. I resolved to conduct as much of an investigation as I could about who might be responsible for these thefts.

As a result of my letters to various people, I discovered the whereabouts of a former member of Agape Lodge, one M.[66] who had been very active in Thelema for very many years. She kindly visited me and we talked and talked about the above event and she let me know about some thefts from her own apartment. She had been robbed twice after the death of her husband in the summer of 1965. The first robbery led her to suspect that it was the work of a former student of hers, one J.B., as the apartment showed no sign of forced entry and J.B. held a pass key, as she had been a trusted student for 10 years. Further, when there were two copies of anything, only one was taken and the other was left intact for further use by M.

The lock on the apartment was changed and then a second robbery took place. This time a back window had been jimmied open and much more was taken, including O.T.O. rituals which had been in M.'s possession. This was in 1966 and a little later Israel Regardie's library was also subjected to thievery when Dr. Regardie was out of the house. The fourth robbery was of the house in West Point.

My conversation with M. in due time revealed the fact that due to my advice to Sascha at the time of Karl's death, no one in Southern California had been informed of the event. I had been so busy taking care of my own affairs that I had no knowledge of what my former associates were doing there and had gotten out of touch.

But when M.'s husband had died and when J.B. somehow got wind of Karl's death, probably when she made a trip to England, she proposed to M. that they should start an O.T.O. Lodge together. M. thought, rightly, that she had not been authorized to

---

66. Mildred Burlingame.

do so and backed out. But J.B. went ahead and formed her own group, which was called The Solar Lodge and drew members from nearby U.S.C. In time they owned two or three pieces of property in L.A. near 30th St. and Vermont, and some desert property near Blythe, California.

During the course of my investigation I also wrote to Grady [McMurtry] who resided in Washington, D.C. at the time. As a result of our long and lengthy correspondence from December of 1968 to April of 1969, we decided that we could start a Thelemic College together. He learned for the first time that Karl had been dead for several years, and I learned that he held letters of authorization in regards to the O.T.O. from Crowley which also named him as Caliph and successor to Karl. I sent for him and he arrived in California on April 29, 1969.

In May and June of that same year, the members of the Solar Lodge got themselves into trouble and their story hit the papers across the country.

A little boy in their group, who didn't really want to stay on the hot desert during the summer months, set fire to one of their buildings and as punishment, they locked him in a box where he stayed for many days (accounts differ as to just how long). But it was very sure that the box was very hot and that his potty was seldom changed, thus drawing many flies. He was discovered by some local people who had come by to buy an advertised donkey. Immediately there was the sheriff and publicity and the arrest of the members of the commune. J.B., her husband, the trusted first man of the group and a few others escaped across state lines. The rest of the commune stood trial and the F.B.I. got on the case as J.B. was also wanted for the cruel and impossible treatment of the boy after the fire. She had actually held a match to his hands afterwards and asked how would like to be burned up, along with other threats.[67]

When the story hit the papers, M. and Grady and I got together, and what was previously merely suspicion on our part became more and more close to true fact that all of the thefts had occurred from the same group. Grady drove to L.A. and

---

67. Since Soror Meral published this account much new information on the Solar Lodge and its activities has come to light. A contrasting perspective of the events can be found in Frater Shiva, *Inside Solar Lodge: Outside the Law* (York Beach, ME: Teitan Press, 2007), and Frater Shiva, *Inside Solar Lodge: Behind the Veil* (Los Lunas, NM: Desert Star Temple, 2012). – Eds.

made an investigation of their house on Menlo Avenue. When he returned we both drove to the desert near Blythe to see what we could uncover.

We discovered the property and a remaining shed on it where a local old man was conducting a sale of various items. There was an enlarged photo of Crowley glowering over the scene and a few items which showed they had studied the qabalah, kept diaries, and done various practices. These were indeed the same persons who had the property in L.A., and they presented themselves as an O.T.O. Lodge.

Later, through some conversations with former members of the group, we discovered that a small room near the attic temple was at one time piled high with boxes and books when formerly it had been nearly empty. Also, this witness told us that in October after the Germer thefts, Crowley's robe was pulled out of a box and shown off to the group, and J.B. was heard to remark that they had a right to it.

Another witness identified some of the rare books they were selling for high prices in their bookstore, "The Eye of Horus" in L.A., up to the time of the scandal about the boy in the box. Unfortunately, when Grady and I heard about the bookstore and went to investigate, the group was already gone and the place was shut up and vacant.

Still later, another witness told us of their operation on the desert and how much of the material had been stored in the house that had been burned down by the little boy. He also stated that he had access to the advanced rituals and had read them through. He gave us these facts when J.B., her husband, and others were still at large but were being hunted by the F.B.I.

The law was not interested in prosecuting for the thefts that occurred; they were only interested in the case of the boy in the box. Therefore, when J.B. and husband stood trial, they managed to squirm out of the charges and got off with probation. We never could get the law to take an interest in the thefts. Besides, our evidence was pretty slim in their opinion, since we had not caught them with the stolen goods.

Then I wrote a letter about all this to Sascha, and this time I had no return address on the envelope. There is now evidence that she had opened the envelope and read the story, but she did not contact us. There was nothing to do but wait.

Grady and I investigated the possibility of a lawsuit, but had to back down when the price of such action was revealed to us. Further, we might have had a difficult time in court. However, the then D.A. of Calaveras County, a Mr. Airola, gave us the advice that it might be better to wait for Sascha's death and then see if we could rescue Crowley's literary remains from the estate.

There seemed to us nothing else we could do, but from time to time we would drive to West Point and enquire about Sascha. We also asked the local Constable to let us know when she died. This he did not do. We also had a conference with the Sheriff about the thefts and saw the pictures they had taken of the library.

Sascha died on April 1 or 2 of 1975, but it was a year before we heard of it, as 1975 was not a year when such action seemed to be possible. We were facing other troubles.

H.[68] and I drove to West Point in late April of 1976, and it was then we discovered that Sascha had been dead a year, and that the house had been vandalized three times. Since it was difficult or almost impossible to lock it up, it may have been vandalized more than reported.

But now I must backtrack and tell you of another peculiar incident which fits into this story.

For quite some time Grady had felt that there was an astral watcher in his study. I too felt uncomfortable in this room. Also, one night when he was away, my name had been called very forcibly and had awakened me from a deep slumber. I could not figure out who might have called me, whether the person was living or dead, and enquiries among my friends yielded nothing.

Then a young friend of ours, K., also had a psychic feeling that some presence was in this same room. He tried to clear it out but was unsuccessful. After this I half-heartedly did a Banishing Ritual several times but was mostly curious as to what was there and remarked to Grady that it would be nice if we knew a psychic who could tell what was going on.

One evening after yoga classes which Grady taught and I attended, Grady arrived with a young woman. She had also been to the same classes and had complained bitterly about how tired she was, as she had spent the previous night chanting in a Tibetan yoga retreat and had had only three hours of sleep, and

---

68. Helen Parsons Smith.

then had worked that very day. She excused herself to join Grady in his room and the door was shut. Afterwards she came out looking very pleased with herself and thanked Grady. For what? I wondered. Shortly after they left for Berkeley.

The next week when Grady was again in Dublin, I asked him about the incident and he stated that she had gone into the room to see about the presence there, as she claimed to be psychic. She had ignored the room itself where the presence had been felt by three of us, but went into the bathroom and looked into the mirror. There she stated that she had seen a psychic vampire dressed in white and seated in profile, who had then turned her head towards the young woman and two long teeth at each end of the mouth showed very clearly. It seems it must have been a quite horrendous creature. At this, the young woman took the bracelet off her wrist and struck the mirror many times while she chanted a banishing of some sort—something she had been taught by the Tibetan Buddhists, I think. She then put the bracelet back on her wrist, the apparition seemed to be gone enough to her satisfaction, and they both proceeded to Berkeley where they contacted another young woman who pretended to be psychic. The bracelet was presented to the second young woman to examine and she confirmed the idea that there was a psychic vampire attached to it.

At this piece of nonsense that Grady had been telling me, I laughed and said she had seen herself in the mirror. The lack of knowledge of psychology and psychometry shown by this incident was abysmal, to say the least.

Well, at this, I literally gritted my teeth and said to myself that I needed a real psychic; one who had no knowledge of me or of Grady or of my house and circumstances.

In early March of 1976, the health food store about three blocks from my house was robbed. I was very friendly there as I was a steady customer. A few days after the robbery when I was in the store to buy some supplies, the ladies told me that the day after the robbery a young woman had walked into the store and learned about the event from their excitement. She had then told them what the robber looked like, how he had crouched down behind the counter, in what part of the establishment he had found the money, and which door he had entered. She also pointed out where the fingerprints were to be found. Then she went on to describe events and circumstances of the ladies in the store which she could not possibly have known, as she was a complete stranger.

When I heard all this I enquired after her name and they were uncertain. I asked them to please get her phone number the next time they saw her and that I wanted her to establish whether there was anything in my house from other dimensions. I cautioned them not to describe my troubles or me at all. They were just to say that I would like to contact her. Since they had been very friendly to me over the years, they promised that this would be done. And it seemed to me that this was the psychic I had asked for!

Then one week before H. and I drove to West Point, I wrote to Marcelo Motta and asked if he knew of Mrs. Germer's welfare. I was to regret the exchange of letters that came from this later.

H. and I got together and resolved to find out for ourselves how Mrs. Germer was doing and maybe, we said, we should have done it last year? As it turned out, we should indeed have enquired about her sooner.

When we drove to West Point and conferred with the local Constable, we discovered that Sascha had been dead since April 1 or 2 of 1975, and that the house had been vandalized three times that they knew of. We then drove to see the Coroner and Public Administrator, Mr. Gualdoni. He told us that the library upstairs was strewn with papers, the bookcase pried away from the wall and malicious mischief wrought. He denied having any boxes of Germer effects as had been hinted at by another person, and stated he had only letters of relatives or people whom he might contact to discover if they were heirs to the property, as Sascha had died intestate and no will of Mr. Germer was to be found. He also stated he had a curious ring in his possession which had been found in Sascha's purse and as he described it, H. and I knew it was Crowley's seal ring. We stated that the materials in the library belonged to the O.T.O., and that they had been willed to the Order by Karl.

Mr. Gualdoni hinted that we should perhaps have the books and papers and I stated my worry about them being discovered by certain types of people and told again the story of the thefts in the Germer house. He then referred us to Mr. Robyn, the lawyer in charge of such matters for San Andreas County. It turned out that Mr. Robyn was the very same lawyer Grady and I had consulted previously when he had a private practice, and whose price for suing Mrs. Germer for the Crowley materials had been too high for us.

The gist of our consultations with Mr. Robyn was that we would have to prove Karl had a will and produce it. Since Sascha had left no will, the property would become the property of the State of California and would be sold to pay Sascha's and Karl's last debts for illnesses and burial. The remainder would be used to pay Mr. Gualdoni for certain services, and then what was left would revert to the State. Even if Karl's will could be found the matter would have to go through probate court and even so, the settlement would be difficult and uncertain as Grady would have to prove he was the head of the O.T.O.

He admitted that the personal effects could be sold separately, and this included all books and papers on the property. He told us something of how these were put on public sale and the proceeds would revert to the State.

When we expressed our deep concern over the welfare of materials which did not belong to Sascha nor to Karl, as they had been willed to the O.T.O. from the beginning, and that these things should be placed in a secure storage, he was uncertain of how to proceed. We asked if we could go to the property and clean things up and see to it that they got into a locked storage, even though they might remain in the hands of the State there. I offered to pay for the storage. He answered that we could not go to the property unless Mr. Gualdoni or the Sheriff was with us. We stated we would keep the law and could this event then be decided upon? He stated that no one had any time to go there to clean things up. Both Mr. Gualdoni and the Sheriff were very busy persons. I offered to pay them for their time. I asked whether the house could not be vandalized again and perhaps burned down. He admitted that this might happen. A notice had been posted at the house by Mr. Gualdoni that no one was to have admittance, but that hadn't made much difference to anyone who wished to enter.

H. and I drove home and were in quite a state to think that we should be so helpless. Even though copies of everything Crowley wrote resided in at least two other places, still the handwritten fragments which remained would be of great value sometime in the future to scholars.

My concern was great and I phoned Mr. Robyn a few days later and stated that numerous phone calls to Mr. Gualdoni had not yielded any assistance, and that we were anxious to put the books and papers in a safe storage building. I asked also that if these were the literary remains of Mark Twain, would the County be so indifferent? He agreed that they might not, and I think that the fact that I used the name of a famous American author may have finally made him realize the importance of the things in the Germer house.

By this time, another letter I had written to Motta about the abandoned materials in the Germer house had stirred him to write to a friend of his, J., and to ask him to take action. This J. did, and since he was the representative of an important publishing firm in New York, Mr. Gualdoni was stirred to some kind of action.

It took some time for the fact that a publishing firm in New York was interested in the materials in the Germer house to sink into Mr. Gualdoni's mind. Meanwhile, H. and I phoned him from time to time, begging to be allowed to go up there and box things and put them in storage. He was always too busy or he was not available—often, I think, on purpose. What could two little old ladies make him do after all? I was being driven out of my mind by worry, and H. was no better off.

In fact, she and a friend of hers went to the house and took pictures of the place, every room, just as it was at that time. She kept watch outside for possible arrivals of the Law and he went in and took the pictures. Later she put this collection of snapshots into my hands, neatly arranged in an album.

Meanwhile, on May 8, I had a terrible accident and was put out of commission for a month in this affair of the Germer Estate. During this time or shortly after, Mr. Gualdoni finally found the time to take everything to a recently completed storage place in San Andreas. No, not all, but the bulk of the material that was in file cabinets. It was reported to me that a good deal was left scattered all over the floor of the second story.

The correspondence with Motta about the current state of affairs at the Germer estate continued until the end of May, when he finally wrote such an insulting letter to me that I refused to communicate further with him.

My idea was that perhaps Motta should have a chance to bid on the Crowley materials since he had shown an interest in it. I also thought that our only way out was to bid on these materials also, as hiring a lawyer to take care of our claim against the Germer Estate might be too expensive and far more than we could even round up in the future. Further, Mr. Robyn's answer about finding Karl's will seemed an impossible thing to do. Mr. Gualdoni hadn't found it and we had no way of going through a mound of papers to find it either. Then through communications with J. we found that Gualdoni had promised him access to the Germer property to pick up all the remaining mess of papers on the floor and to see that they got into storage. H. and I were outraged! We had worked for months to get access to the property to do this and had been given the runaround by Mr. Gualdoni. Now here a man from New York and a representative of a publishing firm was going to be allowed to do it!

Then in the middle of all this the psychic, J., again walked into the health food store in early June. They took down her phone number and I telephoned to her. Over the phone she described my appearance, that I had light colored hair, nearly white, that I was of medium height, not fat, that I was older and that I wore glasses sometimes. She told me of the colors in my house, white, gold and blue and gave me a rundown on the meaning of these colors. I confirmed this. Then she stated that I had called her because of a shadow in a room in my house with a large window. She said that the shadow moved to a corner opposite the window, and then often stayed in the corner near the window as it was darker. I again confirmed that there was something there and I needed help with it. She stated that I helped many people, that I had highly developed talents, and that I had been on this earth before many times, and in view of this, she would be glad to help me. She also said something about my personal life which was true, and that my health was bad at this time. I admitted to the broken bones from the accident and my recent bout with tiredness. At this she said I had been traveling on the astral at night and that I must ask that my energy not be depleted from this. I said that I had to lie on my back during the recovery and that it was much easier to get out of the body when in this position, but that I did not know that I was on the astral at night. She named a despondent woman who was to phone me soon. (This was true, a friend of mine phoned the next day who was in a despondent mood.)

She then got her Bible, opened it at random and gave me some quotes from it. Later that evening I applied the qabalistic methods against these references and found that they alluded to the number and name of my H.G.A. There were a few other significant numbers as well and some months named that would be important to me. This turned out to be true later.

I asked for an appointment and asked if she could work from photographs, and she stated that sometimes she could. During the whole of this conversation I was taking careful notes and did the same thing on the next evening when she arrived to talk to me. I admitted nothing until she told me about it, then I would admit it carefully. I wanted to be as scientific about the event as I could be. She had been as correct as possible for me to see on the telephone and I had no reason to doubt what she said when we met for the first time.

She got down to business immediately as she was seated, and said that the shadow in the room was someone who had passed over, that is he was dead. I couldn't think who might want to contact me from the other side and was greatly puzzled but she went on with her description. This shadow was going towards the lighted window and was trying to escape, but he was an earth bound spirit. He wanted to say things to me for my well-being about the papers—written papers, and books in a library. All this while when the message was coming through, J. had her eyes closed and her hands spread out on each side of her face, as though they were antennae. She went on to speak as though she was the spirit, who continued that he had a heavy burden and he was so tired and that he wanted to direct me and that it was very hard to get in contact with me and that he wished to go on, and again he complained of his tiredness. At this goose-bumps appeared on my arms and cold up my spine, and I suddenly knew that this must be Karl! Who else could speak like this?

The spirit went on to complain some more that I blocked him out and feared him, that he was tired and heavy and then he insisted, "I am good." (Since I was used to doing the Banishing Ritual of the Pentagram day and night it was no wonder he couldn't get through to me; I have ever deliberately kept out everything from other planes except my own H.G.A.)

J. described him as an old man with an overpowering warmth and love. I said this was true.

There was a little break and a description of a scene of children playing around an old barn and she seemed to think this somehow did not belong to the main message. I couldn't place it anywhere in my experience, either.

J. turned herself back to the matter in hand and said the old man wanted to go to his rest soon and that I will know about many things. Again there was some reference to the Bible opened at random and again some more qabalistic meanings as well as passages connected to my magical work.

Then she said I was to go over running water and would discover many things of importance. This was true, to get to the Germer house by either of the two routes one did have to cross running water.

She said there had been an old woman in the house who was now gone and who was now saying, "I was stingy. I lied." She had feared the house was not going to be hers and she was going to get it somehow. But the old lady was now regretting her actions and she was crying and crying on the other side and she was not with the old man.

J. interrupted herself here and told me that I must forgive her and bless her.

Then J. went on to say that I must get to the papers, and that there were a lot of entities in the house, and that the neighbors called it a haunted house.

She said there was a library and that there were a lot of precious things in it, some of them history, and much that was very important to mankind. She said that I must remove these things from the house as soon as possible, for she saw some danger if I did not do this.

At this, I gave her the album of pictures which H. had prepared and J. smiled, put the album in her lap but did not open it and placed her hands on its cover. She again closed her eyes and began to describe the appearance of the house. She stated that it was a small and old house of two stories, that it was in need of paint, that there was a porch leading up to the door, that it was surrounded with weeds, that there was broken glass, and that there was an old fashioned cupboard upstairs in which I would find some handwritten messages which would be important to me. Again she stressed that I must take away the papers before they were destroyed and that everything would soon be coming to judgment. Who would it be? She described a cynical young man with brown hair and a pointed nose who likes to drink and carouse and that he claimed the house. This puzzled me. I had an idea who it might be, but was not sure this description fitted him.

When I should take care of the house, J. went on, there would be a golden ring all around it. The old man admitted his fault and reiterated that he loves me and that he is sorry. He had a great talent and could have done so much for so many people but he didn't use it.

She switched back to the young man again and said he doesn't want to come here, he corresponds.

She then described that there would be a document of importance and that I would phone and plan to take a trip and that another lady and perhaps a man would go with me and we would find the treasures and gather them up.

She went on to describe an important paper which had been moved around many times and had been protected by the spirits and was hidden in an old fashioned closet with boards going up and down. Later we were to explore this closet but nowhere did I find Karl's will and I did think that maybe Sascha, who had found it, had moved it around often when she was trying to take care of the Crowley materials.

She described that the papers in the house had spiritual meanings and that I would read them and discover things that I hadn't known about before. This turned out to be true. She also stated that the papers did not belong to the old man or the old woman and that the old woman, when she was alone there, had been afraid to destroy anything and knew that to do so would be evil. She had wanted to be a do-gooder but didn't know how and nothing was the result. She was crying on the other side.

As we continued with this, some of it repetition, I thought that J. should see the room she had been describing over the telephone. We got up and went into the room with the large window and the white walls and she smiled at the accuracy of her description. I asked if she would check out the bathroom. She did this, and said there was nothing there, the room was warm. I asked if there was anything in the mirror and she said there was nothing there, and then I described what the young lady had seen. At this,

J. smiled and said the young lady had seen herself.

We went into the living room again and had a long conversation while J. told me about herself. She had learned how to be a psychic three years previously, and had never accepted money for her work. When J. left me she remarked that the shadow had now departed and would no longer bother me. This turned out to be true as there has never been any more trouble with that room. J. also told me many things about my personal life which were absolutely true, and here I can say she did not make any mistakes.

This then, was the psychic I had been hoping for, an unusually pure one, as she did not accept money for her task. I, of course, made sure that I paid my karmic debt to her by doing some astrological work for her.

In very early July, H. and I decided that we had enough of the trouble from Mr. Gualdoni and that perhaps we had better contact a lawyer. We did this, and engaged Mr. Airola, no longer the D.A., but who had still the case of Mrs. Germer in his files. When we told him our story he said that the court could perhaps be petitioned that Grady was the only appointed successor after Karl, and that if he had the papers to prove it, and since the library belonged to the heads of the O.T.O. according to Karl's will as well as to Crowley's will, that there was a good chance that we could gain possession of it. We could not hope for the property, though, as that had been willed to Sascha.

A week later we had a second session with Mr. Airola and Grady, along with all the proper papers. Again, there was no hope that Mr. Gualdoni would go with us to the property to box up the remaining materials. We had to wait.

In the middle of July, J. [of New York] arrived. Since he had been given permission to go to the Germer residence and box the remaining things, and H. and I did not have this permission or an appointment to do this, we decided to drive him there. This was convenient for him and we had a good time together as we all drove to the Germer house. J. proved to be a very charming fellow and quite sympathetic. But did I notice a look of surprise on Mr. Gualdoni's face when he saw us all there together? He also made some remark that he didn't think we were friends and didn't expect to see all of us at the house.

We spent several hours boxing every last scrap of paper that seemed to us to be important; J. remarking and exclaiming about this and that as we worked. It was hot and unpleasant and the house smelled of rats and death but we continued until everything was picked up and placed in Mr. Gualdoni's station wagon. From there it was placed in the newly completed cement block storage place in San Andreas—a little bit out of the town, and we were allowed to help with moving the boxes into storage. They were to remain there under Mr. Gualdoni's care until the court had made a decision. Also, Mr. Gualdoni expressed himself as being relieved that H. and I had engaged a lawyer on our case, as he had doubts that we were entitled to the materials.

On the way back, with H. driving, I was very quiet as I had found a hand written note in the cupboard, and it was from Jane to me. Poor dear, she had been having a terrible time of it in the last two years of her life and she was very unhappy and was trying to write to me so that I would take care of her. But her mind was partly gone and the sentences were disjointed and betrayed disconnected thoughts. I mourned for her passing as she had been a very dear friend over twenty or so years of my life.

H. glanced over at me quickly and then gasped and said that there was a hand on my shoulder. I gulped, tears too near the surface, and remarked that it must be Jane as I had been thinking about her. But no, H. said it was a man's hand. At this, we all marveled at the turn of events and how we had been eventually aided in gathering up Crowley's papers.

Two days later Grady, J. and I went again to the Germer house, but without Mr. Gualdoni. We had been given permission to go in to see that we really had gotten everything. We found a few more items that had been hidden in the cupboard and removed the large library carpet, again with permission. Grady did a banishing ritual and stated that he had heard voices telling him, "Thank you" several times.

We wandered around in the yard and explored the garage, and the roof of the house reflected a golden glow as the sun was just at the right angle. Was this the golden ring that J. had said would appear when I had done the needed work of removing the papers? I couldn't tell, as I am not a psychic myself, but that glow from the roof of the house I shall always remember.

In late July the judge decided in our favor, but left it up to the decisions of Mr. Robyn, Mr. Gualdoni and Mr. Airola as to what other items were to be considered as part of the Crowley heritage. We conferred outside the court about this, and Mr. Gualdoni conceded that the seal ring was part of the library. I mentioned that the three typewriters were also a part of the library, and Grady said that the large electric typewriter had been paid for out of Order funds, but we were ignored. There was silence between all three officials on this point, and I couldn't help but think later that there must also have been collusion.

A few days after this decision, we were notified that all of the paper work had been done, and that we could now go to the storage place and remove all the materials. Grady and I drove to San Andreas, and I gave to Mr. Airola the $1,000 for his fee and over a hundred to Mr. Gualdoni for his part in removing the first load of materials to the storage. I also paid for extra storage which Mr. Gualdoni had not cared for, letting things run late so that I would be stuck with it. All of these sums and much more came out of my private funds.

At the storage place Mr. Airola was with us and stood there reading one of the books from the collection. Mr. Gualdoni drove up with his station wagon and a deputy coroner and nervously took the three typewriters right from under our noses, while our own attorney stood there to see what was done. We protested, but were told by everyone that the typewriters were worth $60.00. We couldn't fight, and I had in mind that the seal ring was not yet in our possession. Gualdoni and helper drove off in a hurry and Grady and I were allowed to remove what we wanted on that particular day. We piled up my station wagon with things that we thought might be valuable, and by now I was suspicious of even the manager of the storage sheds. Then we drove to Mr. Robyn's office, where we were to sign a release and the ring would be given to us. Mr. Robyn kindly handed the seal ring to me in his office, and as we waited to have the release typed up, Grady was given the ring and made promises that he would take good care of it. When the release was ready we read it and after some hesitation we signed it, for it released the State of California from any other responsibility in this affair. I was so tired of the fight we had been through that I indicated Grady should perhaps sign and this he did. But now I think that was a mistake, as we could perhaps have demanded that the typewriters would be returned to us or we wouldn't sign.

In early August a member of the Order helped us to remove all the rest of the materials. Again I had rented the truck, and paid for the gas and all that was necessary for this work. We brought the remains of the Crowley-Germer library to my house in Dublin and Grady took some pictures of our arrival. All that evening Grady worked on the sorting of these materials. He also got on the phone immediately upon our arrival and let it be known in certain quarters in Berkeley that everything was here. I was nervous about this, and told him he had just jeopardized my welfare and perhaps my life. Naturally, I was thinking of what had happened to Sascha when it got about that she was alone in her house. It had happened also that threats to rip off the McMurtrys of certain of Crowley's things had gotten back to me just a few years previous to these events. I knew of the lines of connection between some of Grady's friends and acquaintances, and through them in a chain to certain types of "rip-off" artists. I also knew that Grady was often fooled by certain types of people, and this fact had been proven to me by events in the past. Maybe I was being too nervous, but I considered that I had good reason to be worried. I asked Grady for his protection. He refused.

Grady spent one more day sorting the library materials and removing the better books from those that were of no use to Thelema. He also had access to the files of correspondence. After this was over, I drove him back to his place in Berkeley.

The following day I was alone, and I removed every last bit of the Crowley literary remains, the correspondence, the Germer materials and the parts of the library that were valuable into a storage place quite far from my home. To this day these things are hidden and for good reason, and there are quite a few who know these reasons or can figure them out for themselves. Those who might have access to them in the future shall have proven their honesty and their sincere concern for the welfare of Thelema and for the right use of these materials to the benefit of Thelemites everywhere. To prove these attitudes may take some time and a good deal of testing. My stand is that an untried and unproven Minerval of the O.T.O. is not a fit person to be let loose among these library materials. There is some sensitive matter in the correspondence files, for instance, which involves persons still living, and I do not think that anyone has the right to expose matters which were given to Karl or to Crowley in trust. In due time what has not been published of Crowley's works will be published. This is being worked on at the present. Also, please remember that there is a copy of everything that Crowley wrote in England and quite a few people in that country are interested in publishing Crowley material.

Some of you know of the threats to torture me and of the threats that also came from Grady. But these people have now been eliminated from our circle and so must it be. And now I have told you the truth, and if the truth seems to be incredible, remember that life itself is incredible, especially when a person begins to use magick. Also along his line, remember that every cause or event that we can see on the physical plane, has had its effect. We can trace in this story the various causes which produced these particular effects. I might also remark that there is no guidance so perfect as that of the Holy Guardian Angel and may you all attain to this joy and wisdom!

> Love is the law, love under will.

> > Fraternally,
> > Soror Meral

Carete Fratres et Sorores,[69]

> Do what thou wilt shall be the whole of the Law.

Great religions of the past and great systems of thought break down in time for several reasons. One of the most notable of these reasons is the addition of extra material to the original purity of thought which the Magus or Genius utters. Thus, Christianity through the ages suffered Ecumenical Councils through which it was changed in order to serve the drive to power of the Church. Taoism and Buddhism, the thought of Lao-Tze and Buddha, were changed by the reluctance of the petty magicians using these systems to give up their ancient practices of magic and superstition, some of which were workable and some not, and some of a low magical order which simply led the magician to greater power over others. Great systems such as Freemasonry and Rosicrucianism became bogged down by additions of practice and thought which were not inspired by the genius or

---

69. Originally published in: Phyllis Seckler, *In the Continuum* 2.3 (1978): 1–9.

Magus, but instead, were added because of the drive to power of inferior men — that is, egocentricity became too great a force in the original system.

Even though Thelema is in its very young stages, this type of power urge is at work. People who wish to aggrandize the small ego and thus enforce their own will upon others, people who like to change the original word of the Prophet or the original intentions. People who do not care to study deeply the Thelemic system and divine the true meaning within but who instead take a partial and often a very uninformed view, are at the age-old game of ego-aggrandizement. The true Initiate can indeed laugh at these shallow efforts, but how about the struggling young student?

For instance, there is one deviation which happened so early that Crowley was able to condemn it. But this deviation is still being taught! This is the upside down Tree of Life of Frater Achad.

The Master Therion used those elements from the great and workable systems of the past which could aid the student in his spiritual growth. They had aided the man Crowley to attain to the greatest heights and to form a system which can be counted as the most efficient method of Spiritual Illumination, or of attaining the Knowledge and Conversation of the Holy Guardian Angel that has ever been used on the earth. Some of these elements are the western system of Ceremonial magick, the scientific method of yogic systems from Hindu thought and practice, and the Hebrew qabalah and the Tree of Life for the training and ordering of the mind. For if the mind is in a chaotic state, how then can the aspirant hope to gain Illumination?

Spiritual growth, if it is not to be a monstrous thing, must rely upon the right ordering and control of the body, emotions and mind. The aspirant must rigorously train all of his various capacities to lead to the one end, the Knowledge and Conversation of the Holy Guardian Angel. His will must be one-pointed. He must work constantly to see that he does not lose his balance. He, then, will need to build a broad foundation to his pyramid so that he can maintain this balance. It is possible to build a pyramid with a narrow foundation, skipping some of the essentials of preliminary work, but when the crucial struggle arrives, he falls, usually with a crash and often into insanity.

Achad himself made this mistake, and many other persons who have taken up the spiritual development work in Thelema have done likewise. Crowley warns against such carelessness again and again but even in spite of this, there are many who do not know the words and work of the Master Therion. Their scholarship and practices and understanding are at fault; they are unable to learn and profit; the blindness of the small ego overwhelms them. Perhaps they would rather have a shallow power over others instead of doing the True Work. These persons miss the true import of the Thelemic system entirely, unfortunately.

Let us look at the system and order in the Tree of Life as it has been worked out by adepts over a period of time, and marvel at this structure which mirrors the true order of the Universe, and also the true order of the structure of the human being.

In the following diagram (Diagram H) you will see that there are only numbers on the paths between the spheres. This is done so that you can see clearly how the numbers swing in an orderly fashion and in sequence from top to bottom of the Tree and from Right to Left as you view it before you on the page.

The number 1 appears on the highest path on the right. Immediately to balance this, the number 2 appears on the highest path on the left. In between we have the number 3 as the centre of balance. Then number 4 is a horizontal or reciprocating path; and completes those paths which are above the Abyss. Number 3 is unique in that it leads from Tiphereth directly to the Crown or Kether above the Abyss. Its importance is echoed in these words from *Liber LXV*, Cap. I, v. 9 and 10: "One mounteth unto the Crown by the moon and by the Sun, and by the arrow, and by the Foundation, and by the dark home of the stars from the black earth. Not otherwise may ye reach unto the Smooth Point."[70]

The "smooth point" refers to the Crown. There are also many other references to Gimel (*i.e.*, the number 3) in *Liber VII* and *Liber LXV*, too numerous to mention here. Gimel or 3 is the Moon in this quote, and the clear conclusion is that this arrangement is the only way to achieve the goal! How could Achad be so careless in his scholarship? How is it he thought he knew better than the Master Therion?

Again we swing to the right and notice the number 5 on the inner path which leads to Chokmah, and the number 6 on the outer path leading to the same sphere. This same pattern is repeated exactly as a balance with number 7 on the inner side

---

70. Crowley, *The Holy Books of Thelema*, 54.

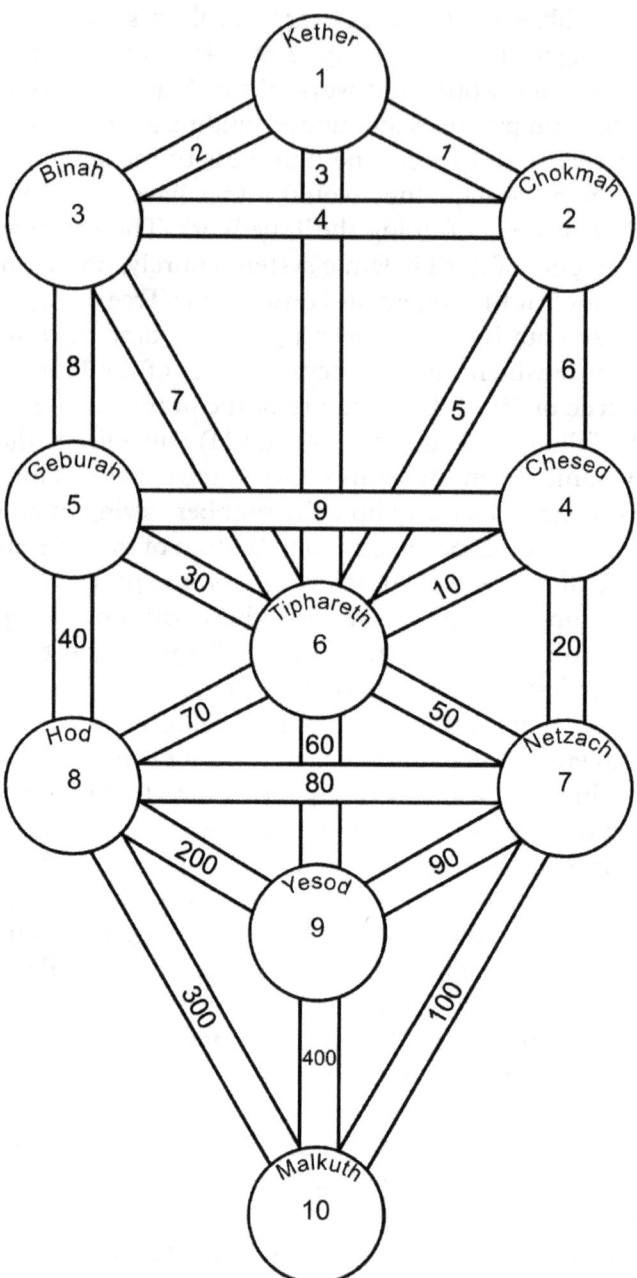

Diagram H.

leading to Binah and number 8 on the outer side leading to the same sphere.

The second horizontal or reciprocating path bears the number 9. Now we have used all the single-digit numbers of our system and from now on we repeat these numbers, adding one or two zeros as the case may be. The fact that we use a system of one to nine is in itself a deep study but we won't take up its significance at the moment.

Again we start on the right side with our numbers that have a zero added and we have number 10 on the inner path from Chesed to Tiphereth and number 20 on the outer path between Chesed and Netzach. Exactly balancing these we notice number 30 between Tiphereth and Geburah on the inner side and number 40 between Geburah and Hod on the outer edge, on the left side.

There is a little change below Tiphereth in that numbers 50, 60 and 70 swing from right to left in order. This is because of the importance of number 60, Samech. It must be in the middle pillar, just as number 3 must be in the middle pillar. In the quote above, Samech is spoken of as the arrow.

Number 80 is the lowest horizontal path. Now add up numbers 80, 9, and 4 and you have 93! And someone wants to change this beautiful arrangement? When you know 93 is a key number in Thelema?

Why is it that some people must insist the earth is flat against all evidence to the contrary? For to insist that the numbers on the Tree of Life can be differently set is to refute the Laws of the Universe, of the mind, and of nature.

We again swing to the right and notice numbers 90 and 100 with the usual pattern of the lower number on the inner side and the higher number on the outer side. Exactly balancing this on the left we have the next two numbers, 200 and 300. In the middle we finish off with the last number — 400, "the dark home of the stars," or Tau.

Now we can add the Hebrew letters which correspond to these numbers; please refer to Diagram I. Thus we have the unchangeable laws of the Universe as much as they can be apprehended by the minds of today. The balance is perfect. We are ever exhorted not to lose our balance on the mystical and spiritual path. Surely this balance should ever be an inspiration to us. Here is a workable diagram showing us how to keep our minds in a similar balanced state. Also notice how easy it is now to memorize this arrangement once you are aware of its perfection and order. Remember again, that genius is well aware of the order of the Universe and this is what makes one man a genius as against the confusion and disorder of lesser men.

Two Tarot cards have been switched on this diagram of the Tree of Life in the New Æon. The Star or Aquarius belongs with Hé on Path 5. The Emperor or Aries belongs with Tzaddi on Path 90. **But this switch does not change the order of the numbers and letters of the Hebrew Alphabet.**

Can you not see now that to do anything else with these numbers and letters is but to mirror forth nothing but confusion and insanity? Universal order is built into the great man and the genius and balance is a necessity if he is to function effectively at all. The Thelemic system has been known to develop genius in those who thought they had none. This is one of the areas—the right ordering of the mind—which is effective in this way.

Those, then, who teach Thelema contrary to the work and advice of the Prophet, the Master Therion, and those who can defy the Illuminated work of the Past Magi or adepts, partake of Choronzon, and we are not to be sorry when they fall! How then can it be stressed more strongly that each should know the work of the Master Therion? Also, how can one "obey" the Prophet if one does not know what he wrote?

Of very great interest to the student is the Way of Illumination that is taught by the placement of the Tarot cards upon the Tree of Life. There is excellent reason why one Atu should be placed as connecting two spheres, and those spheres only, not any other spheres! This is such a long subject that it cannot be taken up now and it is very beautifully written by Crowley in "The Wake World," printed in *Konx Om Pax*.[71]

As we turn to the rituals we learn that they must be "rightly performed."[72] What is the right way? Obviously this would be the way the Master Therion wrote them with their attendant directions. There are reasons for every word and every movement in these rituals. These actions speak directly to the subconscious. A ritual is a way of programming the subconscious so that it will in turn go into action according to the will and work

---

71. Crowley, *Konx Om Pax: Essays in Light*, ed. Martin P. Starr (Chicago, IL: Teitan Press, 1990).
72. Crowley, *Liber AL vel Legis*, 44. [Cap. II, v. 35. – Eds.]

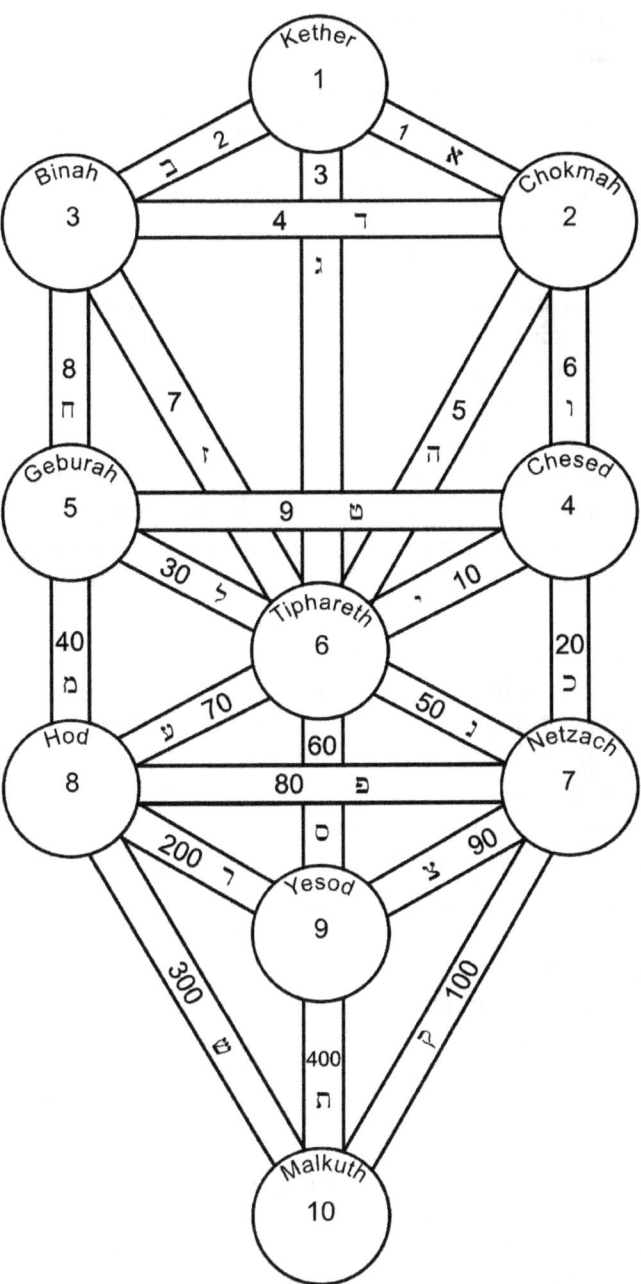

Diagram I.

of the conscious mind and give of its stored or hidden wisdom, which is an accumulation over ages and over many incarnations. This hidden wisdom must be brought out and integrated with the conscious person in all he does and thinks. Ritual has been used in the west for ages, and is actually built into our psyche through our various incarnations and through our ancestral memories. It is a very useful tool to aid us in our work.

We do not always understand why certain figures should be traced in the air, or why the electrical force should be so strong from this tracing that it can be seen by persons sensitive to such fine forces. We do not always understand that the correct vibration of certain words can awaken the powers of the subconscious, of which we were formerly unaware. We do not always know why one should dance or tread a circle in certain directions.

When one is very well informed of all of the works of the Master Therion, some of these reasons begin to dawn on us. We begin to know that the rituals are "half known and half concealed" because it is we who must grow into their appreciation. We must, each one of us, do this for ourselves as we perform them.

A ritual can have little meaning if one is not aware of the significance of its tracings, movements and words. If it has little meaning, it loses its power to inform and enlighten us. To discover this meaning would take long years of study of the work of the Master Therion, and long hours of practice of each ritual that one is prepared to do. Sometimes someone else can help by giving comments and clues as to hidden meanings and even though these comments are incomplete they may be of use. It is to be the work of this publication to do just this.

We often see in the performance of the public rituals of Thelema the same ego-maniac drive to change some of these rituals to suit the passions or drive to power of the operator. In this type of action we again notice the beginning of decay and confusion. How can one who has no Illumination be fit to teach others how to perform ritual? (I might comment here that such a one is not fit to teach anything.)

Our highest help comes from the serious work and writings of the Master Therion and from *The Book of the Law*. We see that the rituals of the New Æon have been "purged" by the Prophet. Very well, then let us perform just those rituals which were treated in this way.

Then we notice that they must be "rightly performed with joy and beauty."[73]

It has come to the attention of this publication and this editor that this injunction is being taken lightly. Is it beauty if the Priestess in the Gnostic Catholic Mass must sit on an ordinary chair instead of on an altar draped in flaming red? Should the Priest look ridiculous with a short garment and with hairy legs sticking out beneath? On this score let me remind all that Crowley favored long flowing robes to the ankle because of their superior grace and beauty. Is the ritual "rightly performed" if there are not 22 candles to represent the 22 Major Arcana of the Tarot and the 220 verses in *Liber AL vel Legis*? Are you speaking to the unconscious to draw forth from it the highest help in your search for Illumination when you slight areas of ritual in this way?

What is this reluctance to gather together all the necessary appurtenances for the right presentation of ritual? If you give it only half of your effort, you will get half or less of the effect it is designed to have on you. If all these beautiful things are too expensive for some, then it is up to you to remedy the matter! Any effort on this line will be worth it a thousand fold. But if you are sloppy in the performance of ritual, if you are careless and uninformed, you are the loser and you are trumpeting to the world that your character partakes of your attitudes.

In this area, let us notice an example set by Crowley. In "John St. John," (from *Equinox*, Vol. I, No. 1), which is an account of attainment by the Master Therion, each detail of his life was done with reference to beauty and dedication to the H.G.A. For instance, when he was ready to work in the evening on this very important Work and do his rituals and practices, he was first bathed and robed. Could we not take a hint from this? Would you offer a body filthy with sweat and the day's work to your Beloved? Is it Beauty to offer filth of mind, emotions and body to the H.G.A.?

In alchemy the student learns that all these parts of himself must be purified. He must visit the interior of the earth and rectify what is found there in order to form the Philosopher's Stone. This is very necessary, for the subconscious, as I remarked before, gives back to us exactly as our actions and minds have dictated

---

73. Crowley, *Liber AL vel Legis*, [Cap. II, v. 35. – Eds.]

to it. The subconscious mind reasons only one way—deductive reasoning—and goes only forward. If we feed it trash in any form, whether of mind, emotions or body, we reap the trash in one form or another.

It is a long study of the self to know just what we are feeding the subconscious but know we must if we are to become truly attuned to our own H.G.A. or even if we are going to take the first step on the path to Knowledge and Illumination. We need to know how the mind works, how its thoughts are precipitated into event by the power of emotions. Presumably one could think and think but nothing much will happen unless the emotion precipitates this thinking into event. This is the power of emanation, the final twist, the Foundation, Yesod, which gives thoughts their material form.

Now these are strong suggestions and put in strong terms. In the final analysis it will be up to you to devise your own aesthetic standards within the framework that the Master Therion has laid down, but devise them you must if you are to succeed. Nuit has given her mandates and her instructions very clearly.

Love is the law, love under will.

Fraternally,
Soror Meral

Carete Fratres et Sorores,[74]

Do what thou wilt shall be the whole of the Law.

With the performance of any ritual it is necessary that the participants know as much as possible about the meanings of gestures, signs, words and magical weapons in order to appreciate the full significance of what is happening. It is true that a ritual speaks to us through the subconscious realms of our Being and may bring out in us attitudes, emotions and memories, etc. of which we were formerly not aware; but it is also a long process to bring to light these hidden parts of ourselves. Our work may be greatly aided by an intellectual appreciation of what is happening, and further, a well-trained mind acts as a corrective to unbalanced

---

74. Originally published in: Phyllis Seckler, *In the Continuum* 2.4 (1979): 6-12.

attitudes and points of view which may lead to various types and degrees of insanity. Who has not observed the religious fanatic who acts against his own and others' best interests? Such a one may be possessed of so-called "spirits," and may even try to force his views on others in the mistaken notion that he is going to "save" them. Need I point out that often some sort of psychic, magical or mystical insanity often exists too, in so-called occult groups? The fact that Crowley stresses again and again the acquisition and use of common sense and the thorough training of the mind is ignored even in our own Order!

Ritual is meant to elevate our consciousness and bring us closer to our own *higher selves* (or God, or Nuit, or the H.G.A., or however you wish to term it). As such, it has been a western tradition to use ritual in the churches with a glory of art and music and costume and gesture and lights and whatever else that can be pressed into the service of the highest aspirations known to men. This attitude is still true for the New Æon of Horus as study of *Liber AL vel Legis* clearly shows. For those who naturally take a liking to ritual and who expect great results from it, this should never be forgotten. As Crowley points out in *Magick in Theory and Practice*:

"There is also a true and positive connexion between the Creative force of the Macrocosm, and that of the Microcosm. For this reason the latter must be made as pure and consecrated as the former. The puzzle for most people is how to do this. The study of Nature is the Key to that Gate" (footnote for Cap. 15.[75])

By the Microcosm is meant the man or woman who mirrors the whole of the Universe. It is our study to purify this Microcosm, to consecrate it to the one Work (or Will), to elevate it and then finally to unite it with the Highest. If the preliminary purification has not been done, the student of the occult arts can get himself into a lot of trouble. There are many ways to carry on the process of purification. For instance, everything you do, say, hear, or have emotions about, will program the unconscious. Later on, when you are not aware, if this programming has been deleterious to the purity of the Highest in you, you may be slammed against the wall (so to speak) and given the most difficult ordeals and experiences, until you perform the necessary purifications of mind,

---

75. Crowley, *Magick Liber ABA*, 132.

emotions and body. If you have stepped out on the path of occult advancement, this is more especially true. You are no longer the man in the street, the ordinary human who lives out his little life unknowing and uncaring of the glories which you seek.

Part of the process of purification can be aided by the right understanding and performance of those rituals which have been purged by the Master Therion according to His instructions in *Liber AL vel Legis*, Cap. II, v. 5. There is a good deal of instruction about rituals in *Liber Legis*, and these should be carefully studied and memorized by any student wishing to work in a ritualistic fashion. Further, the Commentary on *Liber Legis*[76] should also be studied.

All of the things that you need to study and know about your rituals may take you a very long time indeed. You perhaps have to work for a living and your time is cruelly shortened to spend on your own higher development. Further, maybe some of the things you need to know are in books which you cannot find or even afford. So let us see if there can be some help for you in the commentaries on ritual which will be featured in this publication.

Many times the student does not know the significance of the Sphinx in Thelemic rituals. Yet symbols which correspond to the importance of this figure are used by Crowley again and again in his rituals and published works. *Liber Aleph* has some of the most concise and complete instructions on this subject and yet, because of their compact form, it may be difficult for a student who has not enough background to know what is being said.

For instance, everywhere Crowley mentions Life, Light, Love and Liberty, he is referring to the four powers of the Sphinx and one needs to think of some of the correspondences which pertain to this figure in order to understand the true meaning of its use in ritual or literature. Thus, in *Liber CL*, which can be found in the *Blue Equinox* and elsewhere, there is a great deal of instruction as to how to acquire these four powers.[77] Even this can be a lifelong study for some and certainly should be a part of everyday action. The four powers come first in occult development and it is only when one has mastered these that one should go on to build one's pyramid to the stars. Crowley is very clear about this!

---

76. Crowley, *The Law is for All*.
77. See also Seckler, *The Thoth Tarot, Astrology, & Other Selected Writings*, 163-169.

The symbolism of the Sphinx is used clearly in those rituals which have no apparent grounding in the traditional systems used by the Golden Dawn. Thus, we have, on beginning levels, two types of ritual. Those which were inspired (and purged) by the traditions and correspondences arising from the qabalah as used in the past, and those which are purely Thelemic rituals and have been invented for use in our new Æon. The traditional rituals ask you to trace the air pentagram in the east but the purely Thelemic rituals ask you to trace the earth pentagram in the east. This has confused many! Why? the student asks!

The Lesser Banishing Ritual of the Pentagram and *Liber Samekh* both use Golden Dawn symbolism. But *Liber V vel Reguli* and the Star Ruby are new Thelemic rituals and use the Sphinx symbolism.

If you will hold Diagram J above your head and turn it so that Leo, fire, is to the south, you will see that in the east is placed the sign of Taurus, earth. So true to this natural order of the zodiac signs, we then trace the pentagram of earth in that quarter. Notice that in the zodiac, earth is exactly opposite to water. That is, Taurus is exactly opposite to Scorpio. Also, air or Aquarius is exactly opposite to fire, Leo.

Do you see now that you have been following the order of nature in these attributions? What ritual could be effective if it did not use the true natural laws?

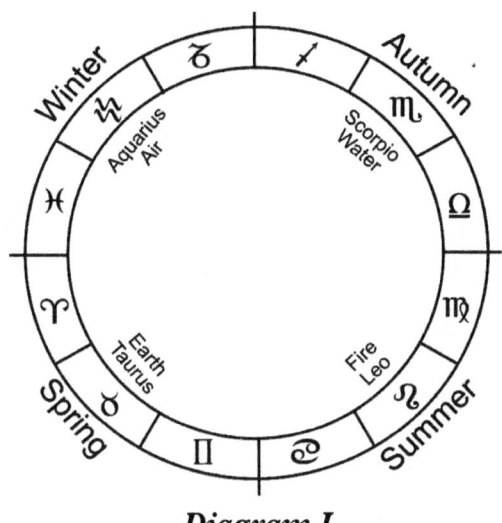

Diagram J.

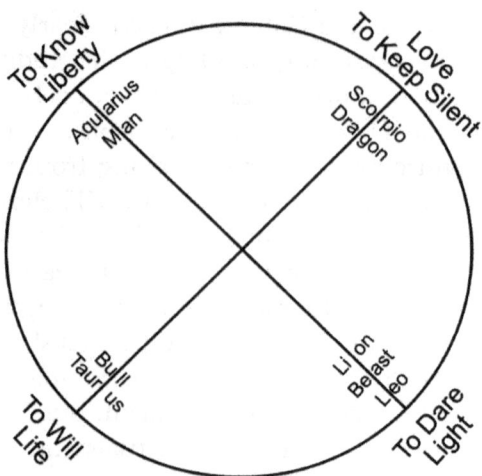

Diagram K.

If the student is south of the equator, his view of the sun, the Father of all Life, will be to the north and not to the south as it is for us in the northern hemisphere. Therefore, he will need to place the diagram at his feet so that Leo, the Sun, is in the north where the Sun of nature shines for him. This will still place Taurus, the earth, in the eastern sector. Now, when this is clear to the mind of the student, we can go on and tabulate the correspondences which comprise the Sphinx.

A further question might arise as to why the cherubic signs are used to make up the Sphinx? The student of astrology would recognize that the middle signs of any season carry the most fixed and immovable forces. The fixed or cherubic signs are responsible for the crystallizing of the element into its final form in manifestation.

In the natural seasons we observe that the greatest force of springtime is in the middle of that season when the beginning growth which started with the Vernal Equinox has crystallized and is in full splendor.

Then in the middle of the summer, we experience the full force of the heat of the sun, of fire. In the middle of autumn, come the rains in most countries, and we experience water falling from the skies. In the middle of winter, nature is asleep and it is like the midnight, where the beetle is quietly carrying the new life hidden and secret. This is where we find the whole is a symbol of how Tiphereth, attributed to *air*, is also the intellect, and the son of fire and water, Yod and He, and that he is also the sun at midnight, unseen and hidden, Khephra, the beetle [see Table B].

This march of the seasons is like the march of the day which we celebrate in *Liber Resh*. So these attributions have also been added to the list. Then the officers of the New Æon are in this list as well. You will probably be able to see the correspondences which exist between the twins of Heru-Ra-Ha (Ra-Hoor-Khuit and Hoor-Paar-Kraat) to the concepts of Therion and Babalon.

Notice that our symbol of the zodiac is a circle and the lines which connect the opposite signs make a cross or an X. Here we have a symbol of very ancient lineage and we are still using it today as it carries a universal truth. The cross can also be thought of as the arms of the cross and the point where they meet as the undefinable point of Hadit. The circle is attributed to Nuit as it has no beginning and no end.

Love is the law, love under will.

Fraternally with love,
Soror Meral

TABULATION OF CORRESPONDENCES
THE SPHINX

	LIFE	LIGHT	LOVE	LIBERTY
The Sphinx	Velle To Will (Energy)	Audere To Dare (Courage)	Tacere To Keep Silence (Soaring Subtlety)	Scire To Know (Intelligence)
Zodiac Sign	Taurus	Leo	Scorpio	Aquarius
Symbol	The Bull	Lion, Beast	Dragon or Woman-Serpent (Scorpion, Snake, Eagle)	Man or Eagle
Tarot Atu	V. Hierophant	XI. Lust	XIII. Death	XVII. The Star
Hebrew Letter and Number	Vau - 6	Teth - 9	Nun - 50	He - 5
Element	Earth	Fire	Water	Air
Quarter	East	South	West	North
Season	Spring	Summer	Autumn	Winter
Part of Day	Dawn	Noon	Sundown	Midnight
Liber Resh	Ra	Ahathoor	Tum	Khephra
Liber Reguli & Star Ruby	Therion	Hadit	Babalon	Nuit
Tetragrammaton	Final Hé	Yod	He	Vau

Table B.

Carete Fratres et Sorores,[78]

Do what thou wilt shall be the whole of the Law.

From time to time we will include letters from Karl Germer which are of general interest. He was not only of very high attainment in the A∴A∴, which Crowley recognized, but he was also the Outer Head of the Ordo Templi Orientis until his death. If he did not do much to expand that Order, there was probably very good reason for it which will be justified by history. After all, Germer was often observed to get decrees and instructions from other planes, and who can say if he did right or wrong with certain actions? There is probably no one alive at the moment who can judge this even though some pretend that they can do so.

Included in this issue are writings by others which are timely and thought provoking. This editor would like to welcome even more articles of the caliber of these.

Usually this type of article is short or non-existent in the Summer but I think a matter has arisen in the last few months which is of prime importance to many people and perhaps it would be best to discuss this matter now rather than wait for the Fall. This topic of interest concerns the A∴A∴.

The reason for this timely discussion of the A∴A∴ lies in the fact that there are many conflicting claims to be a member of this secret order by many people and a beginner, when looking for a bona-fide teacher, is often confused as to who might have a valid claim to this function, and who is less likely to lead him astray and into false and confusing paths.

For instance, as examples, one person claiming high Grades in A∴A∴ asked for money and was a very poor teacher, neglecting his students' needs in great part. Another person never passed the Grade of Probationer, but represented himself by lies as being of higher Grades. Even though he had a real paper and real descent from Crowley, his lies and posturing disqualified him and he is no longer of the A∴A∴. Another person claimed $8°=3^\square$ of A∴A∴, but took a dead man's name and number. Also there was no proof whatever in the outer world (as there must be) that he had accomplished the tasks of $6°=5^\square$ or of $7°=4^\square$. Anyone wishing to see what these tasks are could refer to *One Star in Sight* in

---

78. Originally published in: Phyllis Seckler, *In the Continuum* 2.5 (1979): 1–3.

Magick in Theory and Practice[79] and once one has thoroughly read and assimilated this book, such of those who are claiming these Grades could be laughed to scorn.

So it goes, the frauds are innumerable. Can a person have crossed the Abyss if his ego is still large and unwieldy and there for all the world to see? The answer is not at all!

How is it then, that some people have difficulty understanding *One Star in Sight?* Really, it would be worth anyone's while to try to assimilate this book if they are looking for a real teacher in the A∴A∴. It will have to be the alert person who can spot the frauds and the phonies and apply his own tests and make his own conclusions. Be alert then!

How? Crowley recognized that this confusion might arise and in several of his writings, tried to forestall the efforts of those who might be mad for power over the souls of others and who might like to boast of Grades as a form of ego-aggrandizement.

First then, the aspiring student could be very careful of those who boast of A∴A∴ Grades. He would be justified in thinking that such boasts reveal a person interested only in his own small ego and not in students. Sometimes, the greatest of *adepts*, and I have seen such, will scoff at the idea of Grades. What has this to do with gaining the Knowledge and Conversation of the Holy Guardian Angel? What has this to do with a sincere give and take between student and teacher? Truly, the idea of Grades is very superfluous!

And in *Magick Without Tears* we read this passage in letter 13: "…the A∴A∴ concerns the individual, his development, his initiation, his passage from 'Student' to 'Ipsissimus;' he has no contact of any kind with any other person except the Neophyte who introduces him, and any Student or Students who he may, after becoming a Neophyte, introduce.[80]

Notice that Crowley says a person must first be a Neophyte before taking on another student. This is also clear in *Liber 185* at the back of *Gems from the Equinox*.[81]

---

79. Crowley, *Magick Liber ABA*, 1997, 477-489.
80. Crowley, *Magick Without Tears*, 122.
81. Crowley, *Gems from the Equinox: Instructions by Aleister Crowley for His Own Order*, Ed. Israel Regardie (Las Vegas, NV: Falcon Press 1988), 1107-1134.

What can the student think then, of the Probationer who takes on A∴A∴ students? Is this not the blind leading the blind which Crowley so deplores in several places?

How can the enquiring person know if he has a real Neophyte to be his teacher? This should be possible to verify by a very simple method. The Neophyte in question should be able to exhibit a paper which has been given to him as a result of passing the tasks of a Probationer as given in *Liber 185*. Or, lacking such a paper, as is entirely possible today as a great many things are still in confusion in both of Crowley's occult orders, the student might ask another simple proof by asking his future teacher if he would please recite his chosen Chapter of *Liber LXV*. In the present state of confusion, I am sure any true member of the A∴A∴ would oblige willingly in order to set the mind of the student at rest.

Further proof can be had by other methods. Again a quote from *Magick Without Tears*, Letter D: "By their fruits ye shall know them." You have read *Liber LXV* and *Liber VII*; that shows what states you can attain by this curriculum.[82]

However, many fitted for teaching lower Grades in the A∴A∴ system are not capable of such sublime utterances as those mentioned above. But many teachers do have a work and many teachers can write. Evaluate then, what is written and how the work seems to you. Evaluate the fruits of the teacher in question.

To help you do these evaluations and careful weighing of the evidence, you will find after this letter some pertinent quotes from *One Star in Sight*.[83] Do learn these at least, if you are very serious about a real teacher. When you have prepared yourself by a little solid groundwork, you will be ready for a teacher and it is a tradition that such a teacher will be available to you at that time, but not before.

Further considerations ought to be mentioned for those who wish to work alone and apply Crowley's instructions to all of their work. There is danger in working alone, that the person will be so blinded by his own ego that he will not truly balance himself and apply also processes of psychoanalysis to himself. This is partly the reason why we have such frauds as described above. A good

---

82. Crowley, *Magick Without Tears*, 10.
83. Crowley, *Magick Liber ABA*, Appendix II.

teacher can administer ordeals or point to you things which you, if left alone, would rather not face. This is extremely dangerous as it can leave you a candidate for the insane asylum or otherwise in a very bad situation. Let us hope then, that all of you can find that which will further your own True Will.

Love is the law, love under will.

Soror Meral

Carete Fratres et Sorores,[84]

Do what thou wilt shall be the whole of the Law.

"Every man and every woman is a star" (*Liber Legis*, Cap. I, v. 3).[85]

In the change from the thinking and behavior of the Old Æon to that of the New Æon, there is bound to be a great deal of confusion. As children, most of us had to face and suffer programming by Old Æon thinking; and to some of us, it has been very difficult to change old habits of the past and to let our true selves shine through. Especially in the cases of many New Æon women do we see a great deal of difficulty in this change because of the fact that the past æon, that of Osiris, the dying God who was slain and resurrected, was a paternal or male-dominated age.

That this old paternal æon was exactly parallel to the male sexual responses was not of much aid in understanding the different functioning of the female. Women still produced, preserved and nurtured the race, as has been their function forever, but they were discouraged from participation in government, from artistic and creative work of all kinds, from working with or practicing in any of the traditionally male dominated professions or trades, etc. Even if women had, in their own right, ability for these fields of work, they were forced by the might of custom and male domination to use their intelligence and their abilities for domestic matters and the rearing of children. Only a few women escaped such bonds, a queen here and there, actresses, singers

---

84. Originally published in: Phyllis Seckler, *In the Continuum* 2.6 (1979): 1–13.
85. Crowley, *Liber AL vel Legis*, 25.

and courtesans. The male arrogated to himself all power and action in the world outside the home and women all over the world were reduced to the status of slaves and chattels. They had to comply for the sake of the offspring. They had to adapt in order to survive.

We still suffer today the psychological consequences of these old attitudes, even though women are gradually awakening to their true natures. But this awakening brings with it a great deal of confusion and unhappiness as women struggle to become the star that each one of them is, equal in importance to men, but with a different behavior and point of view. Let us see if we can clear away some of the myths concerning women due to old æon ideas and reorient ourselves to a new view more fitting to the new age.

First, let us view a general over-all classification that Crowley mentions. He divides women into three types; the Isis, the Osiris, and the Horus types.[86]

The Isis woman is all mother, she takes a man as spouse who will be as interested as she is in rearing children. If this kind of woman does not see herself clearly and takes the wrong man, she may end up bringing the children into maturity by herself. This is a very large problem in this age; the number of women having to be both mother and father to the children is uncountable. Male thinking on this score is confused also, due to the fact that this is the Æon of the Child and this child has not grown up as yet. Irresponsibility is one of the hallmarks of children. Also, the Isis type of woman will seek to mother the male to which she is attached, she may even try to mother friends and acquaintances. She is full of good advice, nurturing, compassion, kindliness, you name it. How was your mother to you?

Next, the Osiris type of woman prefers to work with her man in his endeavors and his profession. Her will centers on his will, and children are secondary in her preference. They may be welcomed as an aid to the man's work, or as an aid to his pride in achievement. This type of woman is most valuable to the man who has a great ambition towards his particular work. She can aid with her intuition or with an understanding of psychology

---

86. Crowley, *Magick Without Tears*, 247.

if she has developed this. She is the helpmate, the confidante, the willing helper or whatever it takes for her man to achieve his ambition. This type of woman is clearly seen among the wives of professional men and politicians, for instance. A great many men prefer this type, as is natural, as such men consider that his work is enough for the two of them and she should remain as his sidekick and his helper. If she mistakes herself and finds later that she wants to achieve some ambition of her own, trouble may be brewing.

Last, the Horus type of woman is a woman of the New Æon, just now coming into more prominence than ever before in the known history of the race. She is the one who can challenge a man in his own field. She is creative, she can be artist or writer, conductor of great orchestras, composer, physician, lawyer, judge, governor. She can excel in fields which were often, in the past, the province of men only. Here we see the professional women, those in business for themselves, and again the singers and actresses as prevailed in the past. There are a few of these types in our history: George Sand, the Bronte sisters, Queen Elizabeth I, Queen Victoria, and so on. But now there are many more of these kinds of women; there is a great explosion as women realize that they are no more shackled by the traditions of the past age and by the dominance of men. Often, the male is a consort to this type of woman; inevitably, we see that the consorts of Queen Victoria and Queen Elizabeth II are a great deal in the background, while the Queen is ruler and governor, accepting or rejecting his advice and help. Such a backseat role is distasteful to many men, as male ego and intellect has ruled for so long. It would take a very unusual type of man to be affiliated with the Horus type of woman for very long.

The problem isn't insuperable, though, as nothing prevents the male from carrying out his own will. But he ought not to think that he can dominate the Horus type of woman, and here he may need some help with psychoanalysis to get over his prejudices that males are the favored creatures in the world.

Often successful households can be set up with both partners truly accomplishing their wills. They may hire outside help for domestic duties and the care of children, or they may dispense with this and share the domestic work equally. There ought not to be a need for dependence or superiority on the part of either one in such an arrangement. There is a good chance that they could love without outside considerations, that they could love freely and without bonds. As the New Æon grows, we will probably see a great deal more of this type of partnership.

Please bear in mind that any one woman may play all of these roles in various phases of her life, or she might even combine two or more of the roles at any one time. She might play only one of these roles for all of her life, or perhaps two without the third for the whole of her incarnation. The possibilities are quite a few. However, this simple classification may also be too simple as human nature is invariably more complicated than any classification could be. But at least, with this sort of tool, one can sort out one's preferences and thinking and evaluate how one's reactions to life events predispose one towards this or that role. Perhaps, in many individual instances, some of the confusion will vanish or be resolved in an acceptable fashion.

Next let us consider the natural polarities of men and women as applied to the physical, emotional, mental and spiritual planes. These polarities are an old occult (secret) tradition and mention of them can be found among such writers as Rudolph Steiner, Dion Fortune, many Alchemists and others. There are hints of the polarities in Crowley's writings also. Please refer to the quotes at the end of this article.

On the physical plane we find that men, generally speaking, will behave in a positive fashion. It is men who indulge in feats of strength one against the other, who wage war, who tear down mountains and build them up again. Men like to build cities and tear them down, construct roads, invent new machines which change daily living for all time to come. Men explore new worlds and the space outside of this world, no matter what the cost to the rest of humankind. These are the types of tasks and work conceived by men and mostly carried through by them. Men like to change the face of the earth and often attempt to subvert natural laws in their strivings.

Women, on the other hand, usually behave in a negative fashion on the physical plane. Very seldom will you see a woman interested in displaying pure physical strength against another, or with a great interest in fighting and war. She does not ordinarily have an interest in changing the face of the earth. Women are more oriented towards the preservation of what is on the earth;

they do not care for such changes as will threaten their lives or the lives of their offspring. Women like to nurture and preserve. This can be referred to the form of the cross; the women exert a force more like the horizontal line and seek a level as does water. Male force is more like the vertical line, with great heights and depths, great upheavals and changes.

On the next plane, that of the emotional, women behave in a positive fashion and men behave in a negative fashion. It is women who will pay attention to the feeling relationships between other people. She will spend endless hours with other women discussing emotional reactions to life events. She is not afraid to cry or to give expression to many other emotions. She is well able to descend to the depths of the subconscious world (to hell, the concealed world) and dredge up out of the unconscious those emotional reactions which have had an effect upon her. Thus, knowing and admitting emotions and their power over herself, she is well able to conquer them. Through this sympathy with emotions and her experience of them that is developed through her life, she can often sense the mood of a whole roomful of people, of her spouse or of her children, without one word being spoken. She will know, again without words necessarily, why one person cannot get along with another person. She will often respect these differences in emotional orientation. Through this knowledge she can sometimes rearrange matters so that harmony will prevail in her surrounding group.

A man is more likely to want to act tough; to think it unworthy of himself if he should give way to tears or deeply felt emotions. He is much more disposed to ignore his emotional reactions to others and theirs to him. If matters get out of hand and he is not allowed to express what he really feels about events, he may retreat into repression and feign ignorance that he ever had such an emotion as now threatens his male status. Repression can build up into a dangerous influence as every psychologist knows, and often bursts forth from a man in violence of some sort or another. He can go to extremes and commit crimes and many other types of anti-social acts. This probably explains why we find prisons, hospitals and insane asylums with a larger proportion of men than of women.

Or, when faced with emotional reactions that a man cannot admit, he may retreat into the intellectual world in an effort to escape their influence, as here he functions in a positive fashion. However, many distortions of intellectual thinking can occur too, among such men as do not admit their emotional natures.

There are, of course, exceptions to the above, as there are to all classifications. The horoscope, if it has a predominance of planets in water signs in a male nativity, will make it easier for a man to recognize and control his emotions. The depth psychologists, such as C.G. Jung, Freud and others, spend much energy on the study of the power of emotional reactions. Alchemy and magick practices demand that the student pay attention to these forces. If he does not, as is sometimes the case, he will be in for quite a fall. He sometimes will not know or understand that to control effects of emotions, he must first know what that emotion is, what it does to him, how it controls his life and his fate.

Many thoughts can pass through the mind and come to nothing in the end. It is the emotions which help to crystallize the thought into phenomena. Here is one very potent reason why aspirants to the study of the occult arts should go through a protracted session of psychoanalysis. If they refuse to know about the well-springs of their being, the power of emotional reactions, they may suffer from delusions, obsession, and finally death. Often a woman, well-informed and wise in emotional matters, can be of great assistance to male occultists.

Because a woman accepts and understands the emotional reactions and feelings of others, she is more likely to accept persons as individuals. It would be much more likely that a man would become a dictator in his business or in government, riding over the basic differences of all people in order to establish his own supremacy, or the supremacy of his Ideal or of the State. In the past age many men enjoyed being the absolute dictator in their own homes, showing very little concern for the reactions of wife and children. This still happens today, with unhappy results for all.

On the mental plane, men usually behave in a positive fashion and women behave in a negative fashion. Men can use logic, the powers of reason, the intellect, to solve certain life problems. But because this plane of phenomena is so easy for him, he would like to think that everything can be solved mentally, that his physical and abstract sciences can do nothing but benefit the whole world. That they fall far short of doing this, that they have now posed a bigger problem for the whole world to face and solve, that they have lead to racial strife and personal unhappiness as often as not, is now becoming evident.

Many men would like to stop at the mental plane and claim that nothing else exists. This plane and its proper use proves to him his own superiority over women. Some men like to scoff at the type of womanly reactions they are acquainted with; they like to claim that a woman is not logical, and thinks in ways foreign to their own type of thinking, and therefore she must be an inferior being. But the Age of Reason, which had its highest growth in the 18th and 19th centuries, is on its way out. Here we might refer to the diatribes in *Liber Legis*, especially in Chapter 2, against the unbalanced and exclusive use of reason. Verse 32 states: "Also reason is a lie; for there is a factor infinite & unknown; & all their words are skew-wise."[87]

On the mental plane women have been traditionally negative. They have relied on the two planes in which they function in a positive fashion, the emotional and the spiritual. But in the New Æon of Thelema, the woman has been asked to change her natural way of viewing life events and reacting to them. In *Liber Legis*, Cap. III, v. 11, we read, "Let the woman be girt with a sword before me."[88] The sword refers to intellect, mentality, air. Today we see that women are learning to be positive on the mental plane. They challenge men in their traditional mental occupations; they become doctors, lawyers, judges, business people and now can do just about everything that men arrogated to themselves in the past. Even if none of these modern women has seen *Liber Legis*, the change is nevertheless operative. In due time we shall probably see as great a proportion of women in formerly traditional male occupations as we see of males. Perhaps because women outnumber men, and fewer of them succumb to the ailments and troubles that men do, this would not be too difficult of development, even though some women may prefer a certain time set aside for child bearing and rearing. Certainly with the economic situation as it is, hardly any household can exist without the labor of both spouses.

The question might be asked, that if men refuse to function in a positive fashion on the emotional plane, and that if women now

---

87. Crowley, *Liber AL vel Legis*, 43.
88. Crowley, *Liber AL vel Legis*, 53.

become positive on the mental plane, in what sort of position does this leave men? Will women outstrip men in development? Will women finally rule the world if men refuse to grow and develop either positive or negative functioning on all planes? Is this what *Liber Legis* means when in Chapter I, v. 15, it is stated that in the Scarlet Woman is all power given?

But before we discuss what the Scarlet Woman might be, let us consider the last plane, that of the spiritual. Here women function in a positive fashion and men in a negative fashion.

In the mundane world, we notice that a great many more women than men will support and work with churches; will insist that the family learn something of religion; or will be attending lectures and filling up groups interested in metaphysics, religious matters and anything to do with the spiritual side of life. Even in Thelema, when Crowley wrote *Magick Without Tears*, his letters were addressed to the enquiries of women.

This phenomena has been noticed also, in *Liber VII*, Cap. VI, v. 40 and 41. "There are few men; there are enough."[89] "We shall be full of cup-bearers, and the wine is not stinted."[90] Cup-bearers, of course, refer to the well-known office of the priestess, to behave as a cup to receive the force of the male. She nurtures this force and brings it to birth, whether as a material or immaterial Child. Water is a symbol of the Universal menstruum which brings all to birth out of its depths. As the physical babe in the womb floats in water, so is this reflected on less material planes. The High Priestess of Atu II, Gimel, refers to this fact. The Priestess is herself hidden partly by veils but she is reflected in water, and it is the cup which holds water.

Each plane which the aspirant is desirous of conquering as seen on the Tree of Life, each step upward, is like a male force. The H.G.A. acts like a male force and the aspirant must learn to behave like a cup to receive the influence from on high, from *Mezla*. Women act this way naturally, out of the own natural orientation, but men, being positive on the intellectual plane, must ever strive to learn to receive the influence from on high as a cup. The ruach, or the intellectual plane, is a plane which invites the aspirant to project his or her own forces, to behave in a positive and outgoing fashion. But this plane is not the last one, and must

---

89. Crowley, *The Holy Books of Thelema*, 31.
90. Ibid.

in due time be thoroughly understood as only another tool which is at the moment of consciousness and intellectuality of use to the God within, but must be set aside as the aspirant crosses the Abyss.

We can observe this behavior of each of the sexes in their particular action of the polarities in various of the myths and legends and fairy stories which spring up all over the world. Notice how often the woman is equated with the soul, with the highest spirituality. She is the king's daughter who awaits the arrival of the magician or prince. In his wanderings he has had to purify his aspiration into pure love of this daughter. He has had to become one pointed in his will so that he might achieve union with her.[91] In *Liber Legis*, the formula of Nuit is always this calling of the aspirant, "To Me," she says over and over again. She is also represented as Babalon on a lower plane, the great sea, Binah, the first phenomena which the aspirant must assimilate in order to reach the Highest, Kether.

We see this carefully put before our eyes in poesy and ritual in the beautiful Gnostic Catholic Mass. The Priestess is the representative of Nuit because she is naturally positive on the spiritual plane. She can act like a cup more easily due to her nature and receive the word from Heaven, from Nuit. Then she imparts this message to the Priest who can benefit thereby and grow in spirituality. Hers, then, is the voice of pure intuition and love, which is our Law.

Let us refer to the Tree of Life for a confirmation of this action. Notice that the only purely single-sexed Atu above the Abyss is the Atu of Daleth, Venus, the door, and the symbol of love. Notice that on the symbol of Venus, the whole of the Tree of Life may be drawn. This is not true of the other planets.

The other two cards above the Abyss bear an admixture of male and female; these are 0, the Fool, and I, the Magus which is referred to Mercury, a double-sexed god. Then the one card that leads the aspirant upward from Tiphereth, the center of the whole Tree, and of the ruach, and the center which exemplifies the Knowledge and Conversation of the Holy Guardian Angel, is the Atu of Gimel, the Moon, and a wholly feminine symbol.

Crowley admits in his diaries and in other places that Initiation

---

91. *Parsifal* is a particularly compelling version of this myth.

to Tiphereth was accomplished with the help of male force, of other men, but that his Initiations beyond Tiphereth depended on the right use of the female force, and it was women, the current Scarlet Woman of the moment, who aided him to reach Kether.

Further, let us quote from *The Book of Lies* by Crowley, Chap. 3, "The Oyster":

> The Brothers of A∴A∴ are one with the Mother of the Child. The Many is as adorable to the One as the One is to the Many. This is the Love of These; creation-parturition is the Bliss of the One; coition-dissolution is the Bliss of the Many. The All, thus interwoven of These, is Bliss. Naught is beyond Bliss. The man delights in uniting with the Woman; the Woman in parting from the Child. The Brothers of the A∴A∴ are Women: the Aspirants to A∴A∴ are Men.[92]

And, in Chapter 90, "Starlight":

> Behold! I have lived many years, and I have travelled in every land that is under the dominion of the Sun, and I have sailed the seas from pole to pole. Now do I lift up my voice and testify that all is vanity on earth, except the love of a good woman, and that good woman LAYLAH. And I testify that in heaven all is vanity (for I have journeyed oft, in every heaven), except the love of OUR LADY BABALON. And I testify that beyond heaven and earth is the love of OUR LADY NUIT. And seeing that I am old and well stricken in years, and that my natural forces fail, therefore do I rise up in my throne and call upon THE END. For I am youth eternal and force infinite. And at THE END is SHE that was LAYLAH, and BABALON, and NUIT, being ...[93]

There is much more in *The Book of Lies* along the same themes. This is well worth the study that an aspirant can bring to it.

But is the earthly, everyday woman always the high Priestess, or the Scarlet Woman, or a representative of Babalon and Nuit?

The ordinary, everyday woman is no more a Priestess or a Scarlet Woman than is the man who never bothers to develop his

---

92. Crowley, *The Book of Lies* (York Beach, ME: Samuel Weiser, 1993), 16.
93. Crowley, *The Book of Lies*, 190.

magical and spiritual self, a Priest. Such feminine high offices demand a rigorous training, just as exacting as that which the man undergoes.

It might be objected that the Priestess in the Gnostic Catholic Mass seems not to have to undergo such training but this is only if she is actually virgo intacta. That is, she will never have had sex with a man. There is a peculiar spiritual quality to some virgins, as they reflect the influences from *Mezla*. If she has once had sex this natural purity disappears and from then on, in order for her to be a "Virgin pure without spot," she must be wholly and entirely dedicated to her One Will, that is, the Knowledge and Conversation of her own Holy Guardian Angel.

A description of what it means to be virgin, whether of male or female gender, is given in *Liber LXV*, Cap. 5, v. 9 and 10. Here is the utterance of the Holy Guardian Angel to the scribe, Crowley:

> 9. But I have burnt within thee as a pure flame without oil. In the midnight I was brighter than the moon; in the daytime I exceeded utterly the sun; in the byways of thy being I flamed, and dispelled the illusion.
>
> 10. Therefore thou art wholly pure before Me; therefore thou art My virgin unto eternity.[94]

In *Liber AL vel Legis* we read in Cap. I, v. 44 and 45:

> For pure will, unassuaged of purpose, delivered from the lust of result, is every way perfect. The Perfect and the Perfect are one Perfect and not two; nay are none![95]

Such perfection as is spoken of in the above can be applied to the perfection of male and female as they walk on this earth. This is not easy of attainment and it certainly implies that both male and female have each only one will as above described.

It is true that women naturally have the capacity to act in a positive fashion on the spiritual plane, but women, like a majority of men, have not developed their possibilities and birthrights in every instance. Sometimes negative and uncontrolled passions and emotions stand in the way of their development, as they do

---

94. Crowley, *The Holy Books of Thelema*, 77.
95. Crowley, *Liber AL vel Legis*, 31.

with men. Sometimes early life conditioning in this phenomenal world blocks their capacities; sometimes a past karma and its dreadful results needs to be worked out and rectification established. There are very many reasons why a lot of women would not be able to function as a Priestess or as a Scarlet Woman.

I might remark here that Crowley accepted some of his female lovers as Scarlet Women, and some he did not accept in this way. However, even though he says that some were such, the office of Scarlet Woman goes far beyond the particular incarnation of any woman who had represented this high office to Crowley for such a short span of time. This office is operable for the whole of this present Æon of Horus, which will last for over 2,000 years. Just the same is the office of the Beast operable during this long time.

How rigorous and exacting is the preparation for the office of the Scarlet Woman, a step beyond the office of Priestess, is clearly stated to us in *Liber Legis* in several places in the first two chapters, but most especially in Chapter III. These verses are quite specific:

> 43. Let the Scarlet Woman beware! If pity and compassion and tenderness visit her heart; if she leave my work to toy with old sweetnesses; then shall my vengeance be known. I will slay me her child; I will alienate her heart: I will cast her out from men: as a shrinking and despised harlot shall she crawl through dusk wet streets, and die cold and an-hungered.
>
> 44. But let her raise herself in pride! Let her follow me in my way! Let her work the work of wickedness! Let her kill her heart! Let her be loud and adulterous! Let her be covered with jewels and rich garments, and let her be shameless before all men!
>
> 45. Then will I lift her to pinnacles of power: then will I breed from her a child mightier than all the kings of the earth. I will fill her with joy: with my force shall she see & strike at the worship of Nu: she shall achieve Hadit.[96]

Who is talking? It is the utterance of the God Heru-Ra-Ha, who functions as a twin God, known in his two aspects as Hoor-Paar-

---

96. Crowley, *Liber AL vel Legis*, 61-62.

Kraat and Ra-Hoor-Khuit. This God contains in his name a reference to Kether, Heru, and a reference to the Sun, Ra, or Tiphereth. The whole name adds to 418, which is a number that is a symbol of the Great Work, the achievement of the Knowledge and Conversation of the Holy Guardian Angel.

The first utterance is a stern warning on the subject of how a woman may fail to attain. This is probably due to the fact that very few women attained the Great Work in the past ages, due to their absorption in the affairs and the will of their men. So the woman of today must first of all avoid old sweetnesses out of the past, the desire to relax and be only a cup, not stirring herself in particular on her own behalf, but accepting all that her man has in his mind and behavior for her welfare or otherwise.

Once she has set out on the path to attainment, though, she must then strike out for herself in many ways. It is not that she now spurns a man, far from it, but her relationship to him is now very different. She is no longer merely a wife or a harlot; she must add to these offices and must attain perfection through her own strivings.

The instructions for doing this come in the next verse 44.

Women must raise themselves in pride in this New Æon, and be whole in attainment to the highest spiritual states in their own right. They must no longer allow themselves to be chattel or slaves, subject to the whims of men. They must develop and do their own wills, even if they are in the "Man of Earth" phase of development. This is clear from *Liber Legis*, Cap. I, v. 41, when Nuit demands that the men do not obstruct the women or refuse them to do their own wills.

This attitude is already showing itself even in the mundane world where none of the women now working for women's rights have ever heard of *Liber AL vel Legis*. This struggle is often bitter and confused and fraught with peril and trouble, but victory must be won in time. When a pendulum in human affairs swings too far in one direction, it must be compensated for by a swing just as far in the other direction. This pendulum for over 2,000 years has swung too far in favor of the male, and now to right the balance will take a great deal of difficult work and devotion on the part of women, awake to the peril to the race when the balance between the two sexes is lost.

In order for a woman to first carry out what is her finite will and then to become devoted and virgin towards her infinite will, which would be to attain the Knowledge and Conversation of the Holy Guardian Angel, she must work at the disciplines ordained towards these ends. In the finite will she must be trained in some way so that she can carry out her work in the world. This is just as true for accomplishing the infinite will. She must take up and perform tasks in yoga, magick and ritual, study of qabalah and all the rest of the tasks as prescribed for the Great Work. So her pride, then, would be that pride which is based on honest accomplishment, and not that pride which is seen in lying ego-maniacs who make claims for accomplishments that are not theirs through work.

Next, she must "follow me in my way!"[97] What is the way of this God of the New Æon? His way is clearly stated in the verses in Chapter III and where these are understood, the women can put into action the commands in this chapter. But notice the word understand here! If she does not understand herself, if she has no notion of her H.G.A., she would be making a great miss in trying to follow Ra-Hoor-Khuit. Also, remember that we have already established that this God, Heru-Ra-Ha, more familiarly known or spoken of as Ra-Hoor-Khuit, is a stand-in for the Holy Guardian Angel on this earth. He represents this highest attainment. So to follow him is to attain in this fashion. There is no need to expand on the intricacies of qabalistic meaning in this sentence but the serious student will find some of this inner meaning written down in Crowley's Commentaries on *The Book of the Law*. There is still more which has not been discovered by Crowley or by those who have taken up qabalistic work after him, but in due time this will become very clear.

Then the woman who would attain to be a Scarlet Woman must "<u>w</u>ork the <u>w</u>ork of <u>w</u>ickedness!"[98] The three "w"s in this sentence are underlined to bring out their significance. W [as Vav] is equivalent to six, which is a number of the Sun. Line up the three sixes, and we have 666, a symbol of the Beast. This number of 666 is the sum of all the numbers in the magic square of the Sun which has six numbers on each side. 666 is not especially the man Crowley, it is the sigil of the avatar of this Æon,

---

97. Crowley, *Liber AL vel Legis*, 61.
98. Ibid.

of a God incarnate in a human. 666 would represent the utmost development of the sphere of Tiphereth, the center of any human's Being, and the sphere which represents the Knowledge and Conversation of the Holy Guardian Angel. Clearly then, in this sentence we are asked to make the same attainment as did the Beast.

Further, "Scarlet Woman" in Greek adds up to 667, which is 666 plus one, which is unity. Unity refers again to Ra-Hoor-Khuit. We can check this against the verse which begins "Unity uttermost showed" in *Liber Legis*, Cap. III, v. 37.[99]

Then the word wicked must be looked up in the dictionary. The idea that anything could now be morally bad, which is one of these definitions, has been exploded by *The Book of the Law* itself and further explained in Crowley's Commentaries. Anything is lawful if it is the True Will. But remember, that is One Will, and not several! Remember that it is pure and virgin!

The next sentence asks the woman set upon the highest attainment to kill her heart. That is, she must no longer be swayed by emotional attachment to any one man; she must not hang on to him. She needs to develop intellect and rationality in order to accomplish this task. Would men, then, be out of her province with this accomplishment? Not at all! It is only that in controlling her emotions, her love, she puts these powers under her will! Is not our Law that of Love under Will?

Once she has controlled her emotional attachments, she can then be loud and adulterous and be a true representative of Babalon. Since Nuit and Babalon make no difference, the initiate woman does not make a difference, either. Let her lovers come and go as they please, she has the situation under control and is not overly upset when they depart. This is the attitude of a refined and spiritual courtesan.

Jewels and rich garments can also refer to the accomplishments of the Scarlet Woman. She might be a true artist, or she might be highly developed in the intellectual sphere. At any rate, she has the highest development of her finite will and also of her infinite will. The jewels and rich garments are a sign of this. She is without shame before all men because she now has pride in herself.

---

99. Crowley, *Liber AL vel Legis*, 58.

A woman is just as much of a star as is a man and no longer can she be trampled upon or suffer men's cruelties towards her.

A woman can awaken kundalini as does the man and unite herself with Nuit. In the end, she also attains to Hadit. If she has been termed a hollow star, and the man has been termed a star with a center, she would now attain a center to her star, the same as he has. This is an accomplishment probably far in the future. No woman to date has exhibited signs of this attainment. This is all the more reason for supposing that the office of Scarlet Woman has not as yet been manifested in the body of a woman. This high office is just as much the avatar of a Goddess as the idea of 666 is the avatar of a God.

Verse 45 is more of a promise to the woman when she has attained than it is an instruction. The child promised has, of course, been willed by the Beast, her partner; or we can call him the Magician, or he who has attained to the highest concept of Tiphereth. This child might be a physical child, or it might be a particular work done by these two high officers of the Thelemic Æon. It could even be a creation of the woman conjoined to her own Holy Guardian Angel, that is, a woman who has crossed the Abyss. The meaning of "child" goes far beyond the physical plane, though it is also tied to physical phenomena. This child could even represent Thelema itself.

The Scarlet Woman might bear the seed of purpose of To Mega Therion himself and bring it to birth in the lives and hearts of mankind, even if she does not manifest for some hundreds of years. She might, also, be more than one person, and Crowley seemed to think this was the case. She might be more willing to "Obey my prophet"[100] as is asked of us all in *Liber Legis*, Cap. I, v. 32, because of her own makeup as woman and because she can more easily receive, as a cup, the influence of the highest as it is known to us in this New Æon.

That this might be the case, we must look to the original nature of men. They like too much to change things around to suit their own egos, whether developed or undeveloped. They are always disposed to make new systems, new laws for mankind, even to the point of altering Thelemic intention as set forth in *Liber Legis*. This is even now happening all over the world among men

---

100. Crowley, *Liber AL vel Legis*, 29.

of some attainment who profess to be Thelemites. The women are not so likely to be revisionists.

Could it be that because Crowley had not really penetrated to the meaning of these verses in *Liber Legis*, and because he was a man, and because he had never met a fully developed Scarlet Woman, that he did not fully understand the office of women in the New Æon of Thelema? I think only the future can tell us this when women develop to the highest attainment which can match the attainment of the Beast, 666.

Love is the law, love under will.

Meral

Carete Fratres et Sorores,[101]

Do what thou wilt shall be the whole of the Law.

When reading either the *Magical and Philosophical Commentaries on the Book of the Law*, or *The Law is for All*, the student comes upon some references to Crowley's writings, some of which were written by him before the dictation of *The Book of the Law* by Aiwass on April 8, 9 and 10 of 1904.

One reference is to "The Soldier and the Hunchback," another is to "Time," another to "Eleusis," another to "Berashith." Some of these articles are included in Crowley's *Collected Works*.[102] Some are in *The Equinox* volumes. Many people have been unable to buy any of these books; they are either scarce or too high priced. Therefore, *In the Continuum* has made it an editorial policy to seek out important cross-references and to print them once again for the assistance of the student. The Commentaries on *Liber Legis* are extremely important for every Thelemite. It is very necessary for anyone to understand in as complete a fashion as possible just what is meant by some of the cryptic sentences in *Liber Legis*. Some messages are for future adepts to expound. Some are clearly explained by Crowley and these we must be acquainted with if we are to behave as a true Thelemite and grow and develop under this new Law of the Æon.

---

101. Originally published in: Phyllis Seckler, *In the Continuum* 2.7 (1980): 3-18.
102. Crowley, *The Collected Works*, Vols. I-III. (Foyers, S.P.R.T., 1905-1907).

It is also the policy of *In the Continuum* to publish various poems and other works referred to in the rituals of Ordo Templi Orientis, since this body has gained some activity of late and its members, unfortunately, often work with insufficient knowledge and preparation. Any Lodge Master may write to the Editor of *I.T.C.* and thus ask for a complete list of the poems and articles referred to in the rituals. This list will inform him or her in which issue of *In the Continuum* he can find the desired reprint.

This publication also has as its prime reason for existence, the many and various answers to questions asked by the student. Our policy is to teach and explain. Many times articles are written because questions are asked. Recently, there have been many questions in regard to *Liber O*. Since this is a very important collection of practices and rituals for the student and absolutely necessary as part of his groundwork in magick, the answers to some of these recent questions are of interest to all.

Some have asked about certain details pertaining to the Lesser Ritual of the Pentagram and the Greater Ritual of the Pentagram. For instance, why is air attributed to the east and fire to the south, water to the west and earth to the north?

If we review the work of the Golden Dawn which was basic to Crowley's magical instructions and from which he derived many of his rituals, we will find there many things which he left out of his writings. True, some of the rituals of the Golden Dawn were too verbose, but along with unnecessary words, Crowley also left out many of the reasons for things. My advice to the student is that if a question arises in magick ritual, see if the question can be answered by a reference to *The Golden Dawn* by Regardie.

The explanation for the attribution of various elements to the quarters is stated in *The Golden Dawn* to be due to the winds.[103] Further, as the elements vibrate between the cardinal points, their attribution <u>is not unchangeable</u>. The east wind is stated to be of the nature of air, the south wind of the nature of fire, naturally, for those of us in the northern hemisphere, as the Sun is always seen to the south of us. West winds have moisture and rain and the west is the place of the setting sun. *Liber Legis* attributes this direction to Nuit in the sentence from Chapter I, v. 64, "I am the

---

103. See further: Regardie, Israel, *The Golden Dawn* (St. Paul, MN: Llewellyn Publications, 1993), 280-286 for the text under discussion.

blue-lidded daughter of Sunset; I am the naked brilliance of the voluptuous night-sky."[104]

Water and earth have been attributed to feminine qualities in nature, at least in astrological and zodiacal correspondences. Please refer to Table C. In some of Crowley's rituals, this attribution is switched and air is attributed to the north and is of Nuit, feminine, and earth refers to Therion, or the perfected man [see *Liber V vel Reguli*].

The north winds bring cold and dry air from the pole and the ice sheets there. Here is the *Golden Dawn* table which explains this further, from Volume I, Book 1.[105]

Heat and Dryness	Fire	△
Heat and Moisture	Air	△
Cold and Dryness	Earth	▽
Cold and Moisture	Water	▽

Table C

However, if we place the elements according to the beginning of the seasons in the zodiac, formed from the apparent placement of the sun in the skies relative to earth's equator and the revolution of the earth around the sun, thus making the seasons, we would find that Aries, the season attributed to the east and to the start of life in the Springtime, is a fire sign and therefore we might expect to find fire in the east [see Diagram L]. At the Summer Solstice the sun moves from Gemini into Cancer and is the farthest north of the equator in its travels through the sky. Cancer is a water sign and therefore water would be attributed to the north.

When the sun is at the Autumnal Equinox position, we find that its movement takes it from Virgo into Libra, which is an air sign and, therefore, the west would be attributed to air.

---

104. Crowley, *Liber AL vel Legis*, 37.
105. Regardie, *The Golden Dawn* (St. Paul: Llewellyn Publications, 1993), 50.

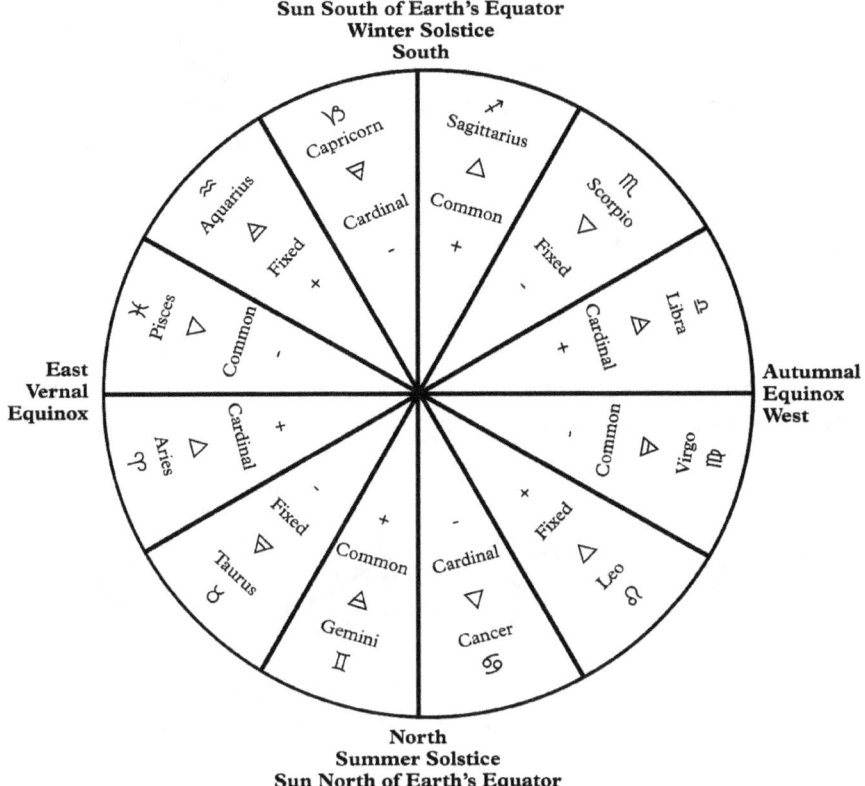

All positive (+) Zodiac signs attributed to △ Fire & △ Air
All negative (−) Zodiac signs attributed to ▽ Water & ▽ Earth

Diagram L.

At the Winter Solstice, the sun moves from Sagittarius to Capricorn and the latter is an earth sign and we would expect earth to be attributed to the south. This is not the system used for the Lesser Ritual of the Pentagram but it is the system for the Lesser Ritual of the Hexagram. Here you have the reason, then, for the placement of the hexagrams to their various quarters.
Please refer to Diagram L.

The Golden Dawn goes on to state that it is better to use the position of the winds in invoking due to the fact that the earth is ever whirling upon its poles. But if working in the Spirit Vision, the book advises that it is better to take the attribution of the elements to the four quarters as they are in the zodiac.

The advice goes on to state that air and water have much in common as one contains the other. Water has a chemical formula of H_2O, and both of these gases are in the air. There is moisture in the air at all times also. Because of this, the symbols of air and water are sometimes interchanged and the eagle, usually of Scorpio's third and highest attribution[106] is often associated with Aquarius instead. In the zodiac, Aquarius is a fixed air sign, therefore the Cherub of air and its symbol is the head of a man. But we note also that this sign is the water bearer. Here then is one of the reasons why the very same top bar is used for air and water for banishing and invoking.

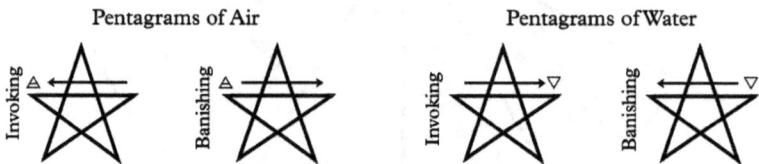

Also, these symbols of the elements as they are placed on the pentagram correspond roughly with the elements of the fixed signs as they are seen on the zodiac wheel. These fixed signs represent the four powers of the Sphinx. For a table with the correspondences of the Sphinx to the zodiac, etc., please refer to Table B.

We can refer these attributions of zodiac and Sphinx to certain sentences in *Liber AL vel Legis*, Cap. I, v. 6: "Be thou Hadit, my secret centre, my heart & my tongue!"

Crowley's Commentary on this reads: "Nuith selects three centres of Her Body to become 'Two' with Hadit; for She asks me to declare Her in these three. Infinite freedom, all-embracing, for physical Love; boundless continuity for Life; and the silent rhythm of the Stars for Language. These three conceptions are Her gift to us."[107] In this sentence he mentions, Liberty, Love, Life and Light (stars).

---

106. The symbols attributed to Scorpio, the Snake and the Eagle.
107. Crowley, *Magical and Philosophical Commentaries*, 94.

We may go further, and as an experiment, not to be taken too rigidly, we could draw a pentagram with Nuit surrounding it and indicate the five points and their attributions to Her words. Remember that the pentagram is a symbol of Hadit and is referred to also in *Liber Legis*, Cap. I, v. 60 as "...The Five Pointed Star, with a Circle in the Middle, & the circle is Red"[108] [see Diagram M].

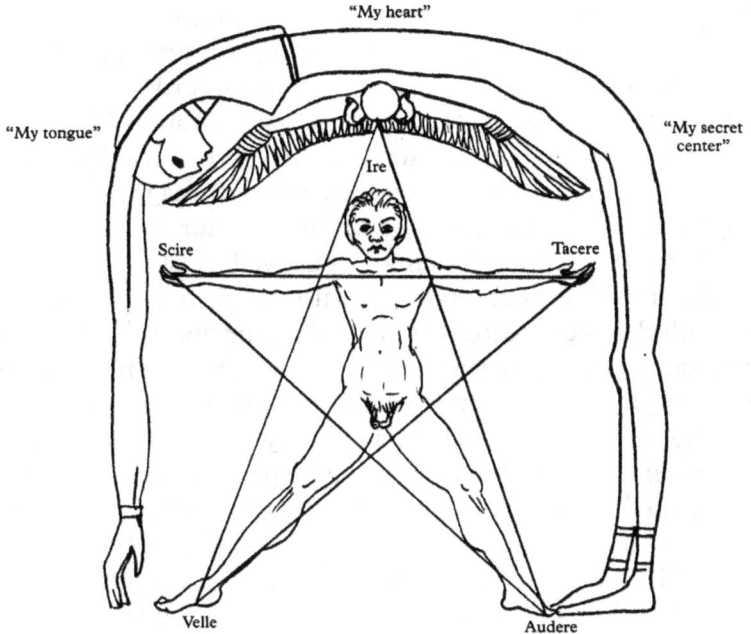

"Her lovely hands upon the black earth."[1]   "Her soft feet not hurting the little flowers."[1]

1. From LIBER AL, Cap. I, v.26

Diagram M.

Next the question is asked, "What use is the Greater Ritual of the Pentagram?" If you are doing *Liber Samekh* you would find that each pentagram traced invokes the proper element in its quarter, according to the winds attribution as before explained. This ritual uses the traditional correspondences of the elements to the quarters. But you have a chance to invoke each element. This is

---

108. Crowley, *Liber AL vel Legis*, 35.

good practice, for you may need this knowledge if traveling on the Astral or scrying in the Spirit Vision.

Further, in *Liber Samekh* you become acquainted with the use of the pentagrams of spirit as you use the invoking pentagrams of "Equilibrium of Actives" and "Equilibrium of Passives." When we count how many pentagrams we have traced in this ritual, we notice that there are six of them. Remember that 5 + 6 = 11, the number of Thelemic magick. This number refers to the union of Macroprosopus, the Universe, and man, the Microprosopus. The active spirit pentagram is a moving towards the H.G.A., a yearning, an active event, which you start in order to invoke and unite with Him. The passive invoking pentagram is like a waiting in passive love, like a cup, for His arrival. In *Liber VII* this idea is written thus: "Nor by memory, nor by imagination, nor by prayer, nor by fasting, nor by scourging, nor by drugs, nor by ritual, nor by meditation; only by passive love shall he avail."[109]

The invoking pentagrams are also used in *Liber V vel Reguli* but with the zodiac attributions to the four quarters, those of the fixed signs, or the Cherubs of air, water, earth and fire. This ritual will give you good practice in using the pentagrams in this way, and should certainly be worked by every Magician in Thelema.[110]

Also, notice that V is an angle of the pentagram. Hence, Crowley's motto, Vi Veri Universum Vivus Vici, (V.V.V.V.V.) translated as "In my lifetime I have conquered the Universe by the force of Truth," is a reference to the complete control of all of the powers of the Sphinx, plus the angle of spirit, and is made up of the five V's to be found at each angle of the pentagram.

For practice in banishing, using all of the pentagrams and hexagrams, the student should refer to *Liber Yod*, "The First Method."

The best learning comes with practice. Intellect is not enough, one must live the experience to know it.

With each pentagram, a Divine Name is given. It would assist in our understanding if we should enumerate these according to the qabalah, and also give the Hebrew spelling.

---

109. Crowley, *The Holy Books of Thelema*, op. cit.
110. Crowley, *Magick Liber Aba*, 561-572.

PENTAGRAM	NAME	PRONOUNCE	HEBREW	ENUMERATION
Spirit, active	AHIH	(Eheieh)	אהיה	21
Spirit, passive	AGLA	(Agla)	אגלא	35
Fire	ALHIM	(Elohim)	אלהים	86
Water	AL	(El)	אל	31
Air	IHVH	(Ye-ho-wau)	יהוה	26
Earth	ADNI	(Adonai)	אדני	65

Referring to *Sepher Sephiroth*, to be found either in *The Equinox*, Vol. I, No. 8, or in *The Qabalah of Aleister Crowley*,[111] we find that *AHIH* is Existence, Being, the Kether-name of God, and that this number, 21, is also a Mystic Number of Tiphareth since it is the sum of the numbers from 1 to 6. Also, if we count the Fool of the Tarot as No. 0, there are then 21 Atu.

AGLA, a name of GOD, is a notariqon of the sentence, "*Ateh Gibor le-Olahm Adonai*" translated as "To Thee be Power unto the Ages, O Lord," or "Thou art mighty forever, O Lord."[112] We can enumerate each word thus:

```
AThH     =  406
GBUR     =  211
Le-OVLM  =  176
ADNI     =   65
            858 = 21.
```

We can find further references to this word in *Book 4*, Part II, Chapter 8, "The Sword." We also can quote from "The Temple of Solomon the King," found in *The Equinox*, Vol. I, No. 5, "A brief explanation of *AGLA* is this: A, the one first; A, the one last; G, the Trinity in Unity; L, the completion of the great work."[113]

---

111. Crowley, *The Qabalah of Aleister Crowley, Including Gematria, Liber 777, Sepher Sephiroth* (New York, NY: Samuel Weiser, 1973). The same collection was later retitled *777 and Other Qabalistic Writings of Aleister Crowley*.
112. Crowley, "The Temple of Solomon the King (Continued)," in: *The Equinox*, Vol. I. No. V. (London: Aleister Crowley / Office of the Equinox), pp. 82 & 100.
113. Crowley, "The Temple of Solomon the King (Continued)," 82.

If we reduce 35, we get 8 and this number is very important in Thelema as it is referred to in *Liber Legis*, Cap. I, v. 46, "...I call it eight, eighty, four hundred & eighteen." I leave it to the student to chase down the meanings of the number eight as Cheth, etc.

ALHIM is thoroughly analyzed in *Magick in Theory and Practice*, Chapter 4.

AL, *IHVH*, and *ADNI* are also analyzed in the above book. Again, let me stress that it is an invaluable aid to the student if he should keep a notebook of important qabalistic numbers which he discovers by his own research. It is too time-consuming to chase down meanings of numbers through various books; these enumerations and their correspondences should be at the finger tips and available at a moment's notice.

Now let us consider the Lesser Ritual of the Hexagram, which has also been the subject of many questions. Many are very puzzled as to just how one traces the hexagram for Sol and it doesn't help that one of the angles has a wrong number on it—the upper left. It should read 2:11 and <u>not</u> 2:4.[114] Here is a diagram which pulls the hexagram for Sol apart and which explains how this is done. However, when tracing this hexagram, one figure is traced right on top of the other.

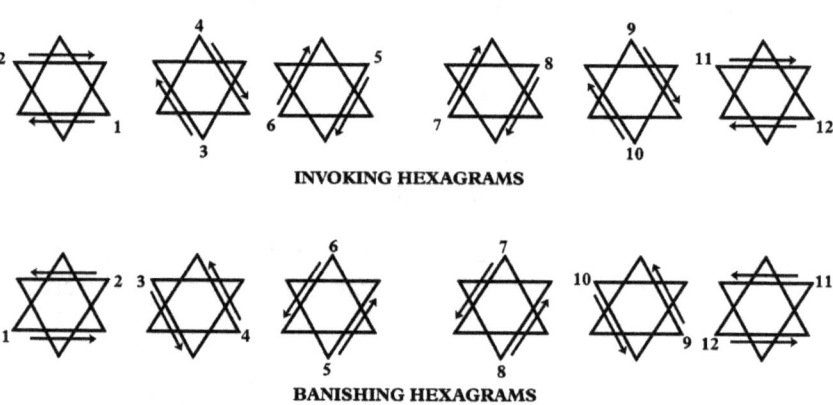

---

114. The error occurs in Crowley, "Liber O Vel Manus et Sagittae," *The Equinox*, Vol. I. No. II. (London: Simpkin *et al*, 1909), and is repeated in most works that reprint or draw from this, including Crowley, *Magick in Theory and Practice* (Paris, France: Lecram Press, 1929), 385.

Trace the sigil of the Sun in the center, of course, as soon as all six of the hexagrams have been traced. Then vibrate the Divine Word *ARARITA*.

Notice that the proper tracing of any of the hexagrams teaches you to think of the proper polarities of the planets or spheres on the Tree of Life. Thus, Mars is opposite to Venus, one planet is positive, the other negative. Mercury is opposite to Jupiter and Saturn is opposite to the Moon. This is a completely balanced use of the spheres and planets. Remember that we should always seek out this balance in everything we do, so as not to become lopsided and fanatic when growing and developing our powers. This is not only true and very necessary for magick, but it is true of all of Life!

Please refer to Diagram N for the placement of the planets on the Tree of Life. The Sun appears in the middle as it is the center of our whole manifestation in life. Saturn is placed at the topmost point as it represents the whole of the Supernal Triad. For further reasons for this type of thinking, the student should refer to *The Vision and the Voice*. Others of Crowley's writings give us the same ideas, but these are too numerous to quote here.

A very fine adept uses the Unicursal Hexagram, especially for this difficult hexagram of Sol (Uni—one, cursal—tracing). This can certainly be done but I am inclined to think that one then misses out on the mastering of something difficult.

Many times students have asked about *ARARITA*. This is a notariqon of the sentence: "One is his Beginning, one is his Individuality, His permutation One." In *Liber 813 vel Ararita*, Crowley changes the word Individuality to the word Spirit.[115] Here is how the sentence breaks down:

One is His Beginning — *Achad Rosh*
One is His Individuality — *Achadotho Rosh, Yechidotho*
His Permutation is One — *Temurotho Achad*

Rosh means head, beginning. Yechidah is a name for a part of the Self, the individual. Temurah means permutation, and Achad = Unity. *ARARITA* is $1 + 200 + 1 + 200 + 10 + 400 + 1 = 813 = 12$.

---

115. Crowley, *The Holy Books of Thelema*, 217.

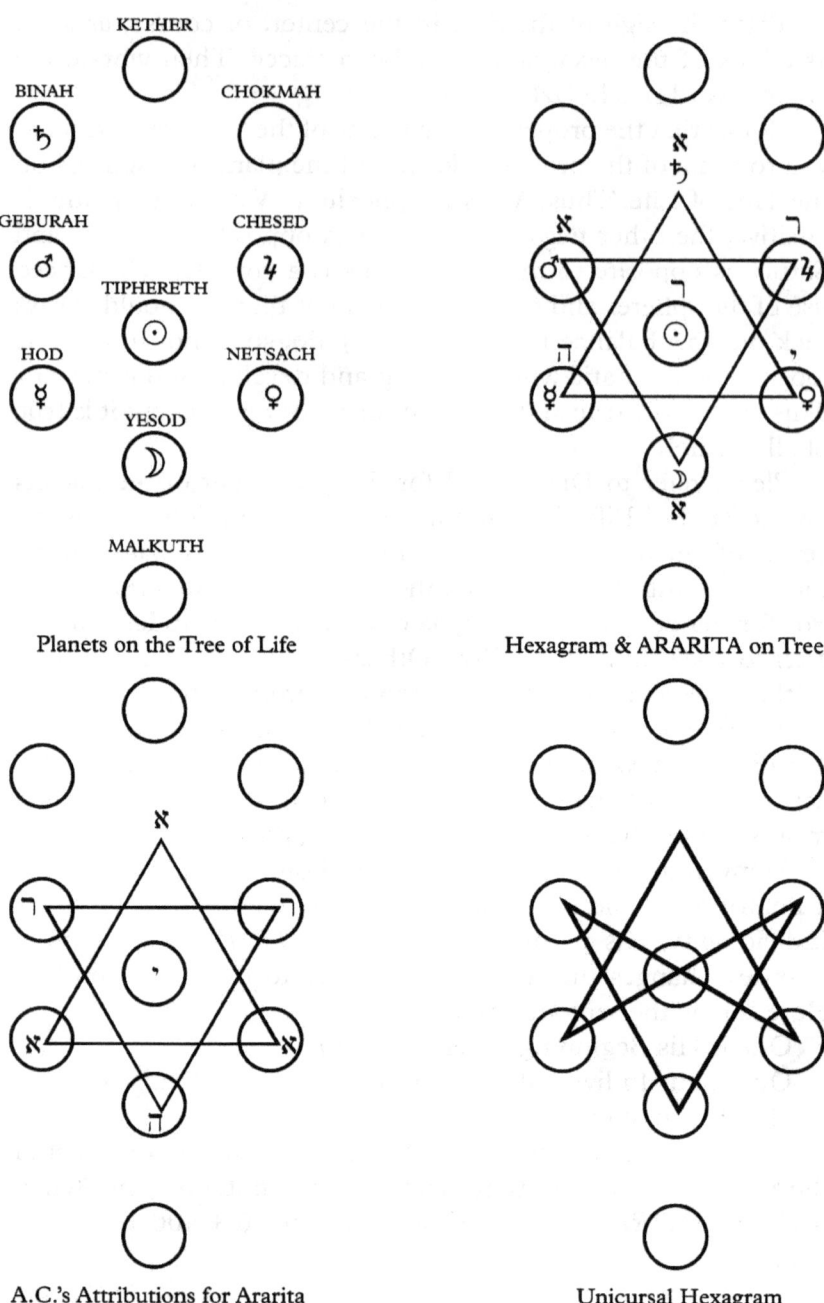

Diagram N.

The traditional attributions of the points of the hexagram to each letter of the Divine Word of *ARARITA* is as follows:

	SPHERE	PLANET	GOD NAME IN ASSIAH
A	3	Saturn	IHVH ELOHIM
R	4	Jupiter	AL
A	5	Mars	ELOHIM GIBOR
R	6	Sun	IHVH ELOAH VA-DAATH
I	7	Venus	IHVH TZABOATH
T	8	Mercury	ELOHIM TZABOATH
A	9	Moon	SHADDAI EL CHAI

These are to be found in *The Golden Dawn*, Book 4. Refer to diagram of the planets on the Tree of Life, No. 3 [see Diagram N].

Crowley has this to say about *ARARITA* in *The Vision and the Voice*, 22nd Aethyr, note 33:

> The use of this Name and Formula is to equate and identify every idea with its opposite; thus being released from the obsession of thinking any one of them as "true" (and therefore binding); one can withdraw oneself from the whole sphere of the Ruach. See *Liber 813 vel Ararita, the Holy Books*. Contrast each verse of Cap. I with the corresponding verse of Cap. II for the first of these methods. Thus in Cap. III (still verse by verse correspondence) the Quintessence of the ideas is extracted; and in Cap. IV they are withdrawn each one into the one beyond it. In Cap. V they have disappeared into the Method itself. In Cap. VI they reappear in the Form appointed by the Will of the Adept. Lastly, in Cap. VII they are dissolved, one into the next until all finally disappear in the Fire Qadosh, the Quintessence of Reality.[116]

---

116. Crowley, et al, *The Vision & the Voice with Commentary and Other Papers* (York Beach, ME: Samuel Weiser, 1998), 82.

Then students have asked, "What is the use of the Greater Ritual of the Hexagram?" Of course, this is used to invoke and banish planets and zodiac signs, but as to the specific design of the ritual, this is somewhat unclear. It is left to the ingenium of the student to devise the ritual.

Perhaps an example made up by a student of alchemy and magick will give an idea of how the student could proceed. Each angle of the hexagram refers to a particular planet and in turn, each planet is referred to a day of the week. A student of alchemy could then devise a ritual which will give him/her practice in the Lesser Circulation as well as practice in magick. Talismans are made up for each day of the week. For an excellent description of how to do this, please refer to I. Regardie's *How to Make and Use Talismans*.[117] Then a tincture is made of an herb which is suitable to the particular day, seven tinctures in all. For instructions on this please refer to Frater Albertus' *Alchemist's Handbook*.[118]

The days of the week are ruled by the planets as follows: Monday, Luna (Moon); Tuesday, Mars; Wednesday, Mercury; Thursday, Jupiter; Friday, Venus; Saturday, Saturn; Sunday, Sun.

Upon arising, the student should perform the Lesser Ritual of the Pentagram in order to purify the atmosphere and clear away the influences of the night. If at the proper time of day, and he/she is a Thelemite, *Liber Resh* can be performed too.

The talisman can be referred to or worn for the ritual or perhaps worn on the person all day. If a Thelemite, some verses from *Liber AL vel Legis* which seem appropriate to the planet can be inscribed as well as the usual God and Angelic names and the Kamea of the planet, etc. This has the effect of reminding the student of the things he should have memorized by now and of course aids in memory. Let me remark here that Crowley had all these details readily for use at any moment and the student interested in Thelema is too apt to forget these methods of magick; and then laughingly, I say, how many times have I seen pretense of high magick powers when the student is so obviously ignorant?

One person I know of even went so far as to wear the appropriate color of the planet for the day as an extension of his awareness of what day it was and what influences could be expected.

---

117. Regardie, Israel, *How to Make and Use Talismans* (New York: Samuel Weiser, 1970).
118. Albertus, Frater, *The Alchemist's Handbook* (York Beach ME: Samuel Weiser, 1987).

In the ritual proper, the hexagram corresponding to the planet is traced and the Divine Name of *ARARITA* is vibrated. Then follows the name of the planet and the names of the Angel and the Intelligence set over that planet and, of course, the God Name as given in the table. The student can make up his own conjuration to suit what he knows of the effects of the planet and what he expects of it during the day. Usually, the name of the spirit is not used due to the advice in *The Golden Dawn*, as it is said the spirits can cause quite a bit of trouble and are mischievous. This whole ritual can be finished off with an appeal that the planet, etc. will bring further knowledge of the Holy Guardian Angel and His workings in the life of the student. This can be followed by the Anthem from the Gnostic Catholic Mass found in *Magick in Theory and Practice*,[119] and after this, the teaspoon of the tincture can be taken.

At the end of the day the ritual can be reversed and the planet is banished, using the proper banishing hexagram and the events of the day are recited as giving important knowledge from the H.G.A. which should be noted. This is then followed by any other appropriate ritual, perhaps Reguli, or whatever appeals to the student, and the whole is finished off with the Lesser Ritual of the Pentagram.

This scheme, as can be seen, gives plenty of practice in the Greater Ritual of the Hexagram. Should the student be working on the astral plane, all pentagrams and hexagrams should be so well known and understood, that they become a part of one and available for use at any moment and under any circumstance. It is only too easy to be led astray by all sorts of visions and experiences on the astral plane as the forces are so fluid there, being made up of very subtle vibrations not usually known to our everyday consciousness. Many are the lying spirits eager to prey on weaknesses in the human aspirant. If the events on the astral are taken too seriously, the student ends up with all kinds of obsessions, difficulties, insanities, etc. which are pretty obvious to the trained observer, but which remain as goads to action and thinking to the poorly trained student. Usually, too, he is entirely unaware of the well-springs of his behavior and often is so poorly fitted for the fight that he goes down with his subtle essences badly maimed for several lives. It may take considerable

---

119. Crowley, *Magick Liber Aba*, 572-586.

incarnations to mend the damage, too. No wonder the occult arts were so carefully guarded in the past!

One use of the hexagrams is to banish astrological effects which may be bothersome and not related to the True Will. One could either banish the negative effects of a planet and invoke the positive and more desired effects, or one could invoke the powers of the planet most likely to offset the negative action of certain planetary aspects to one's own horoscope. For this reason, also, a person should know what happens in his horoscope so as to be really informed on the matter. The horoscope is a map of the present entity and it is also a picture of a series of events which the person can use either to his detriment or to his larger growth and development. Working with such a map is only one part of the work of a real Magician, but it is very essential, nevertheless. It can hardly be stressed too much that one must know what one is doing! The foundations of one's pyramid must be strong and without omissions and weaknesses. The development of the student must be well balanced and even in all directions and in proportion to his capabilities. He must ever see to it that he does not become lopsided, stressing one approach too much over another.

Then remember the injunction in *Liber AL vel Legis* when Nuit says in Cap. I, v. 52, "If this be not aright; if ye confound the space-marks, saying: They are one; or saying, They are many; if the ritual be not ever unto me: then expect the direful judgments of Ra Hoor Khuit!" The underlining is mine to bring it home forcefully to the mind of the student that all ritual (and, as Crowley says, all of our lives) must have the highest purpose. Crowley labored hard to indicate the next step for mankind, and this is to achieve the Knowledge and Conversation of the Holy Guardian Angel.

Ra-Hoor-Khuit is a symbol of this attainment, so when the verse says a person can expect the "direful judgments" they are those of the H.G.A., who administers appropriate punishments, troubles, karmic effects, lessons or whatever else is needed for the person who strays from this purpose.

We perform rituals for the purpose of knowing and controlling unseen forces in nature which reside in ourselves, in our own Hell (*Hélé*, the concealed place, or the unconscious.) The H.G.A. resides in this vast reservoir of unconscious forces. They are the forces also, of the whole Universe, of which we are a part.

The forces of the unconscious have a tremendous power. Some old writers referred to these forces as *Leviathan*, a mighty and powerful creature that lived in water, whose powers, set loose without proper control, could wreck the magician and the world.

We can liken this force and wellspring of power to a mighty engine which can be controlled by the will of the conscious mind. But one needs to know that the powers of the unconscious work only with a deductive reasoning process. This mighty engine can only go forward according to the events and commands of the conscious self. What is programmed into the unconscious mind by what the person allows to happen in his/her life is manifested again into life events. Thus, if one is addicted to programs on T.V. which are strong on violence, one will experience events in the life which mirror what has gone down into the depths. One has <u>programmed</u> the unconscious forces to behave in this manner.

It is the sign of a weakling if he/she will not admit that all events are of his/her own making. True, one cannot at first see the connection, perhaps. Here enters the uses of astrology and psychology to aid the student in understanding. He is encouraged to use inductive reasoning to see how it is he helped a certain event to manifest. Then, when seeing this clearly, it would help considerably to analyze if the event had anything to do with the True Will.

One should never underestimate the powers residing in the unconscious self to produce events in accord with what you are, and what has been fed into this vast reservoir by your actions, thoughts and emotions. Ritual tends to lift brute tendencies to higher purposes of evolution. We perform ritual in order to program the unseen and highly powerful forces of our own unconscious towards more beneficial ends. We work ourselves out of a lower evolutionary state into the "next step." We program unconscious forces to bring about higher states of consciousness, which at our present development we know by the words, the Knowledge and Conversation of the Holy Guardian Angel.

What better way to illustrate this point than by a quote from the Commentary on *Liber Legis* by the Master Therion? Let us refer to the Commentary on Chapter I, v. 37:

Now one more point about the obeah and the wanga, the deed and the word of Magick.

Magick is the art of causing change in existing phenomena. This definition includes raising the dead, bewitching cattle, making rain, acquiring goods, fascinating judges, and all the rest of the programme. Good: but it also includes every act soever? Yes; I meant it to do so. It is not possible to utter word or do deed without producing the exact effect proper and necessary thereto. Thus Magick is the Art of Life itself.

Magick is the management of all we say and do, so that the effect is to change that part of our environment which dissatisfies us, until it does so no longer. We "remould it nearer to the heart's desire."

Magick ceremonies proper are merely organized and concentrated attempts to impose our Will on certain parts of the Cosmos. They are only particular cases of the general law.

But all we say and do, however casually, adds up to more, far more, than our most strenuous Operations. "Take care of the pence, and the pounds will take care of themselves." Your daily drippings fill a bigger bucket than your geysers of magical effort. The "ninety and nine that safely lay in the shelter of the fold" have no organized will at all; and their character, built of their words and deeds, is only a garbage-heap.

Remember, also, that, unless you know what your true will is, you may be devoting the most laudable energies to destroying yourself. Remember that every word and deed is a witness to thought, that therefore your mind must be perfectly organized, its sole duty to interpret circumstance in terms of the will so that speech and action may be rightly directed to express the will appropriately to the occasion. Remember that every word and deed which is not a definite expression of your will counts against it, indifference worse than hostility. Your enemy is at least interested in you: you may make him your friend as you never can do with a neutral. Remember that Magick is the Art of Life, therefore of causing change in accordance with will: therefore its law is "love under will," and its every movement is an act of love.

Remember that every act of "love under will" is lawful as such; but that when any act is not directed unto Nuith, who is here the inevitable result of the whole Work, that act is waste, and breeds conflict within you, so that "the kingdom of God which is within you" is torn by civil war.

To the beginner I would offer this programme.

Furnish your mind as completely as possible with the knowledge of how to inspect and to control it.

Train your body to obey your mind, and not to distract its attention.

Control your mind to devote itself wholly to discover your True Will.

Explore the course of that Will till you reach its source, your Silent Self.

Unite the conscious will with the True Will, and the conscious Ego with the Silent Self. You must be utterly ruthless in discarding any atom of consciousness which is hostile or neutral.

Let this work freely from within, but heed not your environment, lest you make difference between one thing and another. Whatever it be, it is to be made one with you by Love.[120]

Love is the law, love under will.

Fraternally,
Soror Meral

---

120. Crowley, *The Law is for All*, 39-40.

Carete Fratres et Sorores,[121]

Do what thou wilt shall be the whole of the Law.

The structure of much of To Mega Therion's thought, and his instructions for both of his occult orders, the O.T.O. and the A∴A∴, are not at first apparent to the casual student. The Thelemic system of attainment in either order is actually heavily reliant upon the qabalah and the Tree of Life and the system of the Tarot which ties into these.

Many of To Mega Therion's Books, and also chapters within these Books, refer to this structure. A careful study of the Grades in the A∴A∴ as printed in *The Equinox*, Vol. I, and the contents of *Liber XIII, Liber CLXXXV, Collegii Sancti, Liber CD vel Tau, Liber Viarum Viae (DCCCLXVIII)* and many Books almost too numerous to summarize here, lead the student ever onward to a deeper understanding of this structure, which represents that of the Universe and of his own Being. If it was not for order and law within the Universe of our Comprehension, humanity could not have taken the manifold steps towards higher development and knowledge and evolution towards perfection.

To Mega Therion has used the qabalistic system in preference to other systems as it has the cleanest and most orderly mode of training and balancing the powers of the mind. This training is just as important as the training of the emotions, examples of which can be seen in the story of Jane Wolfe and in Crowley's diaries. No student should forget that in order to achieve the highest adeptship possible for him or her in this incarnation, it is necessary to understand and rule the bodily structure, the emotional set and the functioning of the mind. Only in this way can a balanced attainment be achieved. Without this basic work the aspirant can too easily come to grief, be the prey of unknown and misunderstood forces which he has set in motion, or even end up as the inhabitant of an insane asylum. The Guardians have been set before the Temple of Attainment now just as they have always existed in the past. Would that the aspirants to this Temple could always understand this fact!

---

121. Originally published in: Phyllis Seckler, *In the Continuum* 2.9 (1980): 1-3.

But no, there are among us some poor souls who grasp for this or that high Grade in either order without any foundational work as above mentioned. They try to pretend that they are of the highest order of humankind to be found, and they strut around with their pitiful rags of belief instead of true rulership of all that they are or could be in this life.

This is true of many other occult orders, of course, not only the Thelemic. Do we not always have in and among the great body of humanity, quacks in medicine, in astrology, in law, in government and on and on? It is also true that there is a general trend for ego-aggrandizement among unevolved humans who display no real knowledge or Illumination or genius, or the small ego could not be so strong and uncontrollable, all but ruining the life pattern of the person so misled.

The actual proof that any one person is set on the path towards adeptship lies in the work which they have accomplished and not in vain and vacant claims to this or that Grade in our Holy Orders. Whatever work they have done will shine forth in their lives, in the development of their own high genius to the highest mark that the person is capable of in this life. As the ancient sentence so aptly states: "By their fruits ye shall know them." The situation is so chaotic in the occult world in general, and in the systems of Thelema, that we are over-run with these pretenders and quacks; people who claim to be something which they most obviously are not. This is partly because no system has as yet been put into practice for weeding out these lesser types of humanity or of assigning them to their proper function and place in society until they have achieved some real and undeniable achievement. We notice that some of the policies and practices of law and medicine lead to a policing and purifying of the ranks of these practitioners. Though To Mega Therion put forth the path of real attainment for all to see and work by, there are still those who misunderstand and misapply his writings and work, and there is no check to their silly behavior.

I shall not expound on the mistakes made by those of seemingly high rank, those who ought to know better if the Grades they claim are any criteria. This would be an unprofitable path. Instead, this publication is dedicated to informing the aspirant about the necessary steps to be taken in his own advancement towards adeptship. It is what To Mega Therion has done. This publication will back up and explain his system to the best of our ability. It shall then be the task of the student to work and prove what he is in reality, what is his essential genius and what may be his fantastic notions of himself due to his over-inflated small ego may be expunged.

Excuse us if we must laugh now and again at the bumblings of these "Bottoms" in their Shakespearean "Midsummer Night's Dream" as they strut and preen and pretend, showing the most vacant minds in the world and the most uncontrolled emotional life, swamped with the mysterious contents of the subconsciousness. It is no use, either, to criticize and view their bodily ruin when in this race to adeptship the best of health is needed. Ah yes, "Occult to Order," say what Grade you are and lo!, you have it! Those of us who know what true work is, cannot help but be doubled up with laughter!

The path has many and multitudinous guideposts; it is really up to the individual student to work his way to the Supreme Attainment. Let him not forget this injunction from *Liber Legis*, Cap. II, v. 70: "Wisdom says: be strong! Then canst thou bear more joy."[122]

We labor towards the end that each may pursue his greatest strength and Will: those who are of the chosen for the work of illumination or attainment may arrive at their goal; that on the way all do not forget the so necessary balance. Many times we advise the student to consult a knowledgeable teacher or psychiatrist for the troubles of the emotions and their mastery, or to consult a known expert in Hatha Yoga for the work on the material and bodily systems; also experts in the burgeoning fields of nutrition and holistic medicine. This publication can mainly lead to a mastery of the machinery of the mind through the qabalistic system as mentioned and since writing is an intellectual process, there is little we can do for individual problems in the emotional life or for bodily health. We can only indicate what may be studied so that some mental processes may be set above these two lower forms of life and lead them to some coherence of expression, true servants of the imperious will.

Love is the law, love under will.

---

122. Crowley, *Liber AL vel Legis*, 49.

Carete Fratres et Sorores,[123]

Do what thou wilt shall be the whole of the Law.

Almost all that need be said about the abuse of drugs is mentioned in the article "Cocaine" by Crowley.[124] However, there is quite a strong percentage of people who claim to be Thelemites who miss the purpose of Thelema. It is not only self-indulgence on all planes that is the big mistake, but it is also pretense and lies about their so-called high grades in either of Crowley's occult orders. Even apart from such pretense, often these people give no evidence that they know much about self-discipline. They mistake license for freedom.

In *Magick Without Tears*, Letter 70, point 3, Crowley has this to say:

> So much of *The Book of the Law* deals directly or indirectly with morals that to quote relevant passages would be merely bewildering. Not that this state of mind fails to result from the first, second, third and ninety-third perusals!
>
> > When Duty bellows loud "Thou must!"
> > The youth replies, "Pike's Peak or Bust!"
>
> is all very well, or might be if the bellow gave further particulars. And one's general impression may very well be that Thelema not only gives general license to do any fool thing that comes into one's head, but urges in the most emphatic terms, reinforced by the most eloquent appeals in superb language, by glowing promises, and by categorical assurance that no harm can possibly come thereby, the performance of just that specific type of action, the maintenance of just that line of conduct, which is most severely deprecated by the high priests and jurists of every religion, every system of ethics, that ever was under the sun!
>
> You may look sourly down a meanly-pointed nose, or yell "Whoop La!" and make for Piccadilly Circus: in either

---

123. Originally published in: Phyllis Seckler, *In the Continuum* 2.10 (1981): 1-4.
124. Crowley, "Cocaine," *The International* 11.10 (1917): 291-294.

case you will be wrong; you will not have understood the Book.

Shameful confession, one of my own Chelas (or so it is rather incredibly reported to me) said recently: "Self-discipline is a form of Restriction." (That, you remember, is "The Word of Sin"). Of all the utter rubbish! (Anyhow, he was a "centre of pestilence" for discussing the Book at all.) About 90 percent of Thelema, at a guess, is nothing but self-discipline. One is only allowed to do anything and everything so as-to have more scope for exercising that virtue.

Concentrate on "Thou hast no right but to do thy will." The point is that any possible act is to be performed if it is a necessary factor in that Equation of your Will. Any act that is not such a factor, however harmless, noble, virtuous or what not, is at the best a waste of energy. But there are no artificial barriers on any type of act in general. The standard of conduct has one single touchstone. There may be—there will be—every kind of difficulty in determining whether, by this standard, any given act is 'right' or 'wrong'; but there should be no confusion. No act is righteous in itself, but only in reference to the True Will of the person who proposes to perform it. This is the Doctrine of Relativity applied to the moral sphere.[125]

The great stumbling block for beginning Thelemites is to know what the will is really. Crowley states it plainly enough many times in his writings that the next step for mankind is to attain to the Knowledge and Conversation of the Holy Guardian Angel. He states that man is a spiritual being and not an animal bent on pleasure and the glutting of animal appetites: not an animal who can think of nothing but material goods, tied to the earth and dull to every art form, to intuition and the higher matters of the soul symbolized by the ruach in the Tree of Life, and mostly by the Supernal Triad.

One can scarcely attain to such illumination by sitting back and allowing oneself to be blown about by all the winds of chance; no control over the thoughts or over the emotions or body! The

---

125. Crowley, *Magick Without Tears*, pp. 422-423.

God does not choose to dwell in a Temple not prepared or badly prepared.

Thelema, and to be a Thelemite, means hard work. But if the work is to your liking, it hardly matters that you work hard at it. Some of the most successful people in the world work hard at one task—whether to be a financier, an opera star, a violinist or a painter, or whatever else. Here, of course, is a sphere where the average person wishing to become a Thelemite can start with some confidence. Almost everyone has an idea of what type of work they would like to do in the world. If no idea of the 'lesser will' is forthcoming, they can often consult with an astrologer and/or a psychologist for help in the matter.

But to gear oneself up for a series of disciplines in yoga and magick is entirely a different matter. Here the great bulk of humanity would rather wish than will. They think how impossible is the task! They think, "But I have to earn my daily bread and this means certain hours at the task and I have no time left over for the Great Work."

Then these people are observed to waste their time in a multitudinous number of ways. This sort of thinking and behavior has happened again and again among the students of the College of Thelema, as well as among members of both of Crowley's occult orders.

There are ways to use the time efficiently so that the Great Work is not shoved aside unduly. For instance, a person of my acquaintance read one chapter of *Liber AL vel Legis* every night for a year. This took only about 10 minutes before she slept. When the year was up, the chapter was memorized. She went on to memorize all the other chapters of this Book, all of *Liber LXV* and all of *Liber VII* in the same way, meanwhile holding down a difficult job and acting as head of her household. Memorizing is here emphasized as it seems to be the worst stumbling block for the majority; and yet in the work for O.T.O. and A∴A∴, and the College of Thelema, a certain amount of memorizing must be done.

It is needful for the student to remember that he/she has all of eternity at the disposal and that no task is accomplished right now. It is the little acts of every day, day after day, that decide the issue of whether you shall attain or not. It is the determined performance of 20 minutes of Asana before you go to work in the morning, the determined shutting down of T.V., of the dismissal of acquaintances who waste your time, the determined abolishment of any other distraction which prevents you from accomplishing your True Will. It is the day by day analysis of your own actions as to whether you are on the right path towards the K. and C. of the H.G.A., and if not, the correction of any deviation. Above all, set as a jewel and crown to man, is the pure aspiration to attain to such bliss.

Why then are there so few who have failed to grasp the fact that the Thelemite is an expert in self-discipline and an expert in minding his own business and allowing others to go about their own way to accomplish the will—be it the finite will or the infinite will? Why do we have pretense and lies about grades for which no work has been done? Do not those who behave in such fashion merely make for themselves a harsh karma?

Liber Legis is explicit about slaves and the fact that it is those who are slaves to baser appetites, who refuse to realize man is a spiritual being but who must work to attain his spiritual purposes and overcome the siren call of materiality, who remain on the lower levels of humanity and are subject to the whiplash of circumstance and sorrow and degradation in all forms. Such are never the aristocrats, the masters of humanity, the leaders in any sphere of life, nor are they of those who attain to their highest potential in this life.

If the true Thelemite is aware of this, he could never become an alcoholic, a drug fiend, a criminal who interferes with the wills of others—either to own property or to live or to dispose of the body as the owner desires to do.

A true Thelemite must learn what it means to discipline the self, the little self, full of a thousand whims and wishes, like an amoeba floating with the great currents of the sea, no will of its own other than to reproduce. Does the great bulk of humanity function like the amoeba?

It is up to each person to answer this for him/herself and to analyze and perhaps to seek help in analysis and to aspire to the Highest possible for this life and to work hard to achieve these ends: "The Great Work, the Summum Bonum, True Wisdom and Perfect Happiness."[126]

Love is the law, love under will.

---

126. Crowley, "Liber XV," *The Equinox Vol. III No. 10*, 138.

Carete Fratres et Sorores,[127]

Do what thou wilt shall be the whole of the Law.

It is an unfortunate fact that some people are blocked from performing the Great Work by the influence of other persons upon them. Many students say, "I don't like so and so," speaking of some other member of a group to which they belong, such as either of Crowley's two Thelemic orders, and on this basis will cease work which might aid the arrival at an enlightened state in Thelema.

Jealousy and misplaced ambition, hatred and envy are often rife in all groups, and there is no exception to this just because the group is Thelemic and working together in occult studies. Usually these negative emotions arise because a person does not understand either his finite or infinite will, and so finds it difficult to find his rightful place among his brothers and sisters. Often a person will fail to see that it is up to him to see where the shoe pinches in his own case, and to analyze why he must be so negative, and whether his reactions are going to impede his progress.

In partnerships and groups, and indeed in all human intercourse, a person of lesser development will project his own ways of thinking or behaving onto another person, and for all practical purposes will be demanding that the other person come up to his own standards. Actually, one can only see a trait in another if one possesses the trait oneself. One does not experience in this world what is not within oneself to begin with. We couldn't see, for instance, if we did not have the physical apparatus of eyes with which to make interpretations of phenomena. So it goes for all the senses and for the unconscious makeup as well, which partakes of the vast amount of human experience.

Most people make an idealized image of themselves which does not actually fit the facts of their inner natures, nor of the ways in which they behave. The inner unconscious nature has its expression in the outer material world all the time, often unknown in its manifestations to the person concerned.

---

127. Originally published in: Phyllis Seckler, *In the Continuum* 2.12 (1981): i-ii.

In the case of a Superior in either order, it may be necessary to awaken the student to his own projections and bring him to some understanding of the processes under which he operates, often in a very ignorant fashion. This teaching by the Superior cannot be shirked if the student is to have any training at all.

In Jane Wolfe's story, we find that many ordeals were flung at her in rather rapid fashion. This was Crowley's method of procedure with his students as *Liber Legis* gave him full license to be severe with his ordeals. Jane was able to weather these ordeals, to face the changes needed in herself, to work upon them and change her attitudes, and to grow thereby. Because of this, she won the respect of the Master Therion. She thought she failed in one task, the one most difficult for her, but she triumphed in other tasks without knowing it. It was partly due to her work and her ability to see the task through, no matter what, no matter that she often hated Aleister with a vengeance, that we are now a body of young (it is true) initiates on the west coast.

Many of Crowley's students did not survive such severe and rough treatment—in fact, the great bulk of them did not. It is true, they were probably not ready for the Great Work, and were merely proceeding into this because of their unreal notions about themselves. It is much better to find this out at an early stage rather than to be allowed to proceed with major defects which would only add to the risk the student would run as he attempts higher work. His faults and failings are magnified always as he proceeds into higher levels of existence, and if these are not conquered, his crash might be so great as to cut off all hope of effective work for several incarnations.

Having established the fact, then, that what we object to in others is a part of ourselves and we have the trait also, we should be able to develop the greatest tolerance for our brothers and sisters in Thelema. Any person should busy himself to discover the roots of his own objections to others. He should root out his own intolerance and destroy it, for in the body of Nuit anything and everything is possible. The Great Work does not in any way depend on personalities.

Love is the law, love under will.

Meral

Carete Fratres et Sorores,[128]

Do what thou wilt shall be the whole of the law.

Many times it has been necessary to remind a student on the path to illumination that he/she runs a great risk as soon as even one step up the paths of the Tree of Life has been taken.

This danger has been symbolized in several ways in occult tradition and writings. In *The Sacred Magic of Abramelin the Mage*, we find that as soon as the Great Magical Retirement has been completed and the candidate has achieved the Knowledge and Conversation of the Holy Guardian Angel, he is immediately assailed by the Abramelin Demons and all his work is lost and negated if he cannot control and master them. They are reputed to have so much power as to destroy him.

In the first volume of *The Golden Dawn*, we are shown two illustrations, the first has that of an eight-headed serpent coiled at the base of the cross, which includes the Tree of Life, and the two opposing forces of negative and positive, male and female or nature and man, evenly and carefully balanced.[129]

The second diagram shows that the serpent which was asleep in the qliphothic spheres has now uncoiled and is about to swallow every one of the spheres below the Supernal Triad. The last sphere to be attacked in this way is the sphere of Daath, which, since it represents all knowledge which is impossible of attainment by any one person, does not really exist on the Tree of Life, but is separate from it.

The serpent or hydra is not able to rise as far as the Supernal Triad, as here all that the magician has and is and was has been destroyed, so there is nothing which can be shattered.

The conscious mind is represented by the spheres four through nine, and this is called the ruach. At the center is Tiphereth, which represents the completed and perfected man with all of the various qualities of the other spheres in perfect

---

128. Originally published in: Phyllis Seckler, *In the Continuum* 3.1 (1982): 1-4.
129. First diagram opposite p. 147, and second diagram opposite p. 153 in the 3rd edition of 1970. See also the first two diagrams following page 188 of Regardie, *The Golden Dawn*.

balance and harmony. On a higher plane Tiphereth also represents the attainment to the Knowledge and Conversation of the H.G.A. But here in this central sphere, the angel and the human are still two separate beings. As a side note, the highest development of Tiphereth is represented by 666 and all its attendant explanations scattered through Crowley's works. This sphere is the next step for mankind, which A.C. vowed to make easier of attainment in this next Æon.

The Supernal Triad is brought into action when the aspirant and the angel become one entity, inseparable forever. This description can be followed in *Liber VII*, *The Vision and the Voice*, and in other works by A.C.

The little ego is developed along with each step in spiritual development and advancement. This is pride, envy and a host of other negative emotions and thoughts. In psychological language, the process of initiation and of perfection of the human stirs up the contents of the unconscious which, if the person is unbalanced, can threaten sanity and well-being. That is, if the progress has been erratic, if the steps towards illumination are not balanced, ill health can follow and even insanity and in some extreme cases, a terrible death.

The Greeks emphasized a sound mind in a sound body. They knew only too well the results of development which did not base its action on these foundations. Other philosophical and mystical schools have emphasized the same. Such advice is found everywhere from China and India to the western world. The penalty of imbalance has been restriction and persecution, and the most horrid crimes against individuals that one can imagine.

The sin of restriction mentioned in *Liber Legis*[130] is just the sin of restricting the utterances, the development of the Highest which we call the Holy Guardian Angel. Thus, the conscious intellect can develop and still be a monster, allowing lower passions to engulf even the reason. Reason itself can be monstrous, as witnessed in our own age. We are threatened every time science makes a new advancement in intellectual knowledge and the dictates of conscience are ignored. I use the word conscience as representing the spiritual side of man. Sin, as Crowley points out,

---

130. Crowley, *Liber AL vel Legis*, 31. [Cap. I, v.41. – Eds.]

is the restriction of the little ego and undergoing its domination instead of freeing oneself by attaining to the K. and C. of the H.G.A.

Since the path to freedom from the lower nature is rather difficult, many aspirants give up before the battle is won. They may have heard some of the first utterances, they may have developed the conscious knowledge and reason and know very much about occult matters, but since they never mastered the other sides of themselves, they have become a danger to themselves and those around them.

Many examples of this are all around us today. In one case, a person is publishing with the purpose (so he states) of purifying and strengthening the O.T.O. and the A∴A∴. But he has never joined either order, and thinks that his published criticisms will do the job. It is evident that he does not know how to work magick, since he cannot control such an ego that has no knowledge of the actual work being done, but the intellect looks only at the surface of things and a small flaw is noticed, and this person is off on some rather hilarious writings. That is, they are funny when one knows how little the person actually knows about the true state of affairs.

Another example is similar to this, but this person publishes the most grotesque libels about various people in Thelema, attacking almost everyone that he knows who is interested enough in this subject for a long enough time to become generally known. In this second case, the person can tolerate no view but his own.

Then we had, at one time, a bunch of nuts running around claiming to be the reincarnation of Aleister Crowley. These soon faded into the background when they found out there were others who claimed the same thing.

These are extreme cases; more subtle ones can be met with every day. Some of these are those who take degree after degree in O.T.O. and have done almost no work along spiritual lines and remain in a great state of ignorance even about what Crowley wrote for our guidance. These have not even begun to control the manifestations of the passions and the little ego. There are also the unbalanced ones who have no real connections with A∴A∴, have not done any of its carefully outlined work, but still claim grades in this order!

A person might attain to some knowledge of the H.G.A., without realizing that he is at the mercy of the demonic self in the exact same proportion as his attainment. Perhaps he might compare himself to others not so knowledgeable as he is and his pride and ego are exacerbated. He wishes to shoot out and blast from the heights the words and guidance of the Angel as applicable to all humanity, but he forgets that each person has his own Angel and his own method of achievement, his own Way of Going.

The ego must be destroyed, but this hydra is very wily and has many twisting and turnings, and many false paths to present to the aspirant. These are no more than the contents of the unconscious self, which was necessary in more primitive states of life, still active now, but which must be controlled and put to right use. These depths are so subtle that the student is almost unable to tackle these attacks of the hydra, since he does not know or care to analyze himself meticulously.

In the Tarot this monkey of the reason and conscious mind is represented in the card called the Magus, or Magician, which corresponds to Mercury and Beth. The monkey threatens the Magus, but is powerless, for the Magus is above the Abyss and has had an ordered and balanced development, and is Lord of all his own phenomena.

Below the Abyss this is not the case. The monkey of intellect, of reason, is only too strong and is really never subdued until one crosses the Abyss and becomes a Master of the Temple. This is why *Liber Legis* tells us that reason is a lie.[131]

One needs to proceed carefully then, if this highest attainment has not been reached. There was a reason for the cultivation of humility in some of the older systems. The unbridled intellect, reason, can actually stop progress—not only now, but for several incarnations, depending on how strong and how uncontrolled the demonic self has been.

Let us all then, apply ourselves to the work of thorough-going analysis of our unconscious contents as they arise; of purifying each element of action and thought, each vehicle of the self, of body, emotions and mind. For only thus may we attain to the true wisdom. As it states in the last words of the Gnostic Catholic

---

131. Crowley, *Liber AL vel Legis*, 43. [Cap. II, v. 32. – Eds.]

Mass "...the Great Work, the Summum Bonum, True Wisdom and Perfect Happiness."[132]

Love is the law, love under will.

Fraternally,
Soror Meral

Carete Fratres et Sorores,[133]

Do what thou wilt shall be the whole of the Law.

The Way of the Neophyte does indeed seem to him like a dark path. There is so much to overcome and control. Where does he begin? How does he live up to "Do what thou wilt" as a first step on his path?[134] At first glance much in this sentence and in *Liber Legis* seems like an invitation to complete license. It seems as though every passing whim should be indulged. Does this injunction mean do as you please? If the aspirant sees no further than this, then he has missed the full purpose of Thelema. Actually, "Do what thou wilt" means the most severe self-discipline. Just as a violinist, willing to become the best musician possible, must discipline himself to practice for hours every day. He must give up any action in his life which might interfere with this will.

But this is not always considered by a person first viewing the freedoms of Thelema. Some groups have even earned the comment that all they can think of is drugs and sex. These misguided young people are wholly slaves to the base animal nature, the nephesh in qabalistic terms. True, the energies of this animal nature are of great value, but it is the essence of the purified energy which is of value to the adept. As is taught in alchemy, it is necessary first to analyze, that is, pull apart, the various tendencies of the nature. One must view them with an unbiased eye, with detachment, as though these energies belonged to another person. Only when the aspirant sees his pride, his desires, his ambition, his lust, his ego, his appetites, for what they are, as his most terrible slavery, that he is his own worst jailer and enemy; when he can truly see what he is doing to himself with all lesser

---

132. Crowley, *Magick Liber Aba*, 585.
133. Originally published in: Phyllis Seckler, *In the Continuum* 3.3 (1983): i-ii.
134. Crowley, *Liber AL vel Legis*, 31.

tendencies; when he can analyze these perfectly, extract their energy, purify it and then wed these energies to those of his highest aspirations; only then can he become one of the adepts.

Notice that this task does not mean the repression of the base instincts, for these energies have brought man up the ladder of evolution when they have been used with knowledge and skill. A person still in the throes of a complete surrender to the animal self is dubbed "a dog" in *Liber Legis*. In the process of learning to be a God, to be one of the Highest, the aspirant must face many tasks which to him, as a Neophyte, or as a beginner in the O.T.O., or as an intellectual student, even, of Thelema, might not have been obvious when he first plunged into this work. When he must first face himself and realize how he enslaves himself, the task may seem all but impossible. How does he become a king? Here many stumble and fall, for this task of facing one's lower nature, which already through most of the life, has a stranglehold on the soul, has seemed like a dark tunnel, or like the dark cave which Plato describes. How does one turn to the light and get out of that cave?

The path the aspirant is set upon is a path of self-perfection, not of self-indulgence. When one has steeped oneself thoroughly in *Liber Legis* and Crowley's works, this is more obvious than when one is beginning. The K. and C. of the H.G.A. is attained by the perfected individual, the one who has willed this event and has worked hard to attain it, has done all in his power to control those tendencies and energies which would interfere with this perfection.

This goal was seen as the next step on the path of evolution for mankind, and Therion worked mightily that humanity would accept this and enter themselves into this Great Work. There is no standing still in evolution, one must either go forward and take the next step, or one must slide backwards and join oneself with the animal world and thus be destroyed as a human.

Again, in alchemy, this animal or natural man is the "first matter of the work." In Thelema, we can say that his first task is to live up to "Do what thou wilt."[135] In this process he may need psychological help, for few individuals can see the animal nature

---

135. Ibid.

or the base instincts clearly. The ego makes too many excuses for these, since the ego claims to be the whole man. But the ego is not the whole. The Neophyte needs to learn this, and to listen to the promptings of the higher self, then to those of the H.G.A., and then to surrender completely to the guidance of the H.G.A. when he has attained this step.

Such a process seems insuperably difficult at first to the Neophyte. But one must take a first step, and then another. One must not worry about the goal too much: however, this goal must remain as a shining star and a beacon to lead one on. Each day the Neophyte can gain some small victory, if he truly wills it. The important thing is not to give up the work, no matter how slow or how hard. One must not be frightened by its difficulty, nor become a victim of one's own fears. Blinded as is the Neophyte, he is assured that the Light shines there and that he can attain it. As in *Liber Pyramidos*, he is "under the shadow of the wings."[136]

Love is the law, love under will.

Carete Fratres et Sorores,[137]

Do what thou wilt shall be the whole of the Law.

Is rape to be condoned in a Thelemic society? A recent incident and its aftermath brings this question to our attention. Unfortunately, there is a great deal of ignorance as to the real meaning of various sentences in *Liber AL vel Legis* and, all too frequently, no study of Therion's Commentaries on this has been done by some who profess to be Thelemites. For instance, in *Magick Without Tears* and in the Commentaries, Therion states that man, as in Hebrew times, may go in unto woman as he pleases or wills to do, but that in the Thelemic age, this is now as women also will. This means that women are no longer to be considered as non-persons, as slaves or the possessions of men, to be used as sex objects as some men might wish to do. Women have their own

---

136. Crowley, et al, *Commentaries on the Holy Books and Other Papers* (York Beach, ME: Samuel Weiser, 1996), 67.
137. Originally published in: Phyllis Seckler, *In the Continuum* 3.4 (1983): 1-4.

right to the sex act. Women are "stars" as are men, in their real essence. Let me here remark that not all sex is "unto me" as Nuit demands of us. Sex could hardly be devoted to love, which is the highest spiritual force and the aim of all mankind, if one of the partners is being forced to this act under the threat of injury, the pain of mutilation and/or death, actual or threatened, as is the case with the rapist.

Liber Legis states in many places that love is the formula of the Universe. "But to love me is better than all things:" as in Cap. I, v. 61.[138] And in v. 51 she says: "Also, take your fill and will of love as ye will, when, where and with whom ye will! But always unto me."[139] In the *Magical and Philosophical Commentaries on the Book of the Law*, Therion states:

> We are then particularly careful to deny that the object of love is the gross physiological object which happens to be Nature's excuse for it. Generation is a sacrament of the physical rite, by which we create ourselves anew in our own image, weave in a new flesh-tapestry the romance of our own soul's history. But also love is a sacrament of trans-substantiation whereby we initiate our own souls; it is the wine of intoxication as well as the bread of nourishment. Nor is he for priest designed Who partakes only in one kind.
>
> We therefore heartily cherish those forms of Love in which no question of generation arises; we use the stimulating effects of physical enthusiasm to inspire us morally and spiritually. Experience teaches that passions thus employed serve to refine and to exalt the whole being of man or woman. Nuith indicated the sole conditions: "But always unto me."
>
> ...To us the essence of Love is that it is a sacrament unto Nuith, a gate of grace and a road of righteousness to Her high palace, the abode of peerless purity whose lamps are the stars.
>
> "As ye will." It should be abundantly clear from the

---

138. Crowley, *Liber AL vel Legis*, 36.
139. Crowley, *Liber AL vel Legis*, 33.

foregoing remarks that each individual has an absolute and indefeasible right to use his sexual vehicle in accordance with its own proper character and that he is responsible only to himself. But he should not injure himself and his right aforesaid; acts invasive of another individual's equal rights are implicitly self-aggressions. Such acts as rape and the assault or seduction of infants, may therefore be justly regarded as offences against the law of liberty and repressed in the interests of that law.

It is also excluded from "as ye will" to compromise the liberty of another person indirectly, as by taking advantage of the ignorance or good faith of another person to expose that person to the constraint of sickness, poverty, social detriment, or childbearing, unless with the well-informed and uninfluenced free will of that person.[140]

The sentence "always unto me"[141] also means that one is performing an act of love in any fashion (which may or may not include sex) with the highest dedication to our own Holy Guardian Angel. "Unto Me," or rather "To Me" adds to 418 in Greek. This is a formula of attainment of the Knowledge and Conversation of the H.G.A. Rape would be an abomination of this formula, as it is not Love but aggression. The first step for mankind, and that which A.C. insisted on, was to do all in our power to achieve this K. and C. of the H.G.A. Every act or "ritual" must be done with this in mind. If various acts included other persons, then we would not wish to bring down curses on our heads for our own misbehavior, as this would block the attainment of the K. and C. Further, our own interior conscience must be developed as it is the first whisperings of the H.G.A. Those who have abandoned conscience may easily abandon the Angel and bring havoc to themselves and block their own attainment for who knows how long?

Then, too, let me remind you that love takes many forms. It may be the love of the parent for a child, of an artist for the canvas, of a scientist for his research, of a musician for his sounds and his instruments, of a child for the family, and on and on. As

---

140. Crowley, *Magical and Philosophical Commentaries*, 140-141.
141. Crowley, *Liber AL vel Legis*, 33.

A.C. stated above, love is an elevating force for humanity and it should not be profaned in any way.

In verse 52, Nuith continues: "If this be not aright; if ye confound the space-marks, saying: They are one; or saying, They are many; if the ritual be not ever unto me: then expect the direful judgments of Ra Hoor Khuit!"[142]

Ra-Hoor-Khuit is a stand-in for our own attainable states of higher consciousness, symbolized by the K. and C. of the Angel. He is also a god of war and vengeance as humanity has turned too far away from spiritual values and tries to live only in the exterior world, ignoring the whispers and phenomena of the inner or unconscious world. This pattern must be turned around. The rapist becomes this because he has not done the necessary work to understand his own unconscious forces and these forces, thus ignored, turn and devour him with war and vengeance in various forms. This aspect of Ra-Hoor-Khuit can be likened to the furies of Greek myth who persecuted and pursued those who ignored the laws of their own inner being, thus they came to grief with the wrong kind of actions and were haunted forever afterwards. The furies are the punishments we mete out for ourselves when opposing the True Will, the will to attain to the conversation of the H.G.A.

As Crowley states in his comment to this verse: "Each Star is individual, yet each is bound to the others by law. This freedom under law is one of the most difficult yet important doctrines of this Book. So too the ritual—our lives—must be unto Nuith; for She is the Ultimate to which we tend, the asymptote of our curve. Failure in this one-pointedness sets up the illusion of duality, which leads to excision and destruction."[143]

He continues in this Commentary:

> Whatever your sexual predilections may be, you are free, by the Law of Thelema, to be the Star you are, to go your own way rejoicing. It is not indicated here in this text, though it is elsewhere implied, that only one symptom warns that you have mistaken your True Will, and that is, if you should imagine that in pursuing your way you interfere with that of another star. It may, therefore, be considered improper,

---

142. Ibid.
143. Crowley, *The Law is for All*, 58-59.

as a general rule, for your sexual gratification to destroy, deform, or displease any other star. Mutual consent to the act is the condition thereof. It must, of course, be understood that such consent is not always explicit. There are cases when seduction or rape may be emancipation or initiation to another. Such acts can only be judged by their results.[144]

But who can judge the results of the act of rape? This is not an excuse for rape; it is merely a balancing out of one opinion against another. It would take a very knowledgeable person to guess if the end result of rape would be emancipation or initiation for another—an adept, perhaps. The ordinary rapist is not this; he is, instead, the prisoner of his own suppressed rage and aggression. He is a star deformed by hate, and unless he can do something about this, he may be headed for destruction.

Thelema does not mean license, it does not mean that one can do as one pleases. It means instead, that to be a Thelemite, one must first listen to what one's own True Will may be and then one must discipline oneself to attain to this state. Thelema implies that to "Do what thou wilt"[145] one must also let the other person do as he/she wills. This point can hardly be stressed enough as it is so obvious that young and ignorant Thelemites (or so they claim), spend most of their lives interfering with others in various ways.

This is the results of license, it is not Thelemic in essence. A young person interested in Thelema usually misunderstands the nature of his will. It is a long road to appreciation of this and then to carry out the will in full freedom: a gesture which is guaranteed by Thelemic principles. Often the first step is to learn that one must not interfere with others in any way, and then after that, to go about discovering what the finite will may be. If the life is lived unto Nuit in all its fullness, the infinite will, and the means and way to achieve this, become apparent.

From all this, it can be easily ascertained that the rapist does not wish to extend Thelemic freedom to others. If we have one of this type among us, why do we allow it? Should we not take vigorous steps to disallow such a person? To cast him out from our group? For such a poisonous person can poison too many others and thus we are at the mercy of such a one. If our freedoms are

---

144. Crowley, *The Law is for All*, 64.
145. Crowley, *Liber AL vel Legis*, 31.

not vigorously defended, then we are not free. We become slaves to the aberrations of others.

Let us face it, to be free is to continually fight for our freedoms. There are too many in the world who would deprive us of the freedom and so we must act. Thelema is not a wishy-washy system which enjoins us to turn the other cheek. It is a system that is bold and strong; it is for the strong and followed correctly, it can produce adepts. Let us not wallow then, in ignorance and fear; let us develop our higher selves to the best of our ability and let us remove from our paths, those who would interfere with others.

Love is the law, love under will.

Soror Meral

Carete Fratres et Sorores,[146]

Do what thou wilt shall be the whole of the Law.

It must never be forgotten that we are on a work of Evolution, raising ourselves up from the level of the animal and bestial to the level of the evolved and spiritual type of man and woman. Certainly no political or social action in an occult society such as grabbing for Grades, a criticism of one's fellow members, a display of ego and a desire for power over others will ever aid that evolution. These types of behavior are but toys on the material plane and such should be eschewed by the serious student aiming at the highest development of his soul. His growth and development need not be known to the world at large and if he boasts of it, this may be another ego play, and he may not actually have attained enlightenment as he states. As is known from the study of *The Vision and the Voice* and other inspired masterpieces by the Master Therion, if a person has crossed the Abyss, and has become a little pile of dust in the City of the Pyramids (Binah), there is no one who can boast, as what existed before has been utterly dissolved in the Infinite, or the body of Nuit.

But here is a quote from *The Equinox*, Vol. I, No. 9, the editorial in front, which gives us guidance as to the real attainment and the work to be done.

---

146. Originally published in: Phyllis Seckler, *In the Continuum* 3.5 (1984):3-5.

> Our community has existed ever since the first day of creation when the gods spoke the divine command: "Let there be light!" and it will continue to exist till the end of time. It is the Society of the Children of Light, who live in the light and have attained immortality therein. In our school we are instructed directly by Divine Wisdom, the Celestial Bride, whose will is free and who selects as her disciples those who are devoted to her. The mysteries which we are taught embrace everything that can possibly be known in regard to God, Nature, and Man. Every sage that ever existed in the world has graduated in our school; for without wisdom no man can be wise. We all study only one book, the Book of Nature, in which the keys to all secrets are contained and we follow the only possible methods in studying it, that of experience. Our place of meeting is the Temple of the Holy Spirit pervading the universe; easily to be found by the elect, but for ever hidden from the eyes of the vulgar. Our secrets cannot be sold for money, but we give them free to every one capable to receive them.[147]

Our first step in our studies has been the nature of man, for each of us is human and we each must be fully informed as to our psychology and our own individual inner workings as well as what is common to mankind in general.

In our studies, there are only two processes possible, as Therion states elsewhere. These are analysis and synthesis. In alchemical terms, we state solve for the former and coagula for the latter. Of course we start with the analysis, for without a full knowledge of our separate parts and how they work in relation to each other, no synthesis would be possible. This final synthesis may come as a great enlightenment, as a sudden access of understanding, as a blinding light. It has various and manifold ways of showing itself to the individual, but it is at the end of the process of analysis. So let us proceed with the analysis. We have started in each individual case with a horoscope for each one so that the person may know how the forces of the Universe work through him or her. We follow this up with some psychology when the going gets

---

147. Crowley, *The Equinox*, Vol. I, No. IX (London: Wieland & Co., 1913), x.

tangled or tough. We have tried to lay down a foundation of the study of the qabalah, as each person is a Tree of Life. Sometimes these studies become mere intellectual exercises and the person can become forever stuck in the intellectual world, the world of the ruach. But this is a world of analysis still, a world of division. Eventually with all his strength amassed, all his knowledge as a springboard, the individual must in one life or another, give up all that he is or was and cross the Abyss. This step, however, is beyond the knowledge or the understanding of most of us. Let us labor then in the world of analysis and keep our sights on the khabs or star that we are as we go.

The system of the Tarot ties into astrological knowledge and qabalistic knowledge. It is really surprising how many times the Tarot is mentioned in *The Book of the Law*, either directly or obliquely. Does not Nuit say: "All these old letters of my Book are aright, but צ is not the Star?"[148] In other words, the Book Tarot is accepted and given to mankind as a direct route to the highest Initiations. It is at once a map of the Universe and of nature and a map of man. It seeks to explain in one form or another, the most abstruse facts of man, nature and the Universe as is possible to our level of evolution. It is a guide to the attainment of the mastery of the animal nature and the development of the highest spirituality that the individual may seek. Yet in all this, most of its meaning can be grasped by the average intelligent human. We are going to embark in these pages on an exploration of the Tarot Trumps as a map of the unconscious forces in man.[149] Since the unconscious partakes of the universality of the whole Universe, as Jung states, it is very necessary that we should know what powers and qualities and capacities are contained therein. For the Universe also runs through all of nature and man; for Universe, we may substitute the word God.

Is it not obvious to you, then, that to know yourself, to know man, you are also given a method of knowing nature and man? In the synthesis that you will someday be able to make, all of these three will become one.

Not only does mention of the principles of the Tarot run through *Liber AL vel Legis*, but also through Therion's other Holy

---

148. Crowley, *Liber AL vel Legis*, [Cap. I, v. 57. – Eds.]
149. Seckler, *The Thoth Tarot, Astrology, & Other Selected Writings*.

Books. Further, the steps upward of the brother of the A∴A∴, as he wends his way from the bottom of the Tree of Life to the top, is carefully mirrored in the correspondence of the Books of the A∴A∴ with one path or another, as symbolized by the Tarot Trumps. Here you will see how each Liber is made to correspond with its particular Tarot Trump.

Let me explain a little further. In *Konx Om Pax* there is a story called "The Wake World" where little Lola Daydream learns to leave her ordinary life of dreams and *maya* and to live with her Fairy Prince (the Holy Guardian Angel) in the spheres above the Abyss. Her progress starts at the bottom of the Tree of Life and goes upward over the paths, which are the Trumps, to each of the spheres in turn in an orderly fashion. She leaves no path or Sphere out of her progress and neither should the aspirant to the Holy Wisdom.

When a thorough grasp is made of the ideas behind each Trump, I would advise the student to sit down with other pertinent studies, and when he feels he is ready, he should then meditate on each Trump until he can see it working within himself as clearly as is possible. Also, in our daily lives, these Trumps come alive as well as in our dreams. Can you ask yourself with everyday phenomena: well, I see the Magus was at work here, or this was the Priestess, or this was obviously the Tower, the card of Mars, etc.? When you can do this you are very well on your Way! May you know your own khabs!

Love is the law, love under will,

Soror Meral

Carete Fratres et Sorores,[150]

Do what thou wilt shall be the whole of the Law.

Many students write to me of their sufferings. Let me remark on this from a Thelemic point of view. We all of us have made our own phenomena. We, as stars, weave some dance or veil of illusions so that we may gain experience and in the end wend our

---

150. Originally published in: Phyllis Seckler, *In the Continuum* 3.9 (1986): 1-5.

way back to Nuit, "from whom we came and to whom we go,"[151] as Crowley puts it in his commentary on *Liber Legis*.

If you have chosen a veil of suffering for this life, then it was for a reason and was willed by your true self, the star within you for some purpose. It is obvious from the way in which many of you write, that the first thing you wanted to learn was something better than the environment from which you came or in which you now exist. This environment must have been chosen by you for some karmic reason. Perhaps it was chosen in order to refine your soul and enhance the sense of yearning for a spiritual life.

We all of us choose our own parents and the environment in which they live. This is not an accident. In the willed life of a star there are no accidents. Everything has a message and a meaning and it is up to the person going through whatever it is that he experiences to understand this purpose, this lesson to be learned, and why certain illusions, or *maya*, or veils of the true self were chosen rather than others. No person learns from restful and happy experiences—he learns from sorrow and trouble. He literally manufactures the troubles so that he will be obliged to progress in the work of evolution. He chooses false paths so that he will know the one true path when he finally comes to it.

The work of the person on the spiritual path is to understand himself and thus accept himself, and then to chart his course to a more desirable state. Everyone is like a ship on the waters, and this ship needs a chart to map the waters through which it will go; it needs direction in the form of a rudder; it needs motive power in the form of the will. The waters are those of life and experience, the rudder and sails or engine is the aimed direction. (The bulk of humanity lack engines, sails and rudder and cannot aim at anything at all; they are simply a mass of confusion.) When a person can bring all of the elements of himself into a focused direction, this is the power of will. But this power is never developed unless the person can drop some things inimical to the will and develop others. For this reason, it is wise to know your own horoscope in great detail as it is part of your chart for sailing on the sea of life and shows what you have to work with in this life.

---

151. Crowley, *The Law is for All*. [Commentary on *Liber Legis*, Cap. I. v. 52, 65. – Eds.]

But it is for only one life, remember, and in the next several lives into infinity, there will be many other horoscopes, as there have been many for the various incarnations of the past.

The horoscope tells you what is possible and what is not possible in this life. For instance, a person may yearn for a purely spiritual life for ages, but if his karma which he has generated by himself, the horoscope and environment do not concur, then it doesn't happen in that particular life. There may be, instead, a karmic lesson to learn or a debt to work out or some other factor which must be taken care of first before one can become wholly spiritual. For instance, I have seen many a would-be Thelemite ruined because he or she couldn't and wouldn't do the foundational things like earning their own living, taking care of their own children, doing the simple everyday practices recommended by A.C., reading and learning, working on educational matters and so on. Their aspirations simply did not tally with reality.

First things come first. You no doubt heard me say that it was first necessary to get a roof over your head and food in your mouth before you could contemplate the Great Work. Indeed, these things are part of the Great Work and must not be shirked. Some people move fast in certain lives because they have somehow learned the basics and can move through them without too much trouble. This they may have done in other lives. All of our lives are a build-up in responsibility and learning of all that life presents. Some learn what is the True Will easily and others must struggle through all of the blocks on the path that they have put there by themselves. But in the end, the reward is for everyone. All must take the next step in evolution or fall back into savagery; none may stall on the path and remain forever the same. But one must not be unrealistic about what to expect in any given life.

One thing everyone can do without any strain is to purify the aspirations unto the Knowledge and Conversation of the Holy Guardian Angel. You can think of this matter while driving to and from work, while fixing or eating your meals, and in every moment of life. You can be ignorant, or well-learned and knowledgeable, and still you can do this. The more pure is the aspiration, the sooner will the Angel appear. One needs to purify the vehicle of the self, the emotions are for Him only and not for any selfish personal reason; the work of the body is to glorify Him; the thoughts in the mind are of and for Him. This is what is meant by purity, one-pointed will, chastity. This is a preliminary step to knowing Nuit as described in *Liber Legis*. You see, the H.G.A. resides at Tiphereth and so this step is between you and the play of Nuit and Hadit as described in *Liber Legis*.

But when one becomes selfish and ego-oriented, and sees the ego as the end of all, when the ego usurps the place of the H.G.A. and of the pure spirit, when one strives for accolades from one's fellow travelers, when one distorts the truth out of emotional predilections and distortions, when one harms another either mentally or physically, in short, when one lives like an animal like a dog, then the veil separating you from your own spiritual path will never lift. Mankind must live to the highest purpose, or forever be doomed to his sorrows and tribulations.

There is also a lesson to be learned each time one loves another person on this earth. Love is an expression of the H.G.A. and of all creation—call it God if you wish. "Love is the law," but it must be expressed under will or it can go in the wrong direction. Each time you love, it is an expression of the anima for men and of the animus for women. This anima or animus is a picture of all that is perfect for that particular individual. The emotion of love is set into a desire for completion because the lover is expecting the perfection in himself to shine forth in the other. Of course, this is unreal. It is only a projection, and it is only when the projection can be withdrawn, and the lover knows that what he loves is his own higher self, is he then set free to love others and let them be free of his projection. Love fails when it is a projection, because the person indulging in this sooner or later notices that his loved one does not come up to his expectations in one way or another. How can they? They are not the perfect self of the lover! But if the lover can understand that he loves one person for one bit of perfection which is himself, and another person for still another facet of this perfection; when he understands himself, in short, then he can love truly. This is a part of what is meant by "under will."

This is the lesson which I hoped to get across to you by asking you to pinpoint your projections in your diary. For these projections are practiced every day, and the more primitive a person is, the more will they project their own reactions upon others. This process of projections is a hard nut to crack, but if one does not understand it, both as when one hates or criticizes another or when one loves, then it becomes a block to the true understanding of the self and of the H.G.A.

I have had occasion to observe recently how two persons were extremely angry at each other for the very same trait they each had in common. You see, if anything stirs you in an emotional fashion, it is because that tendency or trait lies in yourself and you have tried to block it out, either due to early training perhaps or to other environmental factors. Folks block out the undesirable to such an extent that they lose sight of the fact that this trait exists in them, and was probably clearly visible in childhood.

One needs to know for what one was punished as a child or young adult. This punishment then would lead a person to hide, even to the self, the undesirable part of the self. Therefore, when someone else exhibits this very same trait, a person becomes disgusted, or will fight, or whatever reaction comes to mind and is fairly easy to perform. Everyone needs to know that these reactions are themselves brushing to the surface out of matters repressed in the unconscious. Not to know and accept all that is within oneself is to be only half a human. The path of the adept runs through this knowledge and acceptance process.

With Thelema one must keep in mind that one does nothing to disgust or harm another person. Some traits just may not be lived out in real life, but they can be changed into something more beautiful and productive. All traits and tendencies have power and energy in them and when they are not known, the person does not have access to this power and energy as it remains tied up into the unconscious life. Thus to refuse to know leads to straying far from the True Will and the person will become distorted and alien even to himself. Then through the mechanisms of projection, the person often begins to interfere with others, or to disapprove of them, or to hate them, or to gossip about them, or to seek to rule over others when he doesn't have the real ability to do so, or in other ways to make his ego the ruler in life, and not his spiritual self.

Any would-be Thelemite must then look at his negative reactions to others, for these are the repressed parts of his own personality. He would not know certain traits and tendencies exist in others if he did not have these in himself, for we can only know that which is ourselves, and that which we have not experienced is entirely unknown to us. The universe is our own universe: that which we can know is that which we have made out of our own raw materials, the five senses, and so on. But remember that this experience runs from life to life. The bigger a star is, the more experience it has accumulated through all its incarnations, not eschewing or negating any lesson to be learned, not turning the back on any phenomena which he himself has created, but trying to learn and understand all that is in him and all that he has gone through.

Some stars have to learn the same thing over and over again because they refused to learn the matter in the first time around. They limit themselves with complaints, fears, stubbornness, blindness, folly and on and on.

Everything is designed to lead on to the next step in evolution and this next step for all in this æon is the Knowledge and Conversation of the Holy Guardian Angel. One cannot ignore one's littlest complaint or dissatisfaction, one's hatreds and fears. These are all grist for the mill of initiation. All that happens must be understood and assimilated, and all of the energies of the physical, emotional and mental life must be put to a wise use.

This is the path of the adept—this is what we mean by initiation.

For initiation does not happen in a room full of other people who are putting you through a ceremony. It does not happen because a person says he is of a certain grade in an occult order; it does not happen from mere wishful thinking; it does not happen through power complexes—the desire to lord it over others and to be at the top of any organization. True initiation does not happen if a person will not work with their own universe, their complexes, their hidden unconscious motives, their loves, hates, fears, their everyday lives that they have created for themselves, in short, all of their own created phenomena.

It is not necessary to take a retreat on a high and lonely mountain. Instead, the thing that is necessary is to observe the self going through its own phenomena, and then to act like a magician to use all of one's own energies and capacities wisely, and thus to make change to occur according to the True Will. For if change is not directed from on high, from the supernal triad in each person, then one is simply staying in the same spot and going around in circles and not getting anywhere.

Your emotions are a powerhouse to set you on the right path if you do not let them get the better of you and control you, and thus lead you astray by their clamor. They have to be controlled, even as the body has to be controlled. When these two take their rightful places, then one must work on mind control — to think the thoughts of the True Will, other than those thoughts which interfere with this purpose and goal. This is somewhat harder than control of body and emotions, but it can be done anywhere — it does not need a retreat. One does not retire from life, as life gives the phenomena by which one can know oneself. A person could hardly notice what it is that he has reactions about if he removes all sources that cause these reactions.

Now then, to work, and work every day. Spend some time after the day is over in assessing your gains and your new knowledge.

Love is the Law, love under will.

Soror Meral

Carete Fratres et Sorores,[152]

Do what thou wilt shall be the whole of the Law.

Many times it has come to my attention that a person is working with Enochian, or they are perhaps tackling some very advanced ritual written by Crowley, or they are perhaps claiming to have the secret of the IX° O.T.O. and go around telling others that they can teach it and work it. There are a great many dodges which the uninformed egoistic person uses to draw attention to himself and perhaps to encourage emulation.

But when I investigate to see if the person has any background in these advanced works and practices, there is nothing there. Let me tell you of an experience which was told to me by an acquaintance of mine. He had called up Niksa, the King of the Element of Water and indeed had gotten results, so that his wife, his children and the animals in the house were very frightened. After his ritual this person then tried to dismiss Niksa, but he was very unsuccessful and the spirit refused to go. For a long time,

---

152. Originally published in: Phyllis Seckler, *In the Continuum* 3.10 (1986): 1-2.

then, this person suffered the results of his foolhardy action, for his water pipes in the house burst, his cooling system refused to work (he lived in a hot climate), the radiator on his car burst, there was trouble with the plumbing. All of these calamities happened within a short period of time so it could hardly have been coincidence! Fortunately, none in the family had occasion to swim in that part of the year.

My acquaintance wrote to me about these events and I used a little common sense and asked him why he would want a King of the Element of Water to serve him? Wasn't this somewhat as though he had asked the President of the United States to come at his bidding? If any person did that, various agencies would look into it and make trouble! Was it any different on the other planes of being? Was it not that what was below was like that which was above? And also, did not this King of the Element of Water have his own work to do and would he not resent it if he was called from this by an ignorant person? My acquaintance was stupefied, he had never thought of things in this way.

Crowley always extols common sense, and in his writings he is often extremely critical of those persons who have none, but who instead rely on a bloated ego in order to seem important in the world.

As to the claims that a person can work the IX° of O.T.O., this too is dangerous and perhaps laughable. I have had experience of persons trying to work this and have seen the results. All who made this claim had not mastered the beginning tasks which lead to control of body, emotions and mind. So when they got hold of this power, worse than a high voltage wire, they immediately harmed themselves irrevocably and went down in ignominy. Had they really understood the Master Therion, when he said it might be easy to get an intellectual knowledge of this power but it was not easy to work it? In fact, Crowley states clearly it can't be worked unless the person has mastered yogic practices (the eight limbs of yoga) and is an accomplished magician as well. Then too, one must always do any ritual whatever "unto Nuit" as is clearly stated in *Liber Legis*. If it isn't done "unto Nuit" a person can expect the direful judgments of Ra-Hoor-Khuit. What are these? The trouble that your own Holy Guardian Angel can send you in order that you might learn not to be such a stupid person!

There is an explicit grading of tasks which will take those who work from the realms of nephesh, where a great many people have the roots of their behavior, and up the Tree to the perfection of a master. So if, again, a person gets into trouble or has no results at all from some of the very advanced rituals in Crowley's Books, it is not to be wondered at! There will be no results if there has been no groundwork from the easiest rituals to the more advanced, and also if there is no groundwork in some of the powers that must be developed in ritual. Two most important techniques are visualization and concentration. Besides this, one must know how to make the voice vibrate as one intones the names of Holy Beings. Other techniques are indicated which are of use in some rituals but not in others. Indeed, as in life, one works from the more simple to the more advanced things.

But who wants to work? Ah!, many would claim to be Magicians, and those many have not much work to prove it! Again, *Liber Legis* reminds us "...a beggar cannot hide his poverty!"[153] So now what? Is ego going to be your stumbling block? Or are you going to enter the path to the Light with a humble heart and work on from the easiest to the more advanced. After all, you are not a born magician or a born genius. To gain the most from the best in life, one must work at it! The Light of the spirit will be well worth all your efforts!

Love is the law, love under will.

Soror Meral

Carete Fratres et Sorores of the College of Thelema,[154]

Do what thou wilt shall be the whole of the Law.

As we seek to know ourselves, we must remember that each person is a combination of several factors. Each has a karmic past which must register somehow in this life. Each has been influenced by the position of the planets at birth and this is known through the study of astrology. Each has had an environmental background and this is known somewhat through the study of

---

153. Crowley, *Liber AL vel Legis*, 47. [Cap. II, v 58. – Eds.]
154. Originally published in: Phyllis Seckler, *In the Continuum* 4.9 (1991): 1-4.

depth psychology. Then there is the inheritance of family traits which is different for each person, even in the same family, and this has been a subject of scientific research which will probably expand in the future.

But no one person can be known from a study of just one of these factors. To try to do so would seriously unbalance the understanding of oneself and of the understanding of others. We cannot write here of the inherited traits, as each person must know this somewhat for themselves. Nor can we write of karmic effects in this paper, though some occultists have attempted this subject broadly. But again, this is purely private and individual, and each must study the subject for themselves. Sometimes dreams and visions give a clue, and sometimes experiences that one has been in a certain place before or has known certain people before. There are good techniques for contacting the old records for each life, and some occult schools demand that one do this work at some time during the development of the individual. Of course, some methods appear in Crowley's *Liber Thisharb* which can be found in *Gems from the Equinox*.[155]

The best studies done for depth psychology and the effects of the environment on the individual can be found in the works of Carl G. Jung and of his students and others who have been directly influenced by his work. These studies are multitudinous and it is up to each person to at least begin some study of depth psychology.

What I want to touch on in this paper are some facts about astrology. For one thing, this is a very vast field of study, as no two horoscopes are ever the same; the planets do not repeat the same patterns or aspects in something like 2,400 years. Further, the study of the positions of the planets, sun and moon has a very ancient history. New knowledge is being added all the time as well. No single astrologer can know all that is known in this field—it would be impossible. The known and proven effects, even, are as diverse as human nature. Think only of the billions of people on the earth and about their various backgrounds, genetic pools, karma and so on, and you get an idea of what is facing the astrologer as he tries to interpret a horoscope. Yet because this study is so old, certain things have become quite obvious.

---

155. Also published in: Crowley, *Magick Liber ABA*, 637-642.

One of the most obvious studies is the placement of the Sun, and secondly, of the Moon. This is because the Sun is so huge in comparison to the earth that its position in relation to the earth is the most important factor in the horoscope. Further, its light and heat radiate in extreme fashion compared to the influences of the planets. The young tyro could even be satisfied with a description of the sign his Sun appears in, and this might suffice for some time as to some of the characteristics of his nature.

The Moon is next in importance, as it is so close to the earth and exerts a strong gravitational pull so that the tides are affected when in certain positions in relation to the Sun. When the Moon is overhead, it is even known to cause the surface of the North American continent to rise by six inches. Here too, the study of the Moon's effects on human nature is very old. When one begins the study of one's own horoscope, the placement of Sun and then Moon and then their relations to each other, or the aspects they make, should come first for the student.

After this, a consideration of the planets nearest to earth can be tackled. These would be Mars and Venus, adding Mercury after this. The ancients knew only seven planets (counting the Sun and Moon, or the lights, as they are sometimes termed) in the array. Jupiter is important as an influence as it is very large, and then Saturn, which is also large. These are near enough to be seen with the naked eye, and so their effects have also become a part of ancient and modern astrological lore.

But if you look at the chart with the sizes of the planets and their distances from the Sun, you will see that Uranus and Neptune have a smaller effect on humanity, as they are so far away and are fairly small compared to Saturn and Jupiter. When these planets were discovered, only in recent times, much began to be conjectured about them by astrologers. But not enough data had been gathered to prove the assertions that astrologers made. Through the mists of imagination a few facts about their effects on humans have surfaced. Some astrologers have been extremely cautious about these two planets beyond the orb of Saturn, and have said that they affect only those souls who have developed their higher natures, or who have evolved to the point where such subtle influences can be felt. If the soul has a lower rate of vibration or the evolution is fairly low, these two planets can cause their most negative side to be felt in the life of the native; or sometimes, it might be likely that they have little or no influence on the person.

What then, should we think of all the writings about Pluto, who scientists say does not fit into the same flattened orbit about the Sun as do all the other planets, and is also thought to be a frozen speck of ice which might possibly be a Moon of Neptune? Does it have any influence at all on human life? Common sense would say that the astrologers are being extremely imaginative when they attribute so much influence to Pluto and write so much about it! Actually, there have been too few years since the discovery of Pluto to build up a body of evidence as to its effects (if any) on human character. All that you read at the present is pure speculation or imagination.

This is just the sort of pitfall which awaits the beginner in his study of astrology. There is a lot of claptrap and unproven statements in the world of astrology, but one could steer clear of the worst of these ideas by using a little common sense. This is also why a student should consult quite a few astrologers, either through their books, their computer charts, or personally, in order to get some idea of his own horoscope. When consulting a good astrologer personally, it is often the case that certain intuitional moments will surface and the astrologer will even surprise himself by his reading of the chart. The development of this intuitional quality may take years of study and years of working with various clients or students. Or it might be a gift which surfaces fairly early in the career of the astrologer. The set-up of a certain type of horoscope chart may be the inspiration of certain intuitional moments which cut across all sorts of difficulties in the study of that chart.

When working with books, or computer charts, or with a good astrologer on a personal basis, one must be very honest with oneself as it is only too easy to build up an entirely erroneous idea of one's character and personality. Character and the way one reacts to life events are revealed by a horoscope. It is not necessary to view a difficult aspect as an inevitably defeating influence. Every type of aspect and every position of every planet has its helpful and its deleterious side. Here is where human will comes to the fore. One should know what might be a painful reaction to events, and one should then try a turn-about in attitude so that the event or trait does not harm, but is instead a necessary lesson which has somehow been earned through one's conduct from life to life, or one's conduct in this life. We build our own karma—no one does this for us—and we are responsible for our own attitudes, beliefs, and reactions to the life phenomena we have built up for ourselves.

Too many "easy" aspects such as trines and sextiles might make a person lazy, either mentally, physically or spiritually. But if these sorts of aspects are combined with squares and oppositions, which have been termed difficult or challenging, then there is a way out of the difficulties which might not be evident in a chart belonging to a person who has nothing but difficult aspects, and who shows a tendency to give up the fight.

Remember that a lot of famous persons have had difficult aspects, and these served as a challenge to be overcome, so that the person was strengthened and achieved a great deal. We are here on this earth to learn—this is a school—and lessons should not be shirked, or they will come back again in another life until we have mastered them and what they mean to our own soul growth. We must evolve towards a greater spiritual life—this is our task from life to life—and this is why we are here to suffer what we have brought down upon ourselves, and to solve our very own problems. We all have strengths and weaknesses, and our task is to bolster and emphasize the strengths and to master and control the weaknesses.

We hear a great deal about magick, but no magician deserves the title unless he can control his own reactions and his own immediate environment. It is impossible to be a magician and thus control or "cause change to occur in conformity with will"[156] as Crowley puts it, if one cannot control oneself. So it is best to stop speculating or talking about magick and best to start to work right away with the aid of one's horoscope. We have a long job ahead of us to turn the raw material of life into the spiritual gold of the alchemists.

Soror Meral

---

156. Crowley, *Magick Liber Aba*, 128.

Carete Fratres et Sorores,[157]

Would you try to attend high school without ever accomplishing the work given in grade school? In most cases you would say, "Of course not." You have been taught by your experience that first steps are necessary, and lead on to further learning and growth.

Yet when it comes to occult studies and work, too many people think they do not need the basic tasks and learning. They are inclined to plunge right in and call up entities from other realms. Of course, the sad result of this is that such a brash person soon becomes an occult crazy or a complete occult burn-out. Since such a person cannot control himself, he is soon controlled by subtle energies of which he was not really aware. It is like walking into a forest of wild animals, all ready to attack and kill in one way or another.

Often, in these cases, there have been no background studies, no knowledge of how to approach the astral or subtle planes, no basic protective practices, and above all, no purity of aspiration to the Highest.

Such foolishness and ignorance does not go unpunished. One person called up the King of the Undines and frightened his family and pet dog half to death. Then the radiator in his car burst, the swamp cooler leaked water through the ceiling, the plumbing system went awry and a pipe burst without any reason. It is fortunate that none of his family went swimming, or he would have lost some of them. As it is now, this person is through with occult work for life.

Another person called up an entity and again the house atmosphere was polluted, the dog and cat cowered under the couch, the family of mother and father, when they came home, were terribly upset. The end of all this was that a knowledgeable Catholic priest had to be called in to quiet things down, to do ceremonies, and to bury certain items far out in the woods.

Then there were many persons among my acquaintances who tried to use certain subtle forces they had read about in Crowley's writings. These acted like a boomerang. One person experienced a bad accident, declared bankruptcy in his business and finally lost that and to end it all, lost his wife.

---

157. Originally published in: Phyllis Seckler, *In the Continuum* 5.2 (1992): 1-5.

How many deaths were caused because of the misuse of this knowledge? I am inclined to think quite a few went down because of selfish attitudes and a lack of self-control and self-knowledge. One person under my observation talked to entities on the other plane and was attacked by them so that he was miserable and half-demented for quite a long time. He, of course, could not take the basic first steps to learn about his true self and to control that part of himself that would hinder his progress. In short, he was an alcoholic. His scanty knowledge of occult subject matter was part of his undoing as well.

Failure to succeed with occult studies is more pronounced with young people. The first duty of any person after leaving the parental home, or when grown up, is to put a roof over the head and food in the mouth solely by one's own efforts. If this is not done, then the pursuit of what is called the occult becomes mere foolishness, and will lead to trouble sooner or later. One needs a firm base of self-discipline in order to succeed at anything, and this is also true for occult studies.

The first thirty years of a person's life are generally meant to settle the basic necessities of life. Not only shelter and food, but the other necessities: A mate, and maybe children, and the fulfillment of oneself with daily work which accords with one's basic nature; hopefully, work which is loved. This ties into the finite will, which deals with education, occupation, avocation, hobbies and the like. If this is poorly known and a person is miserable at what they are doing, the matter should be straightened out before ever attempting occult studies.

Further, a decent education which encompasses work in college is a requirement for further understanding of the occult world. (Occult means only secret, and such secrets have been misused so much in the past that they have been closely guarded.)

Let us stop for a moment and mention what might be in an occult study course. There would be astrology, qabalah, Tarot, yogic disciplines such as asana, pranayama and other practices which could lead to samadhi. Then there is ritual and meditation of various sorts. There should also be a profound love for the Holy Guardian Angel, or at least some purity of aspiration which brings to life the spiritual side of the self. Then the advanced student might try astral travel, and perhaps join an occult order where he can meet with a teacher. If there are excessively negative traits shown in psychological analysis or by the horoscope, it may be that the student should do no more than acquire an intellectual knowledge of the field. Much reading could be done, but the person also needs to understand what is read. Without an education, the results might be ludicrous. Indeed, this has been observed many times, how some people will twist known facts due to a difficult inner character.

Astrology and depth psychology are difficult subjects to master, but each person could at least work on his or her own horoscope. The danger here is that the mask the person has built up over the years may become a detriment to understanding the self. Most people have too much ego, and build up a pretty picture of themselves which is often far from inner truths. Pride and ego have to be disciplined and controlled, or the person may become an occult crazy or some sort of failure. Dream work is also indicated to know what is at the core of the self. This too, is difficult and one needs guidance from a trained person in this matter.

To know the self is no child's play; usually it takes the first thirty years of life to get embarked on this project. This is why young people may drop out of occult studies at an alarming rate. Self-discipline is too difficult if one has not had discipline in home and school, or if one is naturally self-indulgent.

Helena Petrovna Blavatsky, a pioneer in melding the spiritual studies and work of eastern and western religions, actually discouraged occult work. Learning the basics in an intellectual fashion was the main thrust of her work. Theosophists to this day are apt to stress the fulfilling of karmic duty and the paying of karmic debts before embarking on the more difficult practices, which would involve astral travel or the raising of kundalini.

Perhaps she was right, for when I view the occult wrecks that I have seen — young persons attempting Enochian work before they have ever mastered any of the basic studies, or perhaps entering the astral world without safeguards or any knowledge of how to deal with such forces, or perhaps calling up entities from the unseen world and then not knowing how to control or banish them — it seems that this secret world may be too much for such undeveloped persons, and their ill-prepared dabbling may ruin progress for not only this incarnation but for several incarnations to come.

Since a graduate of a university has already developed and trained the mental powers, such a person could continue with his training in a mental way and study various occult works. Surely we see a vast growth of interest in occult subject matter. So much so, that more and more books are being published and read on this subject. Then, if the mind can be trained by study and reading, surely the emotions should also be trained. And if one is really serious, the body should be trained to match and to balance the learning.

The Golden Dawn system is an excellent method for intellectual study. But only a teacher can lead the student into an appreciation of what must be done to control the emotions. For wrong emotional attitudes can stop all progress in a hurry, and this has been quite a stumbling block for a large number of students.

If a person cannot understand and control the self, it then becomes impossible to control entities from the unseen realms. Enochian work, for instance, is for the person properly trained in the Golden Dawn system, with a mastery of several branches of learning and a mastery of the various parts of the self.

Such mastery is rarely seen in persons just entering their study of occult subject matter. Fascination and perhaps ego-gratification has called them to this line of study. It is in a person closely approaching what is known in astrology as the Saturn return that some self-discipline and self-mastery can be seen. This is about the age of 29½, when transiting Saturn reaches the point in the zodiac where it was situated at birth. By this time, the person should ideally be engaged in his most appropriate and enjoyable line of work, and should have solved most of the problems concerned with home and family. In other words, the student is pretty well settled in a life pattern. It is at or near this age, also, that some major spiritual experience can happen. For instance, Crowley had *Liber AL vel Legis* dictated to him by Aiwass when he was 29½ years old. It was almost an exact Saturn return. There are innumerable experiences of an expansion of consciousness in Dr. Bucke's book *Cosmic Consciousness*. Surely every student should be familiar with this work. But such an expansion of consciousness does not occur if the person is not ready for it. Sometimes being ready for this experience may involve past lives and the work done in them to lead up to this moment. The mind and emotions and body should have enough strength to undergo the experience. There have been cases where a person became unsettled or partially insane because the preparation was not done.

A broad and solid base must be established upon which a person can develop the more subtle powers. The student should not shirk what seem to be difficult and maybe even boring tasks, such as sitting in an asana for a prolonged period. As a developing child, each person had to learn to crawl before walking and walk before running. It is the same with occult studies. If he leaves some task undone due to weakness or disinterest, then surely that weakness will interfere greatly with his strivings, and impair his progress toward the highest attainment which is possible for him.

Such an expansion of consciousness is really the aim of properly understood occult studies. One is never the same afterwards. Some appreciation of universal meanings and of one's place in the scheme of things may change the life dramatically. With the experience known as the Knowledge and Conversation of the Holy Guardian Angel, one becomes the outer manifestation of that Angel in due time. One swears to obey and one does the work which is dictated.

But those who develop occult powers of various sorts, such as are known as the siddhis in the Hindu tradition, may become lost to the real purpose of the life. Pride and ego may stop progress for a very long time and even in future lives.

What are these occult powers or siddhis? We can list several from *777*. Such are the power of becoming invisible, of transformations, evocation, bewitchments, transmutations, crystal gazing, necromancy, telepathy, clairvoyance, clairaudience, divination and fortune telling. Some of these are lower forms of magical powers and should never be used to harm other persons. The list goes on: enchantments, casting the evil eye, attending the witches sabbath and so on. To become enamored of, misuse or overuse any of these so as to neglect the balance of growth in the soul, is to become lost and deformed. This is true unless such powers are used solely to carry out the work mandated by the Holy Guardian Angel, and should only be indulged in to accomplish His work in the world.

For the bulk of humanity, there is only one aim to occult studies, and this is what Crowley calls the Knowledge and Conversation of the Holy Guardian Angel. Even certain cosmic consciousness experiences and other types of knowledge of subtle planes, of experiences of death and revival, bear witness to this fact.

Even for the more mature student, failure is likely to occur if there is a challenge to the ego or to some treasured aspect of identity. Many people cannot bear to have their favorite illusions shattered.

If the student is a member of an occult study group or of a practicing ritual group, or perhaps in a commune of those interested in the subject and who have a common background, there is always the problem of personality clashes. Quite a few project their own ideas of what might be right for others who are in this work upon those around them. As a result, there is often a lack of acceptance of people as they are. It is all too easy to forget that no other person can be the ideal of anyone else. Intolerance can be a major stumbling block to learning from others who might have something valuable to give or to teach. What would the intolerant person be able to learn from Blavatsky if this person met up with her habit of swearing like a trooper and smoking marijuana? What can be learned from Crowley by the snobbish and closed-minded person when they learn of his difficult habits? Was he not noted for different sex habits, drug dependency and foul smelling perique tobacco?

Then we have the history of various occult or commune groups breaking up because of personality clashes. One most notable example was the break-up of the Golden Dawn as Crowley knew it. The examples of this sort of event are too numerous to mention. Ask yourself, does your disapproval of some persons stifle your progress in occult studies?

Now I have listed several warnings concerning your progress on the occult path, and have given you one shining star to which you may cling when the going gets rough, as it most surely will. You have only one duty to yourself, and that is to achieve the Knowledge and Conversation of the Holy Guardian Angel.

Love is the law, love under will.

Soror Meral

Carete Fratres et Sorores,[158]

Do what thou wilt shall be the whole of the Law.

In our present century, we are bombarded from all sides by the media. There are talk shows, dramas and advertising on T.V., and in the magazines and papers some of the same themes prevail. Advertisers seek to sell their products by appealing to an untamed sexual instinct in the consumer. As a result, there is a good deal of confusion in the minds of many persons who equate love with unbridled sex, pornography, or simply the pride of being male or female and how one attracts the opposite sex.

But there is a difference that many people do not see between love and the animal sexual urges. For instance, one can love one's family, one's parents, one's children, one's friends and co-workers, one's work, one's avocation outside of work, the phenomena of natural things, the growth of plants, the vagaries of weather. One can love sports and a body which feels healthy and strong. Or one could love the earth itself, the sky, the ocean, the land, the animals. One can love one's own higher self or other parts of the psyche and most of all one can love the Holy Guardian Angel—but a person cannot have sex with all these things.

On the other hand, let us review a little what happens when a person is overcome by animal sex. He might become a sex pervert and harm women or little children. He might become violent and add to the sorrows of domestic violence, sometimes leading to murder and death. In a milder form, he may show jealousy and extreme possessiveness and have the urge to be in charge of his family at all times. Many other twisted psychological factors may be in this picture to complicate the matter, but there it is, it is sex gone wild, an animal instinct which has not been faced, understood and controlled. In the final end, the animal in man must be transformed into something higher and better, into a more spiritual and more perfect life.

The Book of the Law has much to say on this subject. One would think that a thorough knowledge of its contents and an attempt to live to its advice would solve some of the problems of the animal person—the "dog" mentioned therein. For it is true,

---

158. Originally published in: Phyllis Seckler, *In the Continuum* 5.6 (1994): 1-4.

as adepts have known all through the ages, that a person must first refine the self, bring to light the primitive animal self which lurks in the unconscious psyche of many persons, hidden from view, and therefore, never faced and purified by work on these primitive urges. In the past such autonomous functions assured man's survival when he faced overwhelming odds in the life and nature around him. But today these functions still exist and are no longer controlled by religions all over the world. Therefore, they break forth and take their toll in human suffering and in lost lives.

It is necessary to have a great experience of love in order to advance from the primitive persons to higher states of evolution. For has not love been declared that it is our Law? Have not old religions stressed this fact, such as the saying in the Bible, "God is love?" Many of the old religions stressed love in very different ways, but most of the time it became an effort to love the more advanced and perfect parts of human life.

When a young person falls in love, he or she does not realize that they are projecting a perfect image of themselves upon another person. In Jungian terms, when a woman is very close to a man's ideal, or his anima, he falls in love with her. The same is true for a woman, when someone comes along who approximates her ideal of the animus, she will fall in love. At first there is bliss, as many of our popular songs attest to, but when the bubble of imagination or projection is broken, the trouble begins. The loved person may insist on being themselves, and at that point quarrels may begin since the partner has been misled, or so this partner thinks.

To truly love, a person must withdraw this projection of his or her own perfect self and see the partner for what he or she really is. When one can allow the partner this freedom and still love, then we can say that this is love and not a projection. This happens over and over again. Those who chase the opposite over and over again are truly in a primitive state and unaware of what they are doing. To complicate matters, primitive urges for sex surface and in some cases this sexual urge must have satisfaction with many different partners. It becomes all mixed up with love and a great deal of confusion results.

But *Liber Legis* seeks to set the matter in a different light. There is much instruction about love and how one should view it.

We are to love Nuit, for one thing. This seems a mysterious saying to those who have no knowledge of higher states of consciousness or who are involved with one person only, or perhaps have been chasing many different partners in a vain attempt to find the star center of the true self.

The vast majority of people have the spirit divided from the body. Many do not know that spirit exists. We have sunk unto a dreadful materialism. The uncontrolled intellect of man has not been guided by spiritual principles or by love, and more primitive unconscious and autonomous factors have held sway. Mankind has given in to uncontrollable greed, inertia and apathy, ignorance, animal sex, aggressiveness and selfishness. There is a primitive urge to preserve the self against the onslaughts of other people and of life itself. In short, in this case, there is little or no attempt at love. Such attitudes would in the end destroy humanity, as the planet is now so overcrowded that these primitive urges serve to destroy rather than to lift mankind to an understanding of the need for evolution, and the greater work and struggle to bring this about. And yet mankind must know, face and understand these animal urges—these autonomous instincts which have been pushed down into the unconscious—and transform their power so that their energy may be used for the benefit of all. Love, one could say, in one sense, is the uniting of things diverse.

In terms that even a child might understand, it is love when one loves one's play or one's work or one's everyday tasks and responsibilities. If a person has a job which he hates, original primitive inertia and laziness must be overcome and the job must be changed to suit the real person which exists within the outer shell. If this cannot be done, then it is of no use to search around for a belief system which will satisfy one's own shortcomings. Such behavior will only lead to psychological imbalance, or in due time, to a good deal of misery, death of the soul and spirit and perhaps end in fanaticism, hatred, insanity and war, either in the outer world or war in the world within the person.

In this century, women are seeking to free themselves from the yoke of male or fatherly domination which was characteristic of the last paternal age. They want to be persons in their own right and to enjoy the privileges of being on an equal footing with males. Though their psychology is different, it does not mean that they should be subdued by male aggression. Women perhaps have paid a great deal of attention to love. Their archetype is known to us through the utterances of Nuit, who is love in its purest essence. They know it is not love when another person indulges in sexual harassment, which often includes invitations to have sex which have not been asked for or even hinted at. The informed person knows that this is only an attempt to prove the superiority of the ego, an attempt to exert power over another person. In some cases, a person may be dominated by sexual urges in such a wild fashion that one suspects that kundalini has been aroused and has stuck at Svadisthana, and has not gone further. The person who has allowed this to happen is in danger of becoming a sexual pervert and of mixing his animal sex in with a deeper love. In recent news this has happened to persons who have pretended to be great spiritual gurus. Obviously, there is no refinement of the sex urge when such a person grooms young girls at the puberty stage to become his "marriage" partners. This is the sad fate of those who do not understand the power of the unconscious forces and who have never tried to understand and purify various factors in their own personality. They do not understand their emotions and they do not understand themselves. This sort of effect has happened often in the history of the world and in a great many cases, too numerous to count, it is the male who goes off the deep end in this fashion.

Liber Legis states clearly in Chapter I, v. 41, "There is no bond that can unite the divided but love: all else is a curse. Accursed, Accursed be it to the æons. Hell."[159] It is indeed a hell of one's own making to misunderstand love and get it mixed up with other extraneous factors, such as pride, revenge, domination urges, mental confusion, animal sex and a host of other factors. Also, hell can refer to the hidden factors in the unconscious which must be brought to light, understood, purified and used in a positive, life-giving fashion rather than in a fashion based on ignorance which in time destroys the soul and the spirit.

The subject of love is extremely vast; it is the very basis of the appearance of life on earth and elsewhere. It is our job in this age to understand it in all its facets and complexities and to practice it in our lives, for this is the path to evolution of the individual, and the transformation of him from a material being into a spiritual being.

---

159. Crowley, *Liber AL vel Legis*, 31.

To this end, a person interested in travelling on the spiritual path should know and practice those sentences in *Liber Legis* which revolve around love, for in no other way can he attain to the Knowledge and Conversation of the Holy Guardian Angel. Each person must perfect himself and refine his instincts, and conquer the animal and unconscious forces which impel him toward a lower order of life. Each person has a spirit which must not be destroyed by wrong attitudes and a misunderstanding of love. In short, this is the main task of those who call themselves Thelemites.

  Love is the law, love under will.

Soror Meral

Carete Fratres et Sorores,[160]

  Do what thou wilt shall be the whole of the Law.

Many times in a season we repeat this sentence, but do we readily know how to live it? Not many would-be Thelemites realize that the above sentence means severe self-discipline. The will is single and is not a bundle of whims, wishes and wants.

  As an example, think of a person training to be a violinist in a great orchestra. This person must practice many hours of the day, no matter the state of health or what may be wished for at the moment. It may be that the musician must give up bad habits which jeopardize his health, for with bad health, he would certainly not reach his goal. He may not smoke, for instance, nor allow himself to be overcome by drugs or alcohol, nor give in to the whims of partying until late at night. He must hold himself to the single task of learning the violin and how best it might express the music to be played by his orchestra. He must study music in many of its forms for many hours of the day, even apart from playing his instrument. All this takes a great deal of self-discipline and most people who utter "Do what thou wilt..."[161] have no idea of such discipline.

---

160. Originally published in: Phyllis Seckler, *In the Continuum* 5.7 (1995):1-5.
161. Crowley, *Liber AL vel Legis*, 31.

Further, our musician must have supplied himself with a roof over his head and food in his mouth. Sometimes when I talk to a beginner in our discipline, they are astounded by such words. But this is only common sense. How can you do your will if you are starving and homeless? So the first step in accomplishing the will, whether it be the finite will as with our musician, or the infinite will which is the next step for mankind, the Knowledge and Conversation of the Holy Guardian Angel, these simple beginning steps must be taken.

Unfortunately, some beginners in Thelema think that the idea of the will does mean whims, wishes and wants, and even worse, they insist on this for themselves and for others. They might say, "This is what I will" as they bother another person or actively oppose another person in their way of going. I have heard that one or two might even say, "This is what I will, therefore you have to obey what I want of you." This is extremely dangerous when applied to the practices of sex. It could lead to violence on the part of one person and enslavement on the part of the other.

With this truth then, that if a person wants to accomplish his or her own will, he or she may not interfere with the rights of others, let us look at the problems of persons who live in close proximity to one another. This could be a shared household, a community, a marriage or any type of liaison between two or more persons. Living by this law of Thelema becomes extremely difficult from day to day when one sees the same person all the time and when one is not informed that the traits and habits one objects to in the other person are probably projections on the part of the person who gets angry or upset.

The problem of projections occurs almost daily, or even hourly, for most people. The trait that makes a person angry is usually a trait he has pushed down into his own unconscious because he is ashamed of it, and has been trained in some fashion that this characteristic is not polite or is not accepted by society or is a flaw in his own character. So when this sort of pressure is brought to bear on any person, the despised trait is pushed down and an attempt is made to ignore it or to pretend it is not there. When such a trait pops up in another person, then he denies its existence in himself but shows anger or annoyance at the other.

Let us take a simple example from a shared household. Each person ideally should clean up after himself and not leave any of his traces of laundry or dirty dishes around. Nor, if he smokes, should he inflict his smoking habits on others. Nor should he play loud music in the night and disturb the sleep of others. Yet I have seen all of these things happen in a so-called Thelemic household. There are many other things which might happen in close quarters which actually deny the rights of others to do "their own thing" as it were. These are all very simple examples and yet in order to really live the law of Thelema, one must pay extreme attention to such small matters. It does not do any good to meditate for an hour if one is guilty of infringing the comfort and rights of others.

Further, in order to truly live this law of Thelema, one must be ever vigilant in small matters before the larger issues may be addressed. This is indeed self-discipline and one must become proficient in the first steps before one can expect to go on with one's will, whether finite or infinite.

In this age, the idea of magick or of mysticism or of doing the Great Work has captured the imagination of a great many persons. These ideas have become glamorous to a large segment of the population. I have heard some say that the Great Work is all that matters to them, and therefore, they will take advantage of anyone who will support or aid them in this goal. But this is not living the law of Thelema in an honest fashion, and each person must be ultimately responsible for himself, and not rely on others to help him, or push him, or whatever the weakness may be.

As explained earlier, the Great Work begins with the perfectly ordinary task of supporting oneself. Then comes the task of learning how to live the law of Thelema in everyday life, hour by hour, and being mindful of the moments when one is upset at other persons due to projections. In short, one must refine the character, but not by the former methods of suppression, and blindness to one's true nature. One must begin to study one's own reactions, and understand and control those reactions and emotions which are veritable stumbling blocks in one's chosen path. Even such work as this is a lifelong task, but if accomplished, surely the whole person will be strengthened. If one is to live the law of Thelema, one must be strong. This is no idle phrase, for in one way or another, this strength or the lack of it will get tested over and over again.

If a person belongs to the O.T.O. or the A∴A∴ the above development of strength becomes crucial. Suppose a person has an ambition to rise to higher degrees in the O.T.O. This is an outer order, of course, and higher degrees mean more and more service is asked of the aspirant. In order to aid other persons, one must be very strong in oneself. The O.T.O. could not do its work in the world if it was led by weaklings and lazy persons. Therefore, when it is part of the ambition of any person to have a higher degree, or to take the next step in the order, his service to the order and to other persons is looked at carefully before the next degree is conferred. Of course, those who operate only on whims, wishes and wants, and who interfere with the rights of others, may not make it to the next step. I have seen many of these problems surface over the many years I have been connected to the O.T.O., and many of the most glaring mistakes have led to expulsion, which is only right. But then, some mistakes of occult crazies or those who do not understand Thelema but are caught by the glamour have also become very laughable.

In the A∴A∴, the service to others is even more demanding and difficult. For each person in this order is led on by the highest of aspirations towards spiritual enlightenment. There can be a very delicate soul problem for each individual that the O.T.O., as it is a political and social order, could not address in an efficient fashion. Therefore, the A∴A∴ remains very small, but the persons who achieve the higher Grades in this order have even more inner power than do many persons in the O.T.O., no matter how high their Grade might be. Further, the work for the A∴A∴, as assigned by Therion, has to do with very serious work upon one's own character, and a mastering of various disciplines which are essential to the path towards the Knowledge and Conversation of the Holy Guardian Angel. For remember that the God will not dwell within a vehicle poorly prepared.

When one begins to get the first whisperings of the H.G.A., it might be through conscience, peculiar to oneself and not dictated by another, and by intuition. These whisperings need to be obeyed if further progress towards spiritual enlightenment is to take place. For instance, if your conscience says you must get up a half hour earlier than usual in order to meditate, then this instruction must be obeyed. Otherwise, a person would get nowhere at all. Now ask yourself, how many times have you ignored the dictates of conscience or of intuition?

These first intimations of the voice of the Angel might eventuate in the actual experience. I can scarcely describe to you the wonder and ecstasy of this experience, but certainly many persons around the world have tried. All of the pain and work that you experienced to gain this goal are as nothing when it occurs. So now in our sentence, after the first experiences have worked their way through you, our sentence becomes a matter of "Do what THOU wilt." One obeys the voice of the Angel, and one does the work in the world which He has foreordained for you. This happens to very few at the present, but it is the next step for mankind, and when more and more persons achieve this illumination, our world will not suffer so much from wars and spoilage of earth, air and water. Some of the selfish interests of those only out for material gain will be balanced by the truly illuminated in all countries.

There is a grave danger here when one has attained to the K. and C. of the H.G.A. Some persons are so unbalanced that they now think they must impose their own experience on others, and thus they form some sort of religious and usually bigoted community which destroys the individual will of the persons within it. This phenomenon has occurred often in modern times. I refer you to the recent news, which describes how others may even die in their slavery to the person who declares himself so spiritually superior that all beneath him must obey. This is pure ego. No one escapes this effect of ego unless the experience of crossing the Abyss is gone through and all that one is and has is destroyed in the manifestation of the boundless depths of the Universe—in our terms, Nuit.

The problem of ego gets stronger and stronger as one advances on the spiritual path. It also gets more subtle and can be observed in various ways. One of these ways is through projections.

When a person criticizes or deprecates the appearance of ego in another person, we can be sure that it is their own ego speaking which is now being challenged. The very idea that one is pure and now free of ego reactions is a false one. Let me repeat, a person could not see any failing on the part of another if he did not have this same failing within himself, at least in potential. As a result, he wishes to push it down or hide it, as he is ashamed of its appearance in his life, his thoughts and his actions.

So the person who has finally achieved the K. and C. of the H.G.A. must immediately face this demon and conquer it from day to day until the final step of crossing the Abyss can be achieved, if it is achieved at all in the same lifetime.

Now I have tried to put down in clear language some of the wonders, the difficulties, and the horrendous pitfalls in this path to spiritual enlightenment. I am making things overly simple perhaps, and certainly many others on this path have done it better and more completely. I can only say to the Thelemic beginner, learn from the best of books, observe and control your own self, work hard with your psychological knowledge not only for yourself but for others whom you must serve, and certainly listen to the voice of your own conscience and your own intuitions. Further, and as an essential part of your work, let Love guide your every move.

Love is the law, love under will.

Soror Meral

Carete Fratres et Sorores,[162]

Do what thou wilt shall be the whole of the Law.

Human nature being what it is, most people have difficulty recognizing or understanding any level of development above their own. Thus, a genius such as Rembrandt, or Gauguin, or Mozart, plus many illuminated persons, many of whom are mentioned in the Gnostic Catholic Mass, are generally misunderstood and ignored by the public at large in their own times. Often, it takes some time after the death of such a person before others in the culture will achieve a similar state of exalted consciousness, and so will understand the work of a past master. In due time, what has been put into an art form, or into writings, or into poetry or into a school of teachings, will spread to a few who have achieved some sort of higher consciousness, and then from them to others, and after a great while, the work of the master will be appreciated

---

162. Originally published in: Phyllis Seckler, *In the Continuum* 5.8 (1995): 1-5.

by those who have also achieved a level of refinement so that they can understand the work of the master.

But the person of genius may not necessarily understand or be able to work with a level higher than his own. He can work with any level beneath this achievement but not necessarily anything transcending it. This is also true of entities on the astral planes. In *The Vision and the Voice*, there are many instances of an angel not being able or allowed to hear or work with an angel of a higher order of being. The inferior angel must disappear before the greater voice and apparition may appear to instruct the seer.

In order to refine the aspirations of those interested in the development of their higher selves, it is a great aid for a person to study the work of others who have achieved. Also, in some cases, memorization of various works aids in the growth of the soul. Thus, Karl Germer memorized *Liber Legis*, *Liber LXV*, and *Liber VII*. When he was confined to a solitary state in a German concentration camp during the time when Hitler was in power, he could recite the Holy Books to himself and this aided him to achieve the Knowledge and Conversation of his own Holy Guardian Angel. When Crowley was informed of this development he confirmed Karl's attainment of the grade of $5°=6^{\square}$ of the A∴A∴. But Karl also had a difficult time of it to understand many subsequent messages from his H.G.A. For once this initial contact is made, many messages dealing with very important steps in the life of the individual are sent by the H.G.A. Karl complained that he was not always open to these messages, but the initial experience was of such great moment that he knew his task in life was to support Crowley and to do his best to publish Crowley's writings. I think it would be of interest to aspirants to read Karl's comments on the H.G.A. which were written to me.

In a letter from November 23, 1951, Karl wrote:

> There is only one thing for each one of us to strive for: the ever closer communication with our H.G.A. To this end, "Ora et Labora" (Pray and Work) is the only method. Follow the subtle instructions which your H.G.A. has given to you, or is giving you. He knows what is needed by you. I should mention, however, that 666 as a super-Hierophant or Initiator is active and operative all along and, as the need arises, He may well take a hand occasionally.

The problem then is to learn to understand the language in which such beings communicate with us. Again, intensive work and preservation of the purity of the soul through regular practices, are essential.

On April 1, 1952, Karl wrote on this subject again:

> In the meantime the H.G.A. sends messengers to train one in a particular job for which one has to become ripe, from time to time, who in themselves have no other purpose but just that, and should be discarded as the lesson is learnt. You understand this clearly, but it does no harm if I express the same idea in another form. It may be years later that you begin gradually to understand the language. A.C. received *LXV* and *VII* in 1909, I believe, but it took years to understand the books. I had a phase of this sort in 1927 and while in the Concentration Camp in 1935. The power of the H.G.A. is unbelievable in going into absurd details. For instance: in the C.C. I was in solitary confinement. When the operation came to a climax, I was changed to another cell with the #175 (which in the German code is the paragraph concerning buggery): and, as you know, it is the H.G.A. who takes the active role in that operation, the magician has to become a bride, and the H.G.A. takes the active role and the magician "was pierced as a thief by the Lord of the garden" (*LXV*, Cap IV, v. 40: see the commentary to this).[163]
>
> Also, paper, ink and a pen or pencil had been taken away from everyone. But when it became necessary that I had to keep a diary, I had all of these; they came to me in the most natural way, without a plan on my part. And there are other instances of the foresight, wisdom and power of those four dimensional beings. Trust Him.

In a letter of May 5, 1952, there was more detail which was meant as an aid to my own strivings:

> It is hard to try to explain in a letter what my ideas are about the H.G.A. You'd ask me again and again. Nobody

---

163. Crowley, *The Holy Books of Thelema*, 73.

explained it to me. I believe everyone has to find out for him/herself. You've got to start from another beginning. You are Phyllis on this plane, but you are also a Star from time immemorial and you have had innumerable lives and represented different types in their course. If you imagine yourself for a moment (to use the imagery of *LXV*) as a Serpent, in which function you would not be operative as Phyllis, but on quite another plane: then there must equally be a Heart around which the serpent has to wind itself. (*LXV*, Cap. II I am the Heart and thou the Serpent; wind they coils closer about me ...) which Heart may at this moment be manifest as a human—or not. It is not very important, because it is not Phyllis that is doing the winding, except as by initiation she gets a reflection of what is going on in her soul as a human being. The Heart (on its plane) will constantly be doing the tickling, if you allow me to say so, the stimulating, the urging towards that goal (the union of the two) which It is longing to accomplish. Once you know the various vv. of the 5 chapters of *LXV* by heart, you will find innumerable passages that keep springing up in your soul and mind to illuminate you.

You should not worry at all, about finding a human partner on this plane to accomplish that union, for it is a mystical union, and a human being would only distract or destroy. Take A.C.: he was looking through all his life for the real Scarlet Woman. It was only at the end of his longing that he found what it was all about. And yet, every one of the Scarlet Women had to convey a message, a lesson to him: but they were nothing but messengers; as soon as he took them to be more, they were torn away from him and ended wretchedly.

Keep affirming in your heart your longing, your devotion, to 65, or the H.G.A.: He is constantly around you, once He has found ingress to your soul. He is watching over you, and the more you begin to perceive His signs, that He is giving you, the more subtle will become your senses and get attuned to His language.

Even the apparent difficulties in your life are part of His plan. One thing that all of us forget is that the clock on higher planes does not go by hours, days, months and years:

the periods are different; the crime is impatience. The moment you stop desiring, in comes 65. Easy to say huh? It is the simple things that are hard!

However, it is the H.G.A. Himself who will set the proper day and hour for the union. Then all will be prepared beautifully and fall in its place. The leisure, the aspiration, the Yoga, the surroundings, the silence, and all the rest. Did I not tell you that He arranged everything for me in the solitude of the Concentration Camp? Learn to abandon yourself with utter confidence to Him. Yet, as it is said: Invoke often! Learn the whole of *LXV* by heart!

False entities or voices, yes, there are plenty. And I must confess to my shame and regret that I have not solved the problem of how to distinguish in every case.

Diary: yes, there are often things or thoughts one is given or urged to write down, that seem outrageous (at the moment). Have you checked such thoughts 3 years later to see whether you do not discover that there is very deep material in them? Don't forget that Truth on the higher planes may look quite different from the conventional truth in which we have grown up.

On May 5, 1953, Karl had this to say:

In the early stages our primitive natures require actual, visible, sensible, proof of an outer being contacting us. I remember in my early period I sometimes asked for a definite sign in order to (a) reassure me in a sort of weak phase, (b) to give evidence that I was on the right track. Yet: (this is important in my case!) I never connected such signs as coming from a definite outer being. I just took it as from "God" or of such things. My conception of the H.G.A. has probably only been condensed after A.C.'s death. Funny? Unbelievable? It is so! The H.G.A. has been taking almost violent, desperate means to bring me to the realization of his existence and presence and operation. But my hide was, and still is, too dense, so that A.C. once in the 1927 period wrote: "instead of a skin you have a carapace!" And this not as a joke, but rather in despair.

Be and feel happy that you are better constituted! Later, the messages become more subtle and so that one cannot distinguish them from what we call 'conscience' in many cases. There are people who carry on definite conversations, they hear voice—or other type—messages; the difficulty remains, however, to verify the source.

Achad got messages to the last; but they were, since his turning away from 666, not from his H.G.A., but its shadow, the Evil Persona. As it is hard to follow the voice of the H.G.A. in later stages, because often things are demanded that seem outrageous, against all morals and ethics, there is the danger of falling prey to the sweet whisper of the other guy (cf. Jesus and the high mountain); in Achad's case it was the promise that he was to be the bloke of *AL* III, 45, (the child), and A.C. seduced him and fortified this conviction (a magical test!) by writing *Liber Aleph*.

"Neglect not the Dawn Meditation!"[164] is one of the most important injunctions of A.C. (I only repeat — I don't do it myself! I can't meditate). It is well to practice this as a routine, so as to be prepared when the H.G.A. arranges a phase for one of the—let me call it—technical initiations or illuminations. Why do I mention this here? Because you write you were deep asleep when you got that one message and only wrote it up, partly, after waking. In my Concentration Camp phase I was alone in my cell (when the crucial weeks came). I worked with hardly any interruption; sleep was broken up so that I never slept more than 3 hours at a time; and that 'sleep' was light, and I snapped instantly back into work. If you read "John St. John" in *Equinox* I, you have the same idea; except that A.C. did his Opus by an effort of will and in 12 days. What I want to say is that such high water marks are secretly arranged by the H.G.A.: then the conditions are right and will bring the result about. But the training of one's mind to waken instantly and fully at a touch, is always helpful.

---

164. Crowley, *The Book of Lies*, 164.

Another comment was in a letter of July 21, 1953:

> Tonight I completed Letter 85[165] and the remarks and observations on the H.G.A. are up to the very end. It'll take years and years to observe, analyze, and dig deeper. The H.G.A., of course, as such, is on another plane altogether. Read the last few 'Letters' where A.C. summarizes: you must not attempt to pull the H.G.A. down to your plane, but by constant, constant and once again, constant work, make yourself capable of—not only visiting that plane on which he is—but of living there more or less when you need Him or want to communicate with Him.

All this is to show that the achievement of the Knowledge and Conversation of the Holy Guardian Angel cannot be faked, even though the experience is different for everyone. Those who have attained to this stage of growth recognize others on the same level and know also a great deal about those on lower levels of development. When a person does not have a high level of development as shown in these letters, nevertheless, this person can be helped greatly by the explanations and writings of others. If one is ever in doubt about the level of achievement by someone else, one needs only to look at the work which announces such attainment. In short, if there is no work, there is no high attainment.

Love is the law, love under will.

Soror Meral

---

165. The letters in *Magick Without Tears* upon which we were working. [– S.M.]

Some Remarks On Death[166]

There is a certain sense of shyness and reticence about events connected with the Holy Guardian Angel, but one event I have often described to students and others. This was the memory of my last death.

It is not certain in what year this occurred or exactly how it happened, but it was a sort of vision while in a waking state. I remembered clearly that I was dying in a sort of garret, as I could see the roof beams above me, which supported a peaked roof. I was suffering terribly from some sort of illness in the abdominal area. My bed was not very clean as there had been no one to aid or help me for quite some time. Also, it was but a single type of bed, the covers crumpled, dirty and wrinkled. The pain became so unbearable that I could stand it no longer when there appeared at my left side a beautiful angel and I then left my body and went to Him. The love he had for me was greater than any love that could ever be on this earth. I can scarcely explain its purity and intensity, as I think no human has ever expressed such a love. Even now, these words are but a poor shadow of the experience. As I thought later about this event, I was certain that I had been an artist in that particular incarnation, and a poor one at that, and that was why I was dying in a garret.

Strangely enough, when I was in my teens, I was extremely interested in art and remarked to my mother that I wanted to be an artist even if I had to die in a garret for it. Sometimes little events like this are clues to who we are. Much later in life several persons suggested that I go to New York and my reply always had been that I would not do so, for I wouldn't want to be caught dead in such a city. This is probably another clue as to the location of my last death. There have been hundreds of unknown and unsung artists in history and I was one of them, barely making a living with some sort of copy work or designs for various businesses, probably just before the end of the nineteenth century.

---

166. Originally published in: Phyllis Seckler, *In the Continuum* 5.10 (1996): 11-13.

But this wonderful and loving experience of the Holy Guardian Angel has left me with no fear of death, and often I remark about going over to the other side, to the horror of family, friends and acquaintances. Too many people have been programmed to fear death in our society. It has become an obsession so terrible, that doctors try every method known to forestall the inevitable. There are organ transplants and machines to keep a person alive, even if in a vegetative state and even if the person is brain dead. Sometimes trying to prolong life leads to suffering greater than any torture device of the middle ages or at other times.

Sometimes even the law will not allow death when a person suffers extremely from some disease. The fear of death has led to a poverty of approach to this matter. Everything that lives has a moment when it lives no longer. That is, the existence is not on this earth but elsewhere. In the case of mankind, since we are so constituted that we cannot remember what it was like on the other side, a great many imaginings are used to explain this lack of memory. In various cultures, a heaven of some sort is dreamed of, and its particulars are different all over the world and follow the beliefs of the local religions.

It is of great profit to the student of such matters to learn how various cultures view the advent and experience of death. In our scientific age, some remarkable events have occurred which give another view of death. Our modern techniques of medicine have brought back some persons from the brink of death after a few moments of the experience. There seems to be a general type of experience for those who died due to accident or illness and which all have told to those who are now exploring just what happens in this other state. Each person coming back from a momentary death describes a long area of darkness and then at the end is a Being of Light. Since it is known by this Being or Angel just what is to happen, that is, the person is to return to earth, there is a discussion of the task to be accomplished in this life just momentarily left. The person comes back with an idea of the Task, the will, and if rightly oriented, then tries to fulfill the instructions. Naturally, this often causes a change in direction, but also a greater joy and sense of fulfillment in the life events.

Every person in the world has a special task, unique to them. Too many have no idea of the task, or finite will, and so they lead a life of despair; part of this despair is the fear of death, of change, of anything new. One could ask if the momentary death due to accident or illness was not a device of the Angel to set one's feet on the correct path?

Since every person must die in due time, what can they say to themselves about the work done to aid mankind? What can they say to the Being of Light about their progress in life? Has it been debilitating, or has it been leading to a high spiritual end? Has the work done in life been to the greater glory of the love between the Angel and the human? Now is the time to ask this question of oneself. Now is the time to experience love in all its forms in order to understand and return the intensity and purity of the love of the Holy Guardian Angel for one's little self in a human body.

And now I will finish this small essay by giving a few relevant quotes.

From "Ode: Intimations of Immortality from Recollections of Early Childhood," by William Wordsworth:

> Our birth is but a sleep and a forgetting:
> The Soul that rises with us, our life's Star
> Hath had elsewhere its setting,
> And cometh from afar:
> Not in entire forgetfulness,
> And not in utter nakedness,
> But trailing clouds of glory do we come
> From God who is our home:
> Heaven lies about us in our infancy!
> Shades of the prison-house begin to close
> Upon the growing Boy,
> But He beholds the light, and whence it flows,
> He sees it in his joy;
> The Youth, who daily farther from the east
> Must travel, still is Nature's Priest,
> And by the vision splendid
> Is on his way attended;
> At length the Man perceives it die away,
> And fade into the light of common day.
> Earth fills her lap with pleasures of her own;
> Yearnings she hath in her own natural kind,
> And, even with something of a Mother's mind,

> And no unworthy aim
> The homely Nurse doth all she can
> To make her Foster-child, her Inmate Man,
> Forget the glories he hath known,
> And that imperial palace whence he came.[167]

From *Liber AL vel Legis*, Cap. I, v. 58:

> I give unimaginable joys on earth: certainty, not faith, while in life, upon death; peace unutterable, rest, ecstasy; nor do I demand aught in sacrifice.[168]

Infinite Possibilities[169]

Do what thou wilt shall be the whole of the Law.

The universe is made up of infinite possibilities. Each star or khabs chooses for itself certain events and thoughts, and makes up for itself a character or mode of behavior. The process of choice forms a layer of several astral or fine bodies. Finally, the whole complex is formed into a physical body which carries all that has been experienced in recent events of this life and in the past. The events of this life may be fairly easy to access when one probes as to the roots of certain behaviors; but far more difficult is the memory of past lives, and the karma that was generated there.

No two stars could ever be the same. There are many marks on the final physical body to show how this might be. For instance, fingerprints are never the same; their variety is endless. Few folks realize how different every star is from every other star. Herein lies a great mischief.

It may be that a certain earth character has built up what he or she thinks is a very fine code of behavior. This code is made

---

167. Wordsworth, William, *Ode: Intimations of Immortality from Recollections of Early Childhood* (Boston, MA: D. Lothrop and Company, 1884), 23-27.
168. Crowley, *Liber AL vel Legis*, 35.
169. Originally published in: *Black Pearl* 1.1 (1997): 8.

up of what the earth person can see in the experiences of the present life, but fails to realize what karma there may be in the ideas that motivate him or her. Of course, the thinking process manufactures certain ideas; but nothing ever manifests unless the power of emotional push brings these ideas into actuality as something worked out on the physical plane. Hence, the code which this person may think is very fine (and which has built his or her character), the person seeks to impose upon others. To the mind of our person, the code of action and behavior has worked fine for him or her, and now must be used to guide the whole earth through compliance with it—because it is so wonderful, and could hardly be improved upon!

This is called projection. We have labored long and hard to bring this fact of existence to your minds. One sees other persons through a fog of one's own ideas and behaviors. In the worst type of scenario, the experiences of the one person are imposed upon another, and sometimes on a multitude of folks. Just look at the events in the world around you. Projections are being imposed all the time upon nations, upon church groups, upon individuals —upon any sort of group. The one who has the most strength of character (and perhaps charisma) can sway a whole roomful of people.

Sadly, a great many persons are not aware of their own secret inner strengths, and are far from being aware of the particular characteristics of their own star. These people will tend to be slaves to the will of a stronger personality. They are not yet free in the Thelemic sense. They hope to benefit from what is being told to them, and do not yet know that the will of one person sways them to do this or that, or to think this or that.

This becomes even more powerful as a form of evil if the person who sways the multitude has built a prison of thought and behavior. In fact, this can be seen all over the world. The prisons are not just in other nations; if you look carefully, you will see they are in our own nation. They are not just in groups of other persons, they are in ourselves!

Thelemic thought bids each person to do his or her will; yet even in Thelema, prisons of thought, ideas, and behavior are being foisted upon the unthinking ones, the enslaved ones. If these poor persons accept someone else's prison of thought, idea, and behavior, then what happens is against their own True will.

As a Thelemite, if one really wants to live this code, one could aid other persons to find their own strengths and weaknesses. One could perhaps lead them to some sort of understanding, so that they can be more acquainted with their true selves. Sometimes a prison of thought and action must be broken down for those who aspire to the higher, spiritual Self. If a teacher or guru cannot do this, then life and karma may take on some form that is a real wallop, leading to unhappiness and sorrow — at least for a while. But then, this personal prison would lead to sorrow and self-undoing anyhow; for it must by now have become obvious that other persons are not going to act on or accept one's own code of behavior. If one is truly thinking in a Thelemic mode, why would one want to put other persons in one's own prison of thought and action?

As I began, so I will finish. Nuit means infinite possibilities for each star, and we are asked to love Nuit. Indeed, there is a great deal of mystery in this statement. I may have only scratched the surface. But I have tried to make clear to you what happens all around you on a daily basis. Perhaps you may be able to stretch your ideas and thinking and accept the differences in others. Perhaps you may finally meditate, and find your own true center, your star or khabs.

Love is the law, love under will.

The Worship Of Nuit[170]

Oh, Light of Life in splendrous rapture of delight / Who fills my veins with life in majesty of might. — Meral, 1982

How does one worship the Queen of Space? *Liber AL vel Legis* gives many clues, but it may take a lifetime before some of its words come to life as actual experience.

Certainly, one must start with love. This may be more than the love of one person for another (though this type of love can be a lesson in itself, even if it doesn't last very long). Love covers other areas of life, and may mean love of one's work or creativity, love for family and children, love for nature, and on and on.

---

170. Originally published in: *Black Pearl* 1.6 (1999): 11-12.

But there is a further love that transcends all loves that we may know while wearing an earthly body. All love, of whatever kind, is a training to experience this transcendent love. Beautiful words have been written to give us an idea of it. One should immerse oneself in such classics as *Liber LXV* or *Liber VII* to begin understanding the love for Nuit, and of Nuit for a human.

There is an intermediate step in this Way of Love. It is the Knowledge and Conversation of the Holy Guardian Angel. Students of qabalah represent this step on the Tree of Life by the central sphere, Tiphereth. At this stage there are two entities, the aspirant and the Angel. Only above the Abyss do the two become one; but such enlightenment may not last long, for it is a state beyond human strength. The aspirant is soon thrown back into the sphere that represents the life's work.

The first stirrings of the Angelic voice may come to us through intuition. If a person isn't open to relying on this deep intuition, it may not be evident that the H.G.A. can speak through the same voice. It is entirely possible to turn one's back on such whisperings and inspirations, especially when one's concerns are mostly materialistic, emotional, or intellectual; but the H.G.A.'s lessons persist. If one becomes upset, unhappy, or miserable due to some behavior, it is certainly the H.G.A. dealing out "tough love" so that one will make changes.

All this I have observed in myself, and when trying to understand others. It provides preamble as I try to write of my own experiences with the H.G.A. .

It was July 1, 1952, when my first acquaintance with the H.G.A. occurred. I was raising my three children alone. Once they were in school, I was also in college, training to become an art teacher. I also had been typing Crowley manuscripts for Karl Germer so they would not become lost.[171]

I was awakened by a light up my spine. I could vaguely understand that instructions had been given to me for some time before my awakening. What I could remember of this was the name of the H.G.A. and His instructions to enumerate this name with the aid of the Hebrew alphabet. Understanding this name took quite a few years; but the voice never really left me after this

---

171. This I did every summer for three years. Karl reproduced this typing on plastiplates from his home in Hampton, New Jersey. [– S.M.]

incident. There have been many occasions when I had help from the voice when it was obviously needed. One goes on living a normal life, working and doing all the things to support oneself and one's children. The voice of the H.G.A. is not needed in everyday circumstances. But one must go on refining oneself and one's reactions. One must study and learn about magical and mystical processes. "The God will not indwell a vehicle poorly prepared," as the ultimate advice states. When major lessons or ordeals were needed, they were supplied in order to continue this growth and refinement.

Prior to this first awakening, I had been writing poetry inspired by various sorts of love that shadowed forth the major direction of my soul. Karl Germer thought that the K&C of the H.G.A. happened in my case because I had a pure aspiration.

The event of the night, which I only too plainly described above, left me with such awe that I could scarcely speak of it without an inner trembling. It was six months before I could even write of it to Karl. Yet he knew from the tenor of my letters that this event surely must have happened. He therefore declared that I was at the level of 5°=6▫ in the A∴A∴.

The poetry continued, for there is not much to say about such an experience in ordinary language. Also, many major contacts were vouchsafed me at various times. The most memorable of these was when I remembered my last death. It was like a vision, in that I was awake and conscious. I was in great pain in that former life, and was lying in bed in what must have been a garret (I could see the sloping roof and the beams above me). My bedclothes were quite dirty, for there had been no one to take care of me during this illness. Nor do I know what caused the pain, only that it was unbearable. Then the H.G.A. appeared at my side. I left the body and the pain, and knew how intense and pure was the Angel's love. Such intensity is never experienced in life, and there are no words to describe it. One can only know that love is the key to such awakenings, and that we are here on earth to learn about this love.

When humans love in this mundane life, too many expectations are usually attached to it. A person may want security, or a partner who will enhance one's importance, or someone to manipulate to show one's power. Human love is usually conditional: Perhaps it is a desire for children, or for companionship that does not fade away. Perhaps a person is afraid to be alone, and requires that someone always be at hand to give support through thick and thin. There may even be a desire for conflict and disastrous situations, allowing for strange cruelties and abuse; but here we have not love, but sexual sadism. Humans mix up the biological urges of sex with what they wrongly suppose is love. *Liber Legis* I: 41 is very adamant about this mistake as no coupling should be experienced unless there is love: "There is no bond that can unite the divided but love: all else is a curse. Accursed! Accursed be it to the æons! Hell."[172]

Love is an intoxication of the spirit, an expression of transcendent spirituality. Sex is related to the lower animal (bodily) instincts. Each person must learn to distinguish between them. Also, for persons incapable of love, sex matters usually predominate. This may lead to abuse of women and pornography. Unconscious forces gain greater power when repressed for too long. Ideally, sex should be an expression of love between two adults, taking on the higher aspects of spirituality. The Gnostic Catholic Mass is a very fine instruction as to the procedures to be followed.

Liber Legis teaches about love in every chapter. It would be well for the aspirant to study this Book very closely. Memorizing it is even better. One cannot experience the higher states of consciousness without the power of love. The love of the H.G.A. is unconditional, and is so intense it could easily burn through an undeveloped soul. That this does not happen is because the H.G.A. is mindful of his client's weakness, and will apply a remedy that will lead to a strengthening of the aspirant.

Learning how to love, what it means to one's very essence as a star, is the major lesson for humans today. When love has been purified—when one learns to love without conditions, and with fervor, purity, and intensity—then one is prepared to love Nuit as we are exhorted to do in *Liber Legis*.

I feel there is no need for me to write more in this space, for many of my poems and other writings have been inspired by the H.G.A. . I, as a small human, do not take credit for all that I have written, said, or done. I have simply tried to follow instructions

---

172. Crowley, *Liber AL vel Legis*, 31.

as best as I can. Yes, when one has this sublime guidance, one must obey—and one does so from the most pure states of love.

Is Thelema A Solar-Phallic Religion?[173]

Do what thou wilt shall be the whole of the Law.

There is a good deal of misunderstanding about the terms "phallic" and "phallus," which Crowley used often in many of his writings. Let us turn to the dictionary for a clarification of these terms.

> **Phallus**: An image of the male reproductive organ, symbolizing in certain religious systems the generative power in nature, especially that carried in procession in ancient festivals of Dionysus or Bacchus. Anatomy: The penis, the clitoris, or the sexually undifferentiated embryonic organ out of which either of these develops.

In other words, both sexes have this generative power of nature. Both sexes have a "phallus."

Before we go further into this subject, I would also like to point out that both male and female conform to the glyph that we call the Tree of Life. When a human takes shape as a physical body in the sphere of Malkuth, then we see that a choice has been made as to whether the soul wants to incarnate as a male or a female. Previous to incarnation, the soul is formed by all the spheres and paths as depicted on the Tree.

There is also a mysterious relationship between sex and the force of kundalini, which lies at the base of the spine in three and a half coils. *Liber AL vel Legis* mentions this force in several places. Mention of it also appears in *Liber LXV, The Book of the Heart Girt With a Serpent*. The term "serpent" has been used extensively in both of these books. In *Liber Legis*, Chapter I, verse 61, Nuit admonishes all humans: "Put on the wings, and arouse

---

173. Originally published in: *Black Pearl* 1.9 (2001): 5-7.

the coiled splendour within you: come unto me!"[174]

The "coiled splendour" refers to the coiled serpent of kundalini. The wings refer to the Ajna chakra, which is always depicted with the two wings (or petals) of the caduceus of Mercury. If this caduceus is properly drawn, it includes all of the spheres of the Tree of Life.

This "coiled splendour" may stop at various of the spheres of the Tree. For most persons, the next step in evolution is the Sphere of the Sun, Tiphereth. Here the attainment is to the Knowledge and Conversation of the Holy Guardian Angel. Persons of either sex can and do achieve this solar attainment. *Liber LXV* is a splendid example of such an attainment. (Tiphereth is associated with the Anahatta Chakra in the heart area.)

In *Liber AL vel Legis*, there is further instruction concerning the force of kundalini. In Chapter II, verses 22 and 26, this force is described as that of Hadit:

> I am the Snake that giveth Knowledge & Delight and bright glory, and stir the hearts of men with drunkenness....[175]
>
> I am the secret Serpent coiled about to spring: in my coiling there is joy. If I lift up my head, I and my Nuit are one. If I droop down mine head, and shoot forth venom, then is rapture of the earth, and I and the earth are one.[176]

There is, indeed, a danger in the careless arousing of the kundalini force. People could burn themselves to a crisp (literally!) from the inside out. There are various accounts of this effect in medical annals. Also, a person could become terribly unbalanced and suffer considerably from various ailments and even insanity. Anyone working with the kundalini force must first be master of the body, of the emotions, and of the mind. Both magical and yogic disciplines must be worked with to achieve such illumination. A good example of kundalini going up only one channel of the spine is given in Gopi Krishna's autobiography,

---

174. Crowley, *Liber AL vel Legis*, 36.
175. Crowley, *Liber AL vel Legis*, 41.
176. Crowley, *Liber AL vel Legis*, 43.

Kundalini: The Evolutionary Energy in Man.[177] He had trouble with the Pingala channel as it was over-developed. He suffered greatly until he could balance it with the Ida channel and direct the force to the central channel of Sushumna eventually.

The three channels of kundalini are shown on the Tree of Life. Perhaps you have noticed that they are also shown on the caduceus.

There is further instruction in *Liber LXV*, Chapter I, verses 9-10:

> Debate not of the image, saying Beyond! Beyond!
> One mounteth unto the Crown by the moon and by the Sun, and by the arrow, and by the Foundation, and by the dark home of the stars from the black earth.
> Not otherwise may ye reach unto the Smooth Point.[178]

"Crown" and "Smooth Point" refer to Kether. The "moon" is Atu II, The High Priestess (Path of ג). The "Sun" is Tiphereth, the heart and central sphere of the Tree of Life. The "arrow" refers to Sagittarius and Atu XIV, Art (Path of ס). "Foundation" is the name of the Sephirah Yesod. The "dark home of the stars" is Atu XXI, The Universe (Path of ת). The "black earth" is the Sephirah Malkuth. The central pillar of the Tree of Life is clearly explained as the only route to the Crown.

Let us consider also verse 14 of *Liber LXV*, Chapter 5 (which is reiterated later in verse 65):

> All this while did Adonai pierce my being with his sword that hath four blades; the blade of the thunderbolt, the blade of the Pylon, the blade of the serpent, the blade of the Phallus.[179]

In his commentary, Crowley attributed the "thunderbolt" to Aleph, but the dictionary definition gives the lightning flash. The "lightning flash" is another term for the qabalistic "flaming sword" that extends from the first Sephirah, Kether, through Sephirah 2, then 3, and on down the Tree in orderly sequence. It

---

177. Krishna, Gopi, *Kundalini: The Evolutionary Energy in Man* (Boston, MA: Shambhala Publications, 1967).
178. Crowley, *The Holy Books of Thelema*, 54.
179. Crowley, *The Holy Books of Thelema*, 77.

is a description of the creation of the universe and of humanity. It is **involution**.

Crowley then attributed the "Pylon" to the letter Daleth, ד, "door." But a pylon is also the two sides of a door, and the two different forces shown on the Tree as the two pillars of Force and Form. This pylon is represented in various lodges of more or less occult persuasion as the two pillars of white and black, or of white and red. All of life below the abyss is made up of opposite forces: sun and moon, true and false, good and bad, etc., ad infinitum.

Crowley attributed the "serpent" to Nun, נ, Scorpio, which, like the Trump that explains it, has the serpent, scorpion, and eagle for its symbols. Another way to view this is as the Serpent of Wisdom climbing the Tree from "The Universe," through "The Æon," "The Sun," and so forth, in orderly sequence. This is the path of evolution, of attainment to the highest, ending in "The Fool," Zero.

He interpreted the "Phallus" as Yod, י, the last letter of אדני. Adonai: "(Yod of I.H.V.H) considered as the inmost and simplest idea." This "simplest idea" is a part of everyone. It is not only the male sex organ. Another meaning is shadowed forth here, furthermore, and has already been shown in *Liber Legis*, Chapter II, verse 26 and in *Liber LXV*, Chapter I, verse 9: The Phallus is the central column of the Tree of Life.

The other meaning of "phallus" in the Great Work is the aspiration to the supreme attainment via the Middle Pillar. Crowley pointed out in *The Soul of the Desert* that there are three main methods of doing this: union of subject and object, which is the method of yoga; union of God and human, which is the method of magick; and union of male and female, which is the Tantric method. All of these methods demand a great deal of work and self-discipline. No matter which path one takes (or perhaps all three?), the consequent awakening of kundalini leads to the development of the greatest genius of which a person is capable.

With these few remarks, perhaps the myth that Thelema is a male-dominated religion can be dispelled. Careful study of *Liber Legis* should certainly bring enlightenment on this matter to everyone.

To sum up, it is best to quote the last verse of *Liber LXV* which gives a description of Adonai as encompassing the whole

Tree with Nuit:

> So also is the end of the book, and the Lord Adonai is about it on all sides like a Thunderbolt, and a Pylon, and a Snake, and a Phallus, and in the midst thereof He is like the Woman that jetteth out the milk of the stars from her paps; yea, the milk of the stars from her paps.[180]

> Love is the law, love under will.

---

180. Crowley, *The Holy Books of Thelema*, 83.

Selected Letters

Letters from Seckler to various correspondents

The first letters included here are addressed to two relative beginners in Thelema who had written to Seckler for advice. Responding to such inquiries was a major focus for Seckler throughout the last several decades of her life. Her exhaustive responses, coupled with a near-obsessive determination to save all such correspondence, have left us with a valuable archive of instructional material conveying the core of Seckler's thinking on diverse matters. These particular letters (along with many of the *I.T.C.* introductory letters presented elsewhere in this volume) were chosen as representative samples of her instruction to beginners.

Rt. 1, Box 122   October 25, 1955
Livermore, Calif.

Dear Mr. Dorey,

Your letter of Oct. 16 was received, also the note of the same date which you wrote to Mr. Germer. He has asked me to answer some of your questions as he is extremely busy at the present. However, he may be in California in December and can then get in touch with you.

You ask what comes first and the only answer to that is a direct quotation from *The Book of the Law*. "Do what thou wilt shall be the whole of the Law."[181] Do you have *The Book of the Law*, or *Liber AL*, as it is sometimes called? If not, please let me know and I can send you a copy.

What does "Do what thou wilt" mean? Obviously it doesn't mean following the personal will but refers to the Higher Will. Just as a pianist must give up certain lazy tendencies and must sit at the piano for hours every day to perfect technique, in many ways also giving up pleasing ideas about how to pass the time in lesser modes, so must the man desiring to follow his will discipline himself. Actually the Law just quoted requires the highest

---

181. Crowley, *Liber AL vel Legis*, 31.

self-discipline ever demanded of men. And please notice how much the self must do on this score. But once the discipline is accomplished, once the body and mind behave and obey the will, the freedom which is acquired is the greatest that can be found on this earth. Yes, freedom does cost something. Those who refuse to work at the will enchain themselves and become slaves. This is one meaning of the reference to slaves in *The Book of the Law*.

So — what is the will? That is the first step. Do you know or have any inkling? As you are on the way to discover it you may come across a finite will, or one belonging to this earth and this life which your real self has formulated. It may have a great deal to do with the profession or again, it may not. However, you may find it difficult to work in any media not really meant for you. For instance, you couldn't make yourself into a musician if you hated music or didn't understand it or didn't have the ability. The finite will is a step towards the infinite but is never the last answer. This all means that a thorough self knowledge is extremely necessary to your progress. What are you capable of in the realm of doing? In the realm of emotions? In the realm of thinking? Of course keeping a diary and submitting it to a Guru or Teacher may help. Also you can help yourself by a good working knowledge of depth psychology. Have you ever read books by Jung?

By the way — I have the data for your astrological chart, which also helps in the task of knowing the self. But, I am sorry to say, my extremely busy life has not allowed of time to make it up. I shall be able to get to it probably by Xmas vacation as I then have a respite from teaching.

About the Order — I quote from Mr. Germer:

"His reference to page vii is from the "Editorial Note" which is not from me but from Yorke. I did not fully agree with the text but let it go. The "Order that does not accept Probationers any more" refers to the "Golden Dawn," not to us."

Yes, there are many systems of reaching the Holy Guardian Angel. I might say there are almost as many systems as there are people. It is up to you to find your own. There are, however, certain useful guideposts. Mysticism is one path, magick another, and the Way of the Tao still another. Sometimes a combination of all three gives the best result. Again up to you. But please keep this in mind — try to maintain a balance. The results of specializing or becoming too one-sided can be disastrous farther on the path.

Yoga is Union. If the result is Zero, why worry? Besides, that is probably too far ahead for you. I might add that Zero or Nothing brings great Joy as a by-product? or as part of the whole process. "Nothing" is merely a code word for something which is entirely inexpressible in language. We simply do not have the proper tools to describe what happens.

I hope this has been a help to you.

Sincerely,
Phyllis Seckler

Rt. 3, Box 479, San Jose   Sat. April 18, 1958

Dear X,[182]

You certainly ask some lollapaloozas of questions. Well, I'll do my best and hope that the books I send to you will fill some of the rest.

Why a soul? If there wasn't one we would be like the beasts. No conscience, etc. Well, an animal has only reached a certain stage of evolution and hasn't gone any farther for thousands upon thousands of years. On the other hand, man acquired a soul and so made the next step in evolution. Sure, it is painful and not peaceful like the animals. All growth has a little pain in it. The better, higher reason is GROWTH. All life is change. Read your evolutionary history and you will find that those animals which couldn't change and adapt to new living conditions on the face of the earth were wiped out. Man would be wiped out for the Next Step if he couldn't change and grow.

People (not the soul) seek enlightenment because they are restless and want to know WHY they must suffer, etc. If they were entirely content they would not ask questions of life. So the Angel throws a little painful lesson once in a while. The higher forces which direct us (much as we direct plants and animals, etc.) wish that we make our next step in evolution. Hence an

---

182. Seckler was writing to a very young female correspondent. Some identifying information has been changed to protect the privacy of a living person. – Eds.

Angel for each. Also for other reasons. Some people fight the very idea and once set in thinking in childhood they will not proceed further. It takes many lives to make this type move on—sometimes dynamite in the form of wars and other calamities.

No, this pity is not another sort of thing. Be careful or you become cruel. It is not right to think so unless the Angel directs it. This is the mistake Hitler made. On the other side of the fence is "Do what Thou wilt." This means that you give each person you meet the right to his or her own will and do not interfere. You can do this best if you know your own will. What if your actions caused interference with another so much that in turn your will to be a nurse was interfered with? This could happen. If you murdered someone because you wanted to do something they didn't want you to do then the law could put you in jail and so interfere with you training for nursing. You must always balance one thing against another. It will not do to act without any thought for consequences. If you don't think—you hurt yourself even more than the other person. In this present case you have done that. So think further—the Angel would have you learn more than ruthlessness. Also, it is not usually up to you to see that another person gets hurt in order to learn. That kind of lesson is for the other person's Angel to devise and not an inexperienced child as you are. The only lawful thing then for you or for anyone is to follow their own will. Nursing is yours, someday children might be a part of it and marriage (I hope) and so you must not jeopardize your own future. No, you never live another person's life, you are right. Not in the slightest do you do that. Further, such freedom is not license to do as you please. Everything you do must be oriented to the One Will. Much later in life you will discover there is a finite will (one's work in the world) and an infinite one. Strangely, the infinite one is the same with all. It is the Knowledge and Conversation with the Angel and also Growth and Development. All one, really, when you understand.

Yes, of course, God is not to be found in a crowd. He is nearest in peace and silence and when you can concentrate on it. Do not just daydream but train the mind on the thought of Him. It can be done—as you know from the experiences I have told you go. Well, look at worship this way. It is a blissful experience of happiness. It is not a "down on the knees" attitude. When you look around at the grandeur of nature then the spirit and peace of nature has a chance to enter the soul. It makes you happy. Whenever you are happy and joyful you are very near to God or the Angel. Whenever you are sad and mean and unhappy or afraid you are very far away from Him. Let me quote. "Dost thou fail, are thou sorry, is fear in your heart? Where I am these are not."

Look up the word worship in the dictionary. It means more than you think. Let me know what you find.

When you have studied various types of thought as I have, whether Hindu, Buddhist, Christian, Taoist, you discover that they are all much alike. There is one type of religious experience in the end but it has individual variations and some people take some paths and some take others. But the Nothing at the end of the path is the same for all — however, everyone thinks about it differently. That is why different religions. They started when communication wasn't good on the planet and each race had to think in terms of evolution or religion (as you will) in the particular idiom suited for that race. For instance, the east wanted stillness and quiet as an expression. The west wanted action and magick. So — religion and beliefs to suit.

No, the super (above) the natural is not of earth. It is the essence of fire. Hence, the Bible speaks of the divine fire. Actually the experience all over the world is a consuming Light. Absolute brilliance. And with it comes knowledge. One knows why one lives, what one does on earth and much else. Yes, your own experience will tell you better than my words.

However, I want you to think deeply and don't act again to ruin the course of your will. Yes, you can be frank with me. If not, what kind of friend would I be? You do have to think how the other person receives your words and actions for he in turn reacts to you and a chain is started which may harm you. You would not spit in the face of the head nurse in the hospital? And yet, some little remark may harm you when it begins to act and react and reverberate around and get back to you again. Sure — it sometimes pays to be cautious. Especially if you are sensitive — or especially where the course of the will must be protected. So you see, one must strive for balance. There can be good feelings if you are frank to the right person and in the right way — always considering how he or she will react to what you say.

Reasons — the mind will tell you many contradictory and opposite things. It is a lying fool, the mind. And the emotions are even worse. You hide within you two criminals to guide you through life. And so does everyone. Well, the only answer is to transcend them both. Remember that the mind always changes from minute to minute—and what you feel today you will not feel tomorrow. If you cry now, there will be reason for laughter later. Yes, the mind will twist and turn and invent in order to escape pain. And yet pain is our awakening into the Real. Just remember that the mind is only a tool which must be controlled and that Experience is your guide. You would not burn yourself on the hot stove two times. Experience taught you about burns the first time.

Yes, Thoreau was talking of life. Sadness cuts you off from the Joy of Living. "Joie de vivre" say the French. And they are right. Always ACT SO THAT YOU CAN ENJOY. You can't enjoy if you interfere with others. But that is the key to life and love of life.

Yes, we are all prisoners of ourselves. But we don't need to be. Reaching outside of oneself—into books, friendships, enthusiasms, art, love, work, tears down the prison bars.

I have tried to answer the most of your questions. Now good luck with your search. The Angel is with you—is waiting for you.

Love,

Phyllis

Sascha Germer, Jane Wolfe, Phyllis Seckler & Karl Germer. 1957.

Sascha and Karl Germer.

The Germer house in May, 1976.

One of the library rooms in the Germer house, May, 1976.

Another room in disarray in the Germer house, May, 1976.

Phyllis Seckler and Grady McMurtry in the early 1980s.

Letters between Seckler and Karl Germer

At the time these letters were written, Karl Germer was the head of both O.T.O. and A∴A∴. While Jane Wolfe remained Seckler's formal Superior in A∴A∴, Wolfe's increasing infirmity and eventual death placed Germer in the role of Seckler's primary teacher-figure in O.T.O. and A∴A∴. These letters contain much of instructional value concerning core Thelemic principles, and convey a sense of the evolving relationship between the two initiates.

11411 S. Federal
West Los Angeles 25, Calif.

April 27, 1951

Dear Karl,

Do what thou wilt shall be the whole of the Law.

It does take a little time to get around to answering letters when there is so much else to do. I am striving for better grades this semester, too, which means more careful and complete study on every subject. I would like to win a scholarship for every semester as it takes off a big financial burden.

Yes, I have read *Heavenly Bridegrooms* and found it very suggestive.[183] I have since debated about Ida [Craddock]'s bridegroom to myself. But you say it was her H.G.A. It would be possible to be another type of being wouldn't it? If it was, could she (or anyone) tell the difference? Couldn't one become possessed by the wrong entity? If this happened I am inclined to think the fullness of joy would not be possible. There might be a flaw somewhere.

I understood your comment on *LXV* when you made them at a Lodge evening, and I also knew why you hesitated on some passages. But, you see, at that time [I had] a partner who somehow materialized the magick, and so to speak, illuminated it. The short cut was in full force at that time. Now I am faced with the

---

183. Craddock, Ida, *Heavenly Bridegrooms: An Unconventional Contribution to the Erotogenetic Interpretation of Religion* (New York: N.P., 1918).

problem of backtracking and trying to achieve the same results on my own. I will always be faced with this and progress seems so slow. I have not the time for yoga, nor the quiet. One of my plans for the future involves a period of retirement when I shall work at it. And I must leave that phase of it there and continue with the task of arranging my life satisfactorily.

There is one thing I can do, and I am now hard at it. That is memorizing. I have already committed one chapter of *LXV* to heart and am now refreshing my memory on it. I am also working on one chapter of *Liber VII* and on *The Book of the Law*. Typical Gemini again! Three things at once! I was told that you accomplished quite a good deal by memorizing, so this spurred me on to it. You see, already you are a good example! And does it not say in *LXV* "and they that sealed up the book into their blood were the chosen of Adonai."[184]

I hope to go on with the whole of both books eventually.

Who or what are the Elephant Gods? You mentioned them in one of your previous letters and I have been puzzling over them ever since.

There is another point I have often puzzled over. In my last experience I discovered that a God was created by the union of two in the physical body. At least I saw it intuitionally. (Or felt it). It seems to me that a purely spiritual process which can be accomplished by working alone, also has its parallel with a more actual base of operations. It seems that this is like producing Adonai. This operation, as I understand it, is sometimes accomplished by the H.G.A. uniting with the incarnate self, thus producing Adonai, and also by this other method of two physical opposites. Now please tell me where and how I err in these conclusions.

I wrote some poetry during this period which was highly inspired and often I found myself addressing Adonai. Sometimes a word would come through that I had no idea of what its meaning was. Later I would look it up in the dictionary and it would prove to be the very word I wanted. This gives an idea of the origin of the poems, as not from me, but as from something beyond my usual self, bigger than I.

As to the diary, I woefully fall down on that point, but your

---

184. Crowley, *The Holy Books of Thelema*, 83.

reminder and Jane's drive me to it. True, intuitional perceptions or lucid thoughts arrive which I can hardly believe consciously. I find it difficult to commit such things to paper, but I shall do so anyhow, come what come may! Do you know the tenor of such thoughts? They arrive out of the ordinary run of thinking, perhaps after an invocation or other concentration of thought on the H.G.A. They bear the imprint of truth. They may even arouse intense opposition from the conscious being, or disbelief. They cause one to wonder if things are getting out of proportion. One doubts, one wonders if the personal ego has gotten blown out of all sense of the future of things. And then one waits to see if they get proven true in the material life, doubting, and waiting.

I have part of *Liber Aleph*, up to page 67.

I wonder if the copy of the Commentary to *The Vision and the Voice* should not be done with a copy of [the main text] along side, so that the notes could be on one page and the text on the other side, facing it. It would be very convenient to be able to refer to the notes without turning a lot of pages, and besides, not everyone has an *Equinox V*. What do you think?

I have a Woodstock machine, standard size. So what number of the yellow masters shall I purchase? I want to start typing when exams are over, about the 10th or 14th.

Are not man and woman created, the Vau and the He final, and is it not she who must awaken the eld of the All-Father, the Yod? A thought which just occurred to me, only a partial view, but is it applicable? The mass comes to mind. Well I must leave this and carry on with the daily labor.

I hope all is well with you and that the business is supplying what you desire.

93 – 93/93

Phyllis

Hampton N.J. November 25, 1952

Dear Phyllis,

 Do what thou wilt shall be the whole of the Law.

Your poems, mailed November 1, came yesterday. They were a revelation in many respects. They are fine, genuine, lofty. They show a great depth of feeling, they come from deep down in the well.

Did you want me to criticize? Of course, you are an artist soul, I must have written this to you or Jane long before. As I can hardly be called an artist myself, with little knowledge of literature, especially in English, I can only make some general remarks.

It seems to me that there is development: the form, rhythm, quality of rime varies, or has improved. The sentiment is always clean and pure, but you do not have attained mastery in riming, rhythm, wealth or vocabulary, (that is number of words, often strange, short words not in ordinary use). How to improve this? I don't know. You surely know the classics in the English language? I might say what I know of A.C.: he knew all English poetry almost by heart; he studied the established meters and science of poetry, set up by the ancient Greeks and modern writers. You have got to know the various poetic "feet" (dactyl, Iambus, trochee, etc. etc.) and master them. Etc. etc. etc. Otherwise your poems, however beautiful, cannot be gems. Sometimes I notice that you want to express something almost inexpressible, and appear to fail. To express subtle, difficult thoughts or conceptions, in language is one of the hardest lessons to learn. It is not a matter of length, quite opposite! It is the art of using what I might call magic words, little used by the common crowd, or by the newspapers, but impregnated by meaning by authors and poems of old. Do not fall into the common American error, that American women are different: they do not have to study the classics as they do in Europe. They are a new race. They can take an airplane and fly right up to the top without having to go through the drudgery of the Europeans.

Don't overlook that it is your genius who inspires you to write poems. If you have not learnt to write and read, even He cannot make His scribe write masterpieces. It is for that reason that all great artists learn the trade first; then learnt facility and get experience. Then at least can the genius get busy, inspire thoughts and forms knowing that a little masterpiece will come out.

A.C. made a deep study of why it is that sometimes poems which don't have a rational meaning, make the deepest impression on soul and mind?—I wish I had the time to go through your poems one by one and indicate what I mean.—if you rime future with nurture you get a painful effect; similarly with innumerable other cases. A.C. had made lists of words for which it was hard to find a rhyme: the problem of increasing his facility was ever present in his mind. Not otherwise can you reach beyond the average scribblers.

Your later poems seem to show that you have begun to Understand: why? This sorrow has to be (caused by separation, I mean); why we must not in despair or disgust at facts of life throw down the lute and refuse to sing. Someday I hope I can let you see A.C.'s diaries where you can see that he never became blasé; that he always, to the end, remained young; kept his impressionality and sensitivity. The oyster can only produce one pearl, caused by the squeezing out of protective material around a piece of foreign matter in its body that causes great pain. Most human beings, and especially women, harden their soul when once it has been hurt to the quick by some experience in love. But "Exceed! Exceed!" means among other things that you have to let your soul grow to ever loftier heights. The next break or separation ought to be faced courageously. After all there is always "that which remains."[185] All great poets have suffered intense pain in their sensitive soul, and it was that phase which produced their immortal pearls.

This is a universal law. Even "heroes" that have their work marked out for jobs in the outer world, do their greatest deeds after their deepest disappointments. Their iron has to be tempered by intense heat, and hardened and shaped by cruel blows.

Have you read the stories of female saints? If not, it would not be loss of time to try to unearth some and study their lives. Or male saints if easier to get by. Only: the women describe often enough their sexual relations with what they call "Jesus" or some other name.

---

185. Crowley, *Liber AL vel Legis*, 39.

One word about "loneliness." As you are Hadit in the final analysis, you are alone; from your point, your look-out on the universe is different from any other, without exception. What A.C.'s diaries showed more than anything else was his loneliness. The higher you rise, the more this becomes intense and acute. See VII, iv, 43 "... rare and far and utterly lonely, even as Thou and I, O desolate soul my God!"[186] And "Into my loneliness comes—"What? A being, or a human being? Oh no! It is "the sound of a flute."[187] He did not appear as a human companion, though it could be argued that later she or he did, for a short phase, so that "the dreadful issue could be fought out."[188]

It is a curse to the soul to strive after something unattainable in nature. It is a boon to the soul to understand at last, how nature, or life are, and not waste any more time to pursue a phantom.

It is quite a different thing to satisfy your physical nature and sip the honey of flowers where your H.G.A. sends them your way, and take your fill, as long as you always keep in mind "But always unto Me!"[189] When your sorrow and need are really serious, and you appeal to your H.G.A., be sure He will send the proper parties, and smoothen the opportunities. You have got to attune your senses to His ways.

Sascha, who is an artist's soul as delicate as yours, read your poems and was moved to the very depth. She planned to write you herself. Whether she does it I don't know. But she has long seen your outstanding qualities.

Let this be all. It is almost too much.

Love is the law, love under will.

Fraternally, with love,

Karl

I'm sending this again through Jane, and hope you won't mind if I leave it open.

---

186. Crowley, *The Holy Books of Thelema*, 23.
187. Crowley, *The Holy Books of Thelema*, 9.
188. Crowley, *The Holy Books of Thelema*, 33.
189. Crowley, *Liber AL vel Legis*, 33.

(1952—no specific date given)

Dear Karl,

Do what thou wilt shall be the whole of the Law.

Thank you for your wonderful letter. I found it very encouraging. Sometimes I would like to believe I am an artist, but I am beset with doubts more often than I can believe it. There are so many Failures, and unpolished works as a result of my brush or my pen; and there is so much drudgery to get out of the way before I can devote any time to an expression, that I feel I could do; that I haven't allowed as much inspiration to work out in art as I would like. Consequently, when I do paint or write a poem, the result is very imperfect owing to lack of application to the matter. The poems you have read were inspired by love, as you know, and that fervor helped to fill in a gap of a lack of good solid study. Now, of course, college is helping fill in that lack to some extent. Next spring I shall also be taking a course called Introduction to the Study of Poetry. This will help polish off my style, should I ever write poetry again. You see, right now, I even doubt that I can. One walks in the shadows at times, and this is one of those periods. I know the quiet periods are necessary and a part of my pattern. I even long to have peace at odd moments. But when these moments come, I resent them, and long to be producing again. Talk about contrary human nature.

Poetry, or art, is only a by-product of something else, and well I know it. It is an effervescence or a spilling over from a capacity for "extraordinary love" as Schmolke puts it. The next time I love, who knows what will result? It may not be poetry at all!

Yes, I know about loneliness too. It has been my companion ever since my early teens. I no longer fear it, for it is as you say, "there is something that remains." Whenever I wish, I can reach out and be assured of that "something." This certainty becomes stronger with each great event or lesson. But your letter may be the needed prod to do some more serious work.

You are right, I swing to the oyster effect, the attempt to cover up a hurt with a hard coating. But I am also very naïve, and jump in for another experience which I know will not be happy. And I also know there is no certainty in life except the H.G.A. I sometimes get the queer effect of pain while at the same time knowing it is only a shadow and temporary. Perhaps it is only negating one attitude with another. I have outgrown the emotions expressed in these poems and I doubt if I shall ever think that way again. Or rather, if I shall ever love that way again.

I feel as though I were struggling to put down ideas again, and am becoming involved. Well, I shall leave it. I am only glad if you got some enjoyment from the poetry.

My new address is above and I am finally settled in and the worst of the work is done. My schoolwork has suffered some from the upset, but fortunately, most of my classes have been easy this semester. I doubt if I shall come off with as many A's as I had thought, though.

It strikes me just now that I haven't sent the whole lot of my poems, only about ¾ of them. Would you like to read any more? Yes, I have copies of them. I only asked for their return, because of a nagging worry that they might fall into the wrong hands and be misunderstood. They reveal too much. To tell the truth, there is too much of a tendency among some of our Thelemites to poke into another person's business and gossip. Or at least I found it so some years ago. I withdrew from contact with some of the worst offenders since then. There is always the possibility that some of them might have improved, but a few will never do so. There, I don't often make comments like that. I don't like to remark about others very much. Also any remark Jane may say doesn't come under this category. That goes without saying. She has my fullest confidence. Jane is balanced and straight, which can't be said of many others.

You mention "the dreadful issue" from *Liber VII*.[190] I memorized this section but was puzzled about just this phrase. What connection does it have with the appearance of the H.G.A. in the guise of another human? Also, when this sort of thing occurs, can not one lay it down to a projection of the H.G.A. onto another, and consequently worship it as such? One later may withdraw the projection and then the other human ceases to exercise the same magic and the affair is ended. Sometimes I think the H.G.A. is very effectively contacted in the projection image. It is a foreshadowing of His nature in the realm of matter and in an

---

190. Crowley, *The Holy Books of Thelema*, 33.

understandable form. This is something of the idea lying behind the poems.

How else can one explain the face of human love? But have I talked about these things before and am I repeating myself? I often mull over these matters, trying to extract the utmost of meaning from love. For after all it is my expressed will.

Now I think I have been confusing enough. I had better stop. There is only one course that remains unconfusing, that is action. It is doing. All thoughts upon it are mere tools, step-ladders to Understanding, but in this end thoughts do not bridge the gap.

With all the best to you.

Love is the law, love under will.

Phyllis

Shall I send *Equ. 5* and *Liber Saturnus* to your present address?

Hampton N.J.   December 7, 1952

Dear Phyllis:

Do what thou wilt shall be the whole of the Law.

Yours of no date.

Inspiration comes, I believe, to different people from varying causes. Love is one. In general I believe one can say a phase of high pressure is needed to make one sit up, and be stirred one's very depth. At least so it may be for people like me. My Concentration period brought me great rewards. There is a German author who wrote a 2 volume book with details of how he experienced a state of Samadhi: he gave the full case history, how he fell in love with a woman, how that woman betrayed him, which shocked him deep most, but as he forgave her from the bottom of his heart, the Samadhi set in and he had the most amazing experience which he set down in detail. I had the book in my library, but it is gone.

Yes: by all means, when you have the time, send me the rest of the poems. I'd like to read them. They will be safe in the steel files, unless you want them returned. Sascha, who understands your soul so well is the only one who has seen them—and admired them.

"The dreadful issue was fought out:"[191] How shall I explain? "As above, so below"—every love is a war between opposites that strive for union. (If Hydrogen and Oxygen want to unite they create the hottest flame known in chemistry.) A genuine love has got to have passion in it. The greater the opposites, the greater the difference is between the two parties, the more passion will probably be created—or call it heat. "With the violent appetite of a beast I hunt thee through the universe."[192] Every fiber must be inflamed to produce the greatest results. You see, it is a natural phenomenon. There are natures who can inflame their souls through their own imagination. Not me. I have none. Each has to discover his or her own faculties and means of getting out of their shell—the word is *ecstasis*. Back to the dreadful issue: that war, I said above, may last for years with suffering to both sides, as long as the mutual passion is kept at red-hot heat. Then the Ibis-fellow may appear, in order to bring Understanding and mutual recognition.

It was wrong of me to talk about the problem as I did in my last. These things each one has to "mull over" for years and years and years, otherwise it may not be possible for the flash of sudden illumination to ignite the dry tinder. I mean: if there is not enough of the latter, it can't be done. You must work it out for yourself.

Yes, please return the books you have to this address, Registered. What is the sign you put ahead of your signature?

Love is the law, love under will.

All the best to you, fraternally,
Karl

---

191. Ibid.
192. Crowley, *The Holy Books of Thelema*, 11.

Dear Karl,
(1953 — no specific date given)

Do what thou wilt shall be the whole of the Law.

Thanks for your letter of the 7th. No, it's not that I mind being corrected if it is objective—detached from other types of observation. It is true, I am perhaps abnormally sensitive to criticism—I've had it ruin my artistic output for long stretches of time. I know all this, know its sources, but have not been able to develop a thick skin towards it yet.

Today I am wondering about the burden Jane is struggling under—am worried too, to tell the truth. You know, of course, that her income is tiny—pension—and yet she sends in her monthly contribution. Maybe she wants to—and might be offended on this presumption on my part—indeed I am presumptuous! But she is nearing quite an old age—and is spry and bright—but somehow I feel she needs a lot of consideration. I am really stepping over my bounds! I hope all and sundry will not think too harshly of me! Not only does this sum go out from her for H.Q., but Mary K is not as spry—needs a lot of attention—drains Jane's energy until I become alarmed! Needlessly? No! I don't think so!

But there it is—and I feel, that is possible, there ought to be help somewhere, somehow, for this situation, even if we can only lighten the burden here and there?

Now then—that subject is extremely delicate—and having unburdened my-self, I turn to another matter.

You mention: "The enemy is waiting at the gate to disrupt it" (as you refer to *M.W.T.*).

What enemy?

I am perhaps singularly short-sighted to make this statement but I firmly believe there is no enemy <u>unless we let him exist</u>. In other words, the enemy would be <u>ourselves</u>! Are we not strong enough magically, to keep all such ideas at bay?

And now to explain this position I am going to quote from my diary.

"Sun. Dec. 21, 1952

Strange—vision? No! Experience.

Was reading Jung's commentary on *The Secret of the Golden Flower*.[193]

---

193. *The Secret of the Golden Flower*, Trans. Richard Wilhelm (New York: Harcourt, Brace & World, Inc., 1962).

As I turned out the light and settled down to sleep I was suddenly in the center of things — and that center was an unmanifest Nothing. It was the true me, but it was nothing.

It was as though I were in the center of a ball filled with air or nothing visible, and all events appeared on the outer shell, connected by a network of red lines, like a cell structure, I imagine.

This experience made me laugh. One lives in the outer shell so much, and becomes involved, and thought processes tell us it is reality, but it isn't not at all!

The real <u>reality</u> is Nothing!

Hence the joke!

Also, when one <u>is</u> the center, the Nothing that allows the outside shell of events to happen, one has tremendous power over them. I had the feeling I could choose to experience any event, or not, as I liked. I could make anything happen.

This is because one event is as good as another and just as unreal.

The Nothing is the "diamond body" or the non-striving of Tao. And what a joke the whole experience was!

It was as though life as I know it had gotten turned exactly inside out and was the exact reverse of conscious thinking processes. Why, the thoughts themselves are the unreality!"

I could then go on and quote several lines here and there to see if this experience has any verification elsewhere. I think it does!

Crowley put it in the Mass:

"Thou that are I, beyond all I am
Who hath no nature and no name"[194]

Etc.

You know it as well as I do —

Also, *Liber AL*, II, vs. 12, 13:

"Because of me in Thee which thou knewest not." (Notice the not! Nothing?)

"for why? Because thou wast the knower, and me."[195]

A direct statement that Hadit was in Crowley— "the core of every star" also is nothing or not—as in verse 15.[196]

---

194. Crowley, "Liber XV" in *The Equinox Vol. III No. 10*, 134. [Note: This text reads: "Thou who art I, beyond all I am." – CM.]
195. Crowley, *Liber AL vel Legis*, 39.
196. Crowley, *Liber AL vel Legis*, 40.

But then the shrine is to be veiled in verse 14.[197] Is the truth too strong to bear? It would seem to me that these verses, my experience, probably other sources, would point to the fact that we are each one of us <u>responsible for our own environment</u> and that throwing the blame for not getting a piece of work done of "magical attacks" or "forces of disruption" or, or, etc might be terribly dangerous thinking.

It is quite another thing if one <u>knows</u> that the particular work is not to be done now, <u>because the Angel orders it</u>.

It is not that I think that you do this type of thinking, but I have seen others around me indulge in it when it was plainly weakness, mere speculation on their part, had no reference to the K. and C. of the H.G.A., but was an excuse to excuse their own mistakes, or laziness!

So though you (and Crowley) have a higher degree of initiation, and could perhaps tell me these forces exist, and that I am too inexperienced to know, etc., etc., still, these remarks about "disruptive forces," "the enemy," "the gods" are sometimes dangerous to the weaker ones in our Order. I think a lot of them need a little stiffening of the spine by an attitude which says,

"What's the matter with <u>you</u>? All that is, that exists for you, was made <u>by</u> you!" Are we not our own enemies? Or otherwise?

By now you probably want to throw me out the door!

O.K., I'll go, but I'll waft you an impertinent kiss, dear brother, to show I mean no harm!

Have you asked yourself lately what your own enemy is doing? We all have them, usually conveniently out of sight in the unconscious.

With this parting shot you'll want to kick me out of the Order!

Who does she think she is?

Nothing! Nothing at all!

Love is the law, love under will

Love,
Phyllis

---

197. Ibid.

Hampton N.J. May 5, 1953

Dear Phyllis:

Do what thou wilt shall be the whole of the Law.

Yours of May 1. I wish I could be of help in qabalah. But I can't. I have no imagination whatever, not the technical knowledge. I have gone through the magical names in Abramelin squares, and can't find any that are like Azar.[198] If you take Aleph, Zain, Aleph, Resh you get 209, 11 x 9, one half of 418, on which you might speculate, or seek light. If you spell ASAR (with its obvious meaning) you get 262 = 2 x 131. The name Asra, or Azra, seems to me biblical (or Ezra)—but I have never read the Bible. Ask Jane, who knows more about it.

Please understand that I make no claims whatever on qabalistic (or technical) magical knowledge or interpretation. I am very opposite to 666 in every respect. Once you get your copy of *Magick Without Tears* you may get some practical help in learning yourself.

However, I will say this, that I dislike your qabalistic counting of words in the ordinary English language, such as "I will to love," etc. English qabalah has not yet been discovered; besides, English does not lend itself to it, anyway. With the older Greek and Arabic and Hebrew, or possibly much older name. I just find, for instance, that Ezra is a biblical name, if you take the letters as here written, they would add to 213, if only EZR = 212 =; but in Greek EZR would be 112 = 2 x 56. You'd have to consult *Equinox* I, VIII, for fuller meanings. I'm too busy now!

I like your spiritual growth. Leave yourself to your H.G.A. and you can find no better guide for further progress.

As to WTS [Wilfred T. Smith]: Never forget: I have never lifted A.C.'s old injunction re dropping all dealings with him. I must say I have looked with [disfavor] and suspicion on the chummy atmosphere that seems to have gradually developed. I made an exception with Jane, because of the Mass. But what

---

198. Azar was the Name of Seckler's Holy Guardian Angel. She had written to Germer to ask for assistance in deciphering the gematria of this Name. – Eds.

has grown out of this is altogether different. From what you say, WTS argues; he has failed to cross the abyss; and so is eternally damned to the clutches of reason and 333. I had thought I could get WTS to do certain things to help, that's why I went along again; I'm afraid I have to reconsider. Please show this to Jane.

I have been, and still am, feverishly working on *M.W.T*. The typist has been working on the loan machine we have had last week, and it turned out that the work she did was meticulously done—BUT it is the wrong roller, the rubber is too soft, the impression is uneven. We have to scrap the masters once more! It is tragic. I won't get another roller before Thursday. And the new machine has been delayed. We need it badly because of the special types, such as '' ^ * ! =, the plus sign, and several others needed. I don't know how far we shall get. If necessary we shall have to print as far as possible, then send the Typewriter to California when [Jean-Ero] leaves and you'd better finish this most important book, and we'd print it in Barstow. I'd ship the Multilith there. We'll see in a week or two, I hope.

Forget about my horoscope: we have so much to do!! And I am far behind in what I have to do! M.W.T. will run to about 400 pages if not more.

<u>May 6</u>. I'll add a few lines.

In the early stages our primitive natures require actual, visible, sensible, proof of an outer being contacting us. I remember in my early period I sometimes asked for a definitive sign in order to (a) reassure me in a sort of weak phase (b) to give evidence that I was on the right track. Yet: (this is important in my case!) I never connected such signs as coming from a definitive outer being, I just took it as from 'God' or such things. My conception of the H.G.A. has probably only been condensed after A.C.'s death. Funny? Unbelievable? It is so! The H.G.A. has been taking almost violent, desperate means to bring me to the realization of his existence and presence, and operation. But my hide was, and still is, too dense, so that A.C. once in the 1927 period wrote: "instead of a skin you have a carapace!" And this not as a joke, but rather in despair.

Be, and feel, happy that you are better constituted! Later, the messages become more subtle, and so that one cannot distinguish them from what we call "conscience" in many cases. There are people who carry on definite conversations, they hear voice-

or other type-messages; the difficulty remains, however, to verify the source.

Achad got messages to the last; but they were, since his turning away from 666, not from his H.G.A., but its shadow, the Evil Persona. As it is hard to follow the voice of the H.G.A. in later stages, because often things are demanded that seem outrageous, against all morals and ethics, there is the danger of falling prey to the sweet whisper of the other guy (cf. Jesus and the high mountain, in Achad's case it was the promise that he was to be the bloke of *AL* III, 45 (the child), and A.C. seduced him, and fortified this conviction (a magical test!) by writing *Liber Aleph*.

"Neglect not the Dawn Meditation!"[199] is one of the most important injunctions of A.C. (I only repeat: I don't do it myself! I can't meditate.) It is well to practice this as a routine, so as to be prepared when the H.G.A. arranges a phase for one of the — let me call it — technical initiations or illuminations. Why do I mention this here? Because you write you were deep asleep when you got that one message and only wrote it up, partly, after waking. In my Concentration Camp phase I was alone in my cell (when the crucial weeks came). I worked with hardly any interruption; sleep was broken up so that I never slept more than 3 hours at a time; and that "sleep" was light, and I snapped instantly back into work. If you read "John St. John" in *Equinox*, I, X, you have the same idea; except that A.C. did his op. by the effort of will, and in 12 days. What I want to say is that such high water marks are secretly arranged by the H.G.A.: then the conditions are right and will bring the result about. But the training of one's mind to waken instantly and fully at a touch, is always helpful.—

Well, I better stop now. This is running into a sermon! It is so easy to talk to you.

       Love is the law, love under will.

                                        Fraternally,
                                        Karl

---

199. Crowley, *The Book of Lies*, 106.

(1953 — no specific date given)

Dear Karl,

93

I am not trying to improve on Aleister's English, which is extremely excellent. So much that I can't believe it if he uses the wrong tense to fit the subject "thou" or uses an incomplete sentence with no verb or leaves out a word or words when quoting from *Liber AL*, *Magick in Th.*, *and Pr.*, or *Book of Lies*, or misspells an important technical term.

I think, perhaps, errors might have crept in through the typists or stenographers who were employed and who perhaps had no Thelemic background, or a background of long working with Aleister or — or —

Every change made is discussed thoroughly with Jane, who <u>does have</u> a Thelemic background, <u>was</u> Aleister's secretary for a time, and who, in cases of doubt, certainly ought to have a basis on which to judge. (You not being out here to consult on these <u>very minor</u> matters.)

It may be true that a word or two might escape her very careful checking (such as the "would" for "should," possibly — I can't tell without the <u>whole</u> paragraph — that Jean reports).

Jean herself notices a funny parenthesis formation, which I had copied exact.

Well, that's what we get for looking at it with an eagle eye, I guess. Four of us doing it! From the secretarial standpoint! Do you know that, I personally, read each letter text three times before the Master leaves my hands? Once to type from it, where lots of details get noticed, once to check immediately after typing, and once to read to Jane while she checks my typing. Then Jean and Ero check. We are bound to notice small details, or errors in this way.

I am on page 227 of the masters I am typing, in the middle of Letter 50, and am not in the least worried about being able to finish before school starts. The proof-reading with Jane will take longer, though. She can only make it down here once a week — it is a great effort for her — (I suspect somewhat exhausting!) and we cannot do too much on that account. However, I would rather have her proof-reading than anyone else's because she too, is very good at English and has the afore-mentioned excellent background.

I have to bow before you and Aleister's superior wisdom as to "Magical attacks" etc. But there is this to say: were not the "dragons" of old untapped powers residing in the "unconscious?" More specifically, the powers hidden in sex—which if misused lay waste the "countryside" or more properly, the individual misusing them. Were not the "monsters" and "Wicked knights" which King Arthur's court valiantly fought, but their own Inertia or dark side, or characteristics which opposed further travel on the "Path of Light ?" And then they had freed the maiden—was not that a freedom won for their souls? Some of the stories even parallel the K. and C. of the H.G.A.

There may be "magical attacks" (I am very unfortunate never to have experienced any other than those I could clearly trace to my own unconscious, or nephesh, or ruach, or what not) but the point that carries importance is that they ought not to be talked of carelessly except where there is <u>proof</u>. If the difficulties surrounding one can be traced to the environment one stubbornly clings to, or to preconceived or set notions in the mind, or to ways of acting acquired from childhood and onwards or to incidents suppressed in the unconscious because of shame, fear, or terror, etc., then I think they ought to be dug out, faced squarely, and actions based on the knowledge and understanding thus gained.

It would seem to me to be very <u>weak</u> to blame many incidents on "enemies" or what not, when all the time it was <u>yourself</u>. I am alarmed, because I have seen others do it, others who offered no <u>proof</u> of enemies, who swallowed whole the myth that their slight troubles came from living near a Catholic Church or what not—and who copied, apparently, related attitudes from you or from A.C.

However, I'm perfectly willing to admit that there are superior powers, and in my own experience I offer the "proof" of my becoming an instrument for forwarding the Work. For I astonish my conscious mind by my determination. But the "proof" is far too long for this letter—so I shall get it set down in the Diary and you shall read it someday. However, I could only become an instrument because of my own peculiar "outer shell" or ruach + nephesh, which was formulated by <u>That Nothing</u> — bringing us right back to responsibility for <u>every event</u> to the Center.

Perhaps it is only more needful that we <u>know</u> and <u>act</u> from that Center? (It certainly swept away with one blow, lots of my fears, inhibitions, or what not. I find myself constantly referring back to it and acting accordingly.)

Also, you say this: (Tiphareth [my spelling] and Kether are in the center column, but right and left are the Sephira that in themselves are unbalanced" (You spelt it "Tipharet").

Is not the Tree Of Life the <u>Whole Man</u>? The unbalanced forces to right and left, yes—but in the <u>individual</u>. Let us only face them squarely, <u>know</u> them and Understand.

I didn't think the experience worth too much, good for turning <u>my</u> life around, perhaps, but if you wanted others to see it, I can't object.

Once I wrote the thing to you, the words had not much more to do with me personally. The reality of it exists elsewhere than in the words. <u>They</u> are clumsy and inept.

Also, who said "Know thyself?" Also the oath of the A∴A∴? dealing with that very subject—"the nature and powers of my own being."

Powerful advice—and I am sure it leads to power over Life—and "enemies"—and "magical attacks."

This must be all—while I rest my back from "typewriter fatigue."

93 93/93

Phyllis

P.S. About H.Q.! Things have <u>got</u> to turn out right. And I notice that if instructions are followed, they generally do, and no broken bones or sacrifices either. Crowley also remarks on this matter in Letter 50. Thelema <u>will</u> be promulgated if we don't fight against it! Sometimes this means a step in the dark—but this inconvenience is more than balanced by the Joy of Obedience.

Rt. 1, Box 122 Oct 15, 1956
Livermore, California

Dear Karl:

Do what thou wilt shall be the whole of the Law.

I have read with interest your last letter and find much to comment on which seems to be bursting to get out. You caused quite some thinking.

Now—on the problem of Kundry. At first what you seemed to say seemed to be an insult to my sex. It is true I am getting (no, have been) very tired of the old Aeon ideas concerning the feminine half of the world which I encounter at every turn. They are so deeply entrenched because of the fact that the last aeon was paternal and it may take a few hundred years to get over them. Meanwhile I shall strike a blow or two for liberty.

It does seem to be an observed fact that a woman now and then turns some aspiring aspirant away from the true path. Why does this happen? Why tell us of the rest of the matter? Why? Why?

Dion Fortune in her book *The Holy Qabalah* gave us a clue here.[200] Correct me if there is a better source which can refute what she says. She says that the true occult tradition is that man is positive on the physical plane, and feminine, or negative on the next plane—that of the astral or emotion-spiritual. Conversely a woman reverses this; she is negative in the physical; positive on the astral or emotional; negative on the intellectual; and positive on the spiritual.

So then, if this be true she is already stronger than the man and spiritually could sway him by virtue of this strength. The old fairy tales seem to point to this when the Prince goes seeking for the Princess. She is meant to represent the soul or the spiritual side of life and once he has united with that principle he is happy ever after. *The Book of the Law* also points this way when Nuit says "To love me is better than all things."[201] Nuit represents feminine principle of nature and she promises all riches in her

---

200. This is probably a reference to Fortune, Dion, *The Mystical Qabalah* (York Beach, ME: Samuel Weiser, 1999). – Eds.
201. Crowley, *Liber AL vel Legis*, 36.

worship. Through various other passages the aspirant is exhorted to "come unto me"[202] and "if the ritual be not ever unto me: then expect the direful judgments of Ra Hoor Khuit"[203] and many other passages which indicate the above matter. We are not exhorted to worship Hadit—but only as referring to his relationship to Nuit. Hadit is the point within us that goes—that accomplishes the act of Union.

Now to get back to man and woman. Any woman might possibly be placed by the Magician on the throne of Nuit, spiritually that is, and worshipped as one manifestation of that great Infinite. Or other aspects of Nuit might be worshipped. "I am above you and in you," for example.[204] If she is worshipped there is no danger. Where then does the danger lie? Not in woman—for she could be the representative of Nuit. If the Magician is powerful enough he could make her so. The answer then lies in the magician himself. Nuit says, "There is no bond that can unite the divided but love."[205] We are divided from realization of her omnipresence by taking a mortal body.

If a man can still love his wife and put her on the Throne—as is done in the Mass—she represents to him no danger of stumbling on the path. To do this he must have controlled sex—must have controlled the astral—or the emotional life within himself and must put every action to the service of the highest ideals—the love of Nuit. Can woman help if he does not do all these things? If she stumbles because of his inability should she be vilified, avoided, enslaved, reduced to the lowest animal life as she has been in the past aeon?

Women have enough Nuit in themselves to rebel against the man who is weak. She will turn and devour him because he does not love her enough. He can't if he has no control. She knows this intuitively. Many a woman dreams of the strong man—the Knight on a charger—the King among men. She would give all she possessed, her soul even, to be associated with such a man. But she is sometimes merciless if he is not spiritual. She is positive spiritually—and this causes her reaction to the weakling. A man must strengthen his spiritual and emotional side.

---

202. Ibid.
203. Crowley, *Liber AL vel Legis*, 33.
204. Crowley, *Liber AL vel Legis*, 26.
205. Crowley, *Liber AL vel Legis*, 31.

Kundry does not like her position. The Magician she serves is at least strong—even if a Black Magician. She waits for the real strong man—and she tests every comer. She hopes she will find one who can exert—who has the real strength to love. NO WEAKLING (she knows) can really love. And when Parsifal leaves his wandering, when he grows up into the Magician, she becomes allied with him, as a representative of the most spiritual in life, she becomes invaluable.

Again, as to marriage. "There is no bond that can unite the divided but love. All else is a curse."[206] Now if the marriages we have discussed do not come up to this rigid standard they should be abolished, and he or she involved would be particularly weak to allow such a situation to go on. We are in the Aeon of Horus—the child—and no longer can we blame the sex of another for what happens. Both are responsible—but each within his or her function. This throws further light on the passage "Oh lover, if thou wilt, depart."[207] The middle stage deals in particular with love, and so all passages in *The Book of the Law* which talk of this subject ought to be referred to.

93 93/93

276[208]

Barstow, Cal.   Nov. 1, 1956
601 Frances Drive

Dear Phyllis:

Do what thou wilt shall be the whole of the Law.

Your letters are different. They force one to go a little below the surface. I'll do what I can, though I am at the moment too much preoccupied with decisive and cranky problems. (The most important is that of Sascha, which seems to be near a first solution.)

---

206. Ibid.
207. Ibid.
208. The enumeration of "Meral."

Dion Fortune's book was sent to me by Jane, but I'm ashamed to say I did not read it. If what you quote is her theory, it seems plausible to me, or could be; I would not say now. That some sort of such a relation exists has long been known to me; may-be she has it from Blavatsky or elsewhere. But why do you say you have to break a lance (or however you express it) for your sex? Look at the Stélé: is not Horus worshipped by the Beast? Do not ever misconstrue the fact that the Head of A∴A∴ is the Silver Star, not the Golden Star. I have an idea that a star can take a male or female body in any particular incarnation. It doesn't make any diff[erence]. But if it takes a female body it just cannot function as the creative genius; yet, even as a female incarnation its accomplishments can be overpowering: compare Semiramis, Cleopatra, Catherine the Great, Elizabeth, Blavatsky, Jeanne D'Arc, and so many others. I could say more, but can only whisper it into a silent ear. Besides I'm yet a learner.

Kundry: the way Wagner shows her I agree with most of what you say. Is she smaller because she functions as a woman? — Would you prefer a reversion to the matriarchal age — because you say the last aeon was paternal?

The root of the matter? (your § 3). I don't know, but here is an aspect. Most men and women are primitive, in an early stage of magical evolution; they have not begun the lesson of control of different functions. But even if they have a long past behind them, if they have skipped one or two incarnations, have forgotten, they have to re-learn the relation between woman and man. So, they have to go through the Than, Theli, Lilith experience slowly, painfully, until they reach the Snake of Emerald stage. (One thing in passing: as you must have found in [*Liber*] *418*, A.C. commented, was it in the 3rd Aethyr, that maybe Alostrael — Leah Hirsig — played the role of Lilith in his life. You see, Lilith has marvelous qualities which baffle even the Magus. Though in this instance I won't be too positive at all. At all. Just food for thought.)

Another aspect: why should men and woman not have to face and pass similar problems and ordeals? Oswald Spengler had a word about women who, independent stars, master sex, and rise above the usual type of men. This, of course, only when they ripen magically, and are no longer slaves. I think many movie stars belong in that category, also "grande amoureuses" of the

French type. I believe it all boils down to the need for a woman to know as many males as possible and for a man equally. In fact, I think a woman has the edge, for she can always, a man, not.—No: we must not worship Hadit! It is He that worships.

"Danger?" That exists for both alike. It may be generally to fall into a rut, to refuse or have fear to make new experiences, to be afraid to face the unknown, to become a habit-human, a bourgeois, to love comfort, to yearn for 'rest.' <u>Every</u> relation between two tends to be habit-forming; stimulus ceases; passion ends; I doubt if—as you write—"if a man still love his wife..." If you live too long with one man it becomes a drudgery, even if he be great. If you are a Queen in your own right and can match his stature, there will come a point when tension stops; that, I believe is the time for her to strike out towards a new mountain peak and climb it.

In other words, my thesis is not yours, that the old Aeon is to blame. The law is for both alike, as it ever has been. Maybe not so in America where matrimony is sanctified by law, habit, economics, and religion. But take the prominent Americans, men or women: they break through this bondage. Except that in other countries marriage need not be dissolved specially, each simply goes her or his way; there is no heart-balm or ostracism to make it impossible, difficult, or profitable.

Kundry: § 3 p. 3. It is a matter, it seems, of what genus or magical family, she or Kundry belongs to. Klingsor belonged to what we call the Black tradition. Kundry essentially to the White. She fell under the power of Klingsor, true, because he was strong. But I say: strength is not the criterion, not alone. Kundry became the servant of the G[reat] W[ork] not because Parsifal was, possibly, strong, but because she was from time immemorial sworn to serve the G.W. If you seek long enough with infinite patience for your Parsifal, he will turn up some day, I'm sure.

Why your constant outburst against, or defense of, your sex? I have no such thought of finding fault with it. There is no mention of "marriage" in *Liber Legis* anywhere. Only love.

Lilith: I wonder whether she can ever be put on the throne of Nuit (your § 1 p. 3). I believe she belongs to the demonic world, at least in her temporary function. As such, the magician has nothing else to do but to learn and understand her function, then destroy her in that function. The Universe is so vast, there are

<u>always</u>, in every case, new men or women appointed to minister to the next phase; and the number of these phases is endless; one hundred years even for one "who does run forward so fast" as A.C., are not enough to go through all of them.

In closing let me say, that my philosophy in all of this is, that the goal for everyone is to become a Sanyasi, or a Sanyasina; were worldly aspirations have ceased or been overcome, so that all personal needs are confined to a rice bowl, a spoon and shoes and dress for walking. Then let the spiritual light shine. Marriage or the lust for living with a companion do not exist; they may be taken up as a temporary burden for one particular job to be done.

Do overcome your inferiority complex re women. There are some women around us who have reached, or are near, the Sanyasina stage, I believe, if they would only begin to realise it and live like it in full consciousness. Then disquiet of mind and false seeking will drop off automatically.

Love is the law, love under will.

Stimulate more letters where one has to dive deeper!

Yours,
Karl

Letters to Israel Regardie

Seckler carried on a lengthy and varied correspondence with her fellow teacher Israel Regardie over the course of many years. The following letters from Seckler show the two initiates comparing notes on all manner of topics, including the state of the O.T.O. and A∴A∴ at the time, and various points of Thelemic doctrine.

P.O. Box 2043
Dublin, Calif.
94566

June 16, 1979

Dear Francis,

Do what thou wilt shall be the whole of the Law.

Thank you so much for your very timely warning.[209] However, if no one in the O.T.O. who claims a Grade here and there has worked for that Grade and we have no adepts, no illuminated ones, or however you want to put it, I certainly don't see how any branch of the O.T.O. can succeed.

In fact, I am led to wonder if maybe the warring factions were meant to destroy each other? Certainly not many care to follow out Crowley's instructions to the letter or even very close attention to *Liber AL* as hardly anyone has the time or will to study it and the Commentaries and *Liber Aleph*, etc. extremely carefully. Instead, most are warring with each other to hold egomaniacal power, and the Berkeley O.T.O. is no exception. The only hope I have is for the branch in So. Calif. and like any mother, I have been compelled to fight for what Crowley wrote, in hopes I can help the truly sincere persons. But maybe I take the wrong tack and who am I to know?

In fact, it may be that I shall drop the O.T.O. and this is a very definite possibility. It begins to look as though it is more of a hindrance to my true Work — the College and A∴A∴, than

---

209. Regardie had written to Seckler several days earlier, expressing concern about the danger Marcelo Motta posed to O.T.O. and A∴A∴. – Eds.

anything else. I really dislike political fights extremely but can fight if I think I have to!

Since O.T.O. has been in my background of training for 40 years, this is a very difficult decision to make. But like you, I too care not much for the ego strivings to hold power over others.

As to what Motta has recently written, I shall not keep a copy of it in my house and shall try to do my work quietly without reference to him. (Naturally!) Yes, he is obviously insane and the seeds of this showed long ago. I have some of his early letters to me still! And you are not an idiot to offer counsel—for all we may know, your words may turn up a tide???? Who can tell? Certainly I admire you greatly for speaking up! Thank you again.

All the best to you and Alice and I often wonder if she found help with Holistic medicine?

Love is the law, love under will.

Fraternally,
Phyllis

Phyllis Seckler (Soror Meral)
P.S. please notice change of name.

P.O. Box 2043
Dublin, Calif.
94566

July 10, 1979

Dear Francis,

Do what thou wilt shall be the whole of the Law.

That was good news in your letter of July 7 that Alice is much better and has moved across the street from you! Please give her my very best wishes.

The threat of the O.T.O. is within and I doubt Motta can do any real harm. He never had permission from Karl or anyone else to start a Lodge or Camp and was trying to get this permission when Karl died. M[otta] was frantic and put some information about this in a letter to me and one to Sascha.

As to the A∴A∴, it doesn't belong to Motta and the more he writes as he does, the sillier he looks. His digs at me don't affect me—I have been laughing all day about what he wrote in his so-called *Equinox*—which someone sent to me just today. Motta is just angry because I refused to acknowledge him as a high muck-a-muck from the very first after Karl died and I only have to publish M.'s letters to me and mine to him to prove this point and make M. look strange! Also, my College is so tiny until I get my teachers trained and will still remain tiny for a long time as it takes a long time to raise a child in Thelema! Same for my efforts on A∴A∴ lines, so it is hardly worth anyone's while to take potshots at my effort. However, even though small, I only want to teach a little and help a person here and there and that is all!

Well, I too had trouble with my health until I pinpointed the cause out of the unconscious. It was all due to my reluctance to eliminate O.T.O. out of my orbit. So once I had again realized that and so on—took steps with myself, that is, things got better. I also had a Dr.'s help, of course, for the physical part of it.

Thanks very much again for bringing Vitvan to my attention. I am going to read through and follow his courses. I really needed it too, as he does more correlating with science than A.C. had time to do. I've already gotten strong insights into Thelemic matters through Vitvan's painstaking work! You know, a real adept is unmistakable and reading and knowing one makes a clown out of Motta! All the very best to you and Alice.

Love is the law, love under will.

Phyllis

P.S. Exactly! The Gods use strange people, ways and means if need be to accomplish what they want! Grades mean nothing to them.

P.O. Box 415 Oct. 25, 1982
Oroville, CA 95965

Dear Francis,

Do what thou wilt shall be the whole of the Law.

Thank you for your words of encouragement over Jane's biography in your note of Sept. 27. I don't know how long it will take to complete this, as there is a huge amount of material which she left to me, which I must read through. She didn't keep copies of letters to Germer in every case, and often a gap will appear which is cleared up, if at all, in some other obscure communication. However, she did keep all her letters in vast amounts in other places and those sent to her, etc.

I am giving a Seminar on the history of the California O.T.O., on Karl and the others, all the things which I observed. Also, I will talk on A∴A∴, which is now being conducted exactly as A.C. wrote it should be in *Liber 13, 185,* "One Star in Sight," and other places. I am happy to inform you that we now have four well prepared Neophytes and one about to go on to Zelator in a few months, and a few Probationers about. I don't tell this to everyone, just to you, so that you might perhaps be heartened by the correct application of A.C.'s instructions. I made up an exam for Neophytes which is a dilly and everyone is hard at work to pass it. You saw part of the Probationer's exam in *I.T.C.* and already commented on it.

The work of the C.O.T. is also going well and I am in the throes of structuring the courses so that they will equal 2 years of college work and in due time maybe we can ask for accreditation. At least the groundwork is being laid—my successors can take off from the work done so far.

The Seminar will be Dec. 18 and 19, '82, and I will also talk about C.O.T. and on the 2nd day will talk on astrology. This will be done at [X]'s house in [location]. He does all right with attracting people into the O.T.O., and is a good man to face the public. We hope he will be the next Caliph. Grady is going downhill even more, if that is possible, don't know where his irrationality will lead him! The grapevine reports that he is off booze for a year but is now on drugs. C'est la vie!

As for you? Are you well? Is your work for Falcon Press still going strong? Are they good publishers? I think of you often and wish there was some occasion when I could visit.

Love is the law, love under will.

Phyllis

P.O. Box 415   Oct. 17, 1983
Oroville, CA 95965

Dear Francis,

Do what thou wilt shall be the whole of the Law.

Your last letter was dated July 18, for which I thank you and it is very bad of me to take so long to answer.

Yes, the later history of Jane, Germer, A.C., does seem to be a mess, but then out of putrefaction comes new growth, does it not? Anyhow, the proof of the pudding is what is happening now. The O.T.O. is now claiming about 700 members—though what kind of members is sometimes of concern to me, but to who else? Also, the College of Thelema has been started and though small, we are working towards accreditation at some future time. To this end, I have been devising courses which will hold their own with any similar college course. I notice too, that now some colleges will teach astrology or Tarot—maybe someday qabalah, who knows? Thelema is percolating through many groups, some of whom do not even know the source of their thinking and behavior.

All this because a handful of folks insisted on publishing A.C. and on carrying forward his thought—even with the then O.T.O. in Hollywood. It is because some endured the bad times that Thelema now takes hold. Also, I sometimes think of Jane as being pregnant with the child of the New Aeon and pregnancy is never exciting but is very painful and full of trouble. Perhaps I shall express this in some of the story about Jane. By now you have the latest *I.T.C.* and so can continue with this story. Jane had some oppositions in her horoscope and so was always dragged this way and that by opposing points of view. I really should write out an analysis of this as part of the story.

What is the news of the Falcon Press? I paid for several books ahead of time, but are they now publishing still? Should I demand my money back or wait? I must write them also, but I think you can give me some of the lowdown? Again, I must thank you on behalf of humanity for all the trouble and work you have taken to get A.C. published. I am especially interested in his *The World's Tragedy*, which I do not have. Also, I enjoy every publication you put out and sometimes use your tapes in teaching the C.O.T. students.

I am busy with a Latin class and with the garden as usual. Also, the writing, which I enjoy as well. Lately we have had some difficulty with personality conflicts and at the end of this month I shall have to see if I have any skill at all in resolving them. There is a great lesson in the early O.T.O. of W.T. S[mith] in Hollywood. Oh, if these people could only learn to live the Law of Thelema and stop interfering with one another! I hope you are very well. Are you writing some more?

Love is the law, love under will,

Phyllis

P.O. Box 415
Oroville, CA 95965

Dec. 12, 1983

Dear Francis,

Do what thou wilt shall be the whole of the Law.

Thank you for the news about Falcon Press in your letter of Oct. 21.

Of those you recommend to me, I must tell them that we do not do this work by mail. It is very imperative that these persons show up here personally and have some personal instructions. All my experience of the past with correspondence has been quite bad as students write what they think will make a good show—you know, they hide things which might be deleterious to ego display. When I called some of them on this by mail, they couldn't understand. Much better to have long hours of conversation and then the students understand what is going on and can present their own point of view. I can also see them better as stars when face to face. Some of those you recommend when hearing that we will not teach by mail or hand out A∴A∴ forms right off are disappointed and never write back. But this is as it should be. We want <u>only</u> workers and those who are eager to do A.C.'s outlined tasks, which is our specialty along with a bunch of astrology and some psychology.

Also, I usually explain that I am older and not only do I want workers and serious people, but that they must first join C.O.T. so that I can get an idea if they are serious and in Course I, they are asked to attend 2 seminars here in Oroville. The latter are going very well, are very deep and instructive. [X] is one of the teachers and so now we have 3 of us who teach as there is one other bright young man besides myself. This makes it easier on me as each teacher has a full day in a 4 day seminar. We have yoga exercises and kindred subjects early in the morning, the middle of the day has about 6 hours of instruction and in the evenings we do rituals, demonstrate them, talk about them, etc.

I appreciate that you send these people in my direction and do not mind doing the weeding out. Sooner or later someone really bright and serious will come along and that will be all to the good.

I had to give a deposition to Motta's lawyer last week. Some funny things happened, like Grady presenting a letter from me which ripped him wide open and which didn't need to be in this case at all! I gave 6 hours testimony and the O.T.O. lawyer said mine was the best testimony. I had more history in an accurate fashion and letters to prove the points, I guess. I have kept track of all that has happened, either in letters or in diaries going back for years.

Someday, I suspect, someone may want to know why and how a certain event came about. Also, the Berkeley Lodge does a good deal of gossip about me which is rather unkind and quite wrong, so this history will someday straighten things out.

I laugh at their misconceptions most of the time but occasionally it can be seen as rather deleterious to the work I am doing and holds some people back, too. But I guess if they have no more sense than to listen to gossip, then they get what they deserve. How well do I know that the Great Work has nothing to do with personality conflicts! It has been proven to me all my life through one event or another.

There is sometimes a way to smooth out conflicts between students and this is with an emphasis on balance and on what is written in *Liber Aleph* and *Liber AL*. One must also have communication skills and assertiveness training. I am picking up a little of this, thanks to [Y], who now teaches psychiatric nursing and has an M.S. in this field.

I am more and more convinced that the first thing to do with students is to teach them <u>how</u> to live Thelema through their everyday events, conflicts, projections, etc. Just reading or memorizing the words is not enough. One has to bring it home with what they have done somewhere and have them look at this clearly and put the mirror of Thelema up to their faces. Little by little, they will come to understand. If not, then they may never be real Thelemites, contrary to their wishes on this matter.

To turn the mores of various students around is a terrific task as they have had years being programmed in non-Thelemic thinking. Some are better than others in being Thelemites, of course, some take to it naturally. Anyhow, there is a good deal of adventure in this task which I do.

The College continues to attract good people and to throw off the non-workers. I could hardly ask for more.

My health continues somewhat precarious. My daughter says I must consult a cardiologist but I prefer holistic physicians as I take plenty vitamins and minerals. So I am casting around for someone decent who won't give me the run-around on the heart condition like I got in the past.

I hope you are very well and enjoying life mightily. Wish we could meet. I remember all those lovely times when we did this and how much I learned from you!

    Love is the law, love under will.

Fraternally,
Phyllis

Letters between Seckler and Grady McMurtry

This correspondence between Seckler and her ex-husband, former A∴A∴ student, and frequent sparring partner, Grady McMurtry, encompasses the three major phases of their relationship: their initial acquaintance in the late 1950s, their collaboration in the work of resuscitating O.T.O. in the late 1960s and early 1970s, and their tense post-divorce cooperation within the still-nascent modern O.T.O. of the 1980s.

It should be noted that Seckler's strong criticism of O.T.O., evident in the later letters, was largely a temporary emotional response to her separation from and subsequent conflicts with McMurtry, and her protectiveness concerning Crowley's legacy. She remained a supporter of O.T.O. to the end of her life—yet as these letters show, she was always willing to supply intense constructive criticism and other feedback as the need arose.

5641 27th Avenue
Sacramento 20, Calif.

Nov 3, 1959

Dear Phyllis,

Do what thou wilt shall be the whole of the Law.

I have not received a reply to my letter of June 27th, but take it that you are as busy as I am. Anyway a number of things have happened recently, so I thought I would drop you a quick note. For one thing, I have a new address, as of above. Also I am spending a great deal of time studying for examinations with the hope of promotion in the civil service. Right now I could sure use the money. As you mentioned in your letter of Dec 6, Karl is getting old and is bedeviled with fear. That may not be all he is bedeviled with, but anyway my relations with him, which have been deterioration for some time, have just reached what I can only refer to as a "crisis stage." As I am sure you know, he loaned money to several of us a few years ago. Apparently Meeka refused to pay him back, I don't know about your status, but I have been paying him $10 a month, as we agreed. Also there was never any question of interest on the loan. I missed the payment in September, but as he had authorized me to deduct $50 from the loan for a *Book of Thoth* I had given him and he had sold to [X], I am way ahead on my payments. Nevertheless he has just written threatening to take the "necessary steps," whatever that means, to have me repay the balance of the loan, amount unspecified and indeed I don't think he knows, "with interest!" What it seems to me, Phyllis, is that he has isolated himself up there on that damn mountain with no one but Sascha to pour poison into his soul and nothing to do but brood on trivial items, such as whether Grady's $10 check will arrive on the first of the last of the month. Apparently the September lapse was just enough to set his fuse. Anyway the upshot is that I am planning on going up to see him Saturday, Nov 7th, and have written him that I am coming. So I thought I would let you know and see if you are also interested, or able, to make the trip at the present time. If you are, and want to drive up, I plan on stopping at the Richfield Station in West Point for a few minutes around 10 AM Saturday morning. If you can't do that but can take the bus, I can meet you at the Greyhound Station in Sacramento Saturday morning if you will let me know what bus you will be in on. I have also dropped a note to [M], so if he is interested you might check with him about pooling transportation. His address is 1019 Hampshire St., Apt 3, in San Francisco in case you may have mislaid it.

Out of all this a great deal of good <u>could</u> come. Who knows what we might be able to arrive at if we got together with Karl in person just so he could have someone besides Sascha to talk to? Also I would like to get together with you for an astrology lesson. After your last communication I decided that the whole thing was hopelessly confused until I could get some personal instruction.

In any case, if you let me know that you might be able to come, and he replies that he will not be home, I will let you know as soon as possible, by telegram if necessary. Must be all for now. I am terribly rushed.

Love is the law, love under will.

Grady

Nov. 5, 1959

Dear Grady,

    Do what thou wilt shall be the whole of the Law.

My answer to you must be hasty as you need a reply right away. But first let me ask you—why the company when you needs must discuss the nature of your payments to Karl?

I don't believe Karl keeps track of $10.00 payments so do you know how much you still owe him? I hope you have been paying by check—a good record. If neither of you has kept track—good grief!

Karl loaned me $200, the year he bought your car for you. I have paid him $210.00 as he lost track of an early $10 payment soon after the loan. (I have the cancelled check). But I wrote and told him he deserved the extra $10 and probably much more for waiting so long to be repaid in full. I finished the last $60 payment last summer. He has only a tiny income and probably needs his loaned money now for publishing or extras—who knows?

To tell you truthfully—it seems to me that you want me to go with you to pull your chestnuts out of the fire. And why M.? Be a man and face Karl alone and try to understand him. Crowley's books are a superhuman burden—the responsibility of the whole thing is beyond anyone's strength now alive. He deserves to be a little afraid—there is reason for it. You work and your wife works—well—you think it over. Have any of us been of much help?

Not only am I disinclined to go with you to talk about your loan—I can't. I am struggling with a heart condition and must see my Dr. on Saturday. Also I expect guests. It is too early to tell—but I hope the heart condition is not going to impair my ability to work.

This letter sounds a little severe, I know. There aren't too many Thelemites around but what few there are ought to be at least very grown up. Develop your heart, Grady. Yes, I know—and I have to quit preaching. But you are my brother in Thelema—how can I remain silent?

    Love is the law, love under will.

Fraternally,
Phyllis

7674 Jasmine Court
Dublin, Calif. 94566

April 6, 1967

Dear Grady,

Do what thou wilt shall be the whole of the Law.

Your newsletter for Dec. 1966 was gratefully received at that time and many times I have thought I would write you some answer. That I have not written before this is either due to despair, laziness or some modicum of respect for Sascha. Probably due to all three factors.

After Karl's death I was able to assist Sascha for a few weeks and then after that there has been complete silence. It's a long story and I must tell it sometime but not today.

However, as you know I like to be frank—(between brethren)—and Karl seemed to think you had "sold out"—to whom I do not know. The fact that Sascha was even worse set in this belief has rather stayed my hand for some time. Of course I would like to know whether you think this way or not.

I seem very isolated from other Thelemic brethren at the present and this is not good. Those in Los Angeles whom I used to know do not appeal to me and so I would like to ask with this letter if you know of anything stirring in a Thelemic way in this sad world of ours.

In your newsletter about Kerista there wasn't much mention of Thelema—or at least I didn't spot it. Is your colony in British Honduras going to be Thelemic or is it going to be your own baby almost entirely? Now that is a difficult question, I admit, but I would certainly like some of your views on the matter.

As for me, I still teach at Livermore High but can retire in 5 more years with a very small sum if I am careful. I want to write, especially a book about Jane's life, as I promised her before she died. I am buying a house at the present and also taking full care of my granddaughter, now 2½ yrs old. Otherwise I paint a lot and sell some of my paintings so that department of my life has improved. Also, I have had the great good fortune to begin some classes in beginning astrology and the kabbalah to some very bright young people.

I must admit that with the aid of LSD and other such drugs America does not seem to be so entirely a spiritual desert as before. Some of the young people I meet actually understand what an expansion of consciousness means because they have been through it. Have you made similar observations? Well, I hope you will answer this letter and end some of my isolation? Since I possess the IX° secret do you know if there is any chance of starting a Lodge?

   Love is the law, love under will,

               Phyllis Wade

---

418 Lodge   June 1, 1983
P.O. Box 415
Oroville, CA 95965

Dear Grady,

  Do what thou wilt shall be the whole of the Law.

Your question this morning over the telephone intrigues me, so I will give a rundown as to who had the IX° in the days of Agape Lodge.
  Karl Germer — direct from Crowley
  Wilfred Smith — got it either from Achad (Jones) or Jane.
  Jane Wolfe — direct from Crowley
  Grady McMurtry — direct from Crowley
  Max Schneider — don't know where he got it, but probably from W.T. Smith, as he was an early resident at Winona Blvd.
  Jean Schneider — got it from Max
  Phyllis Seckler — got it from Germer
  Roy Leffingwell — got it from Max, who was ordered by A.C. to go to the desert with the oath and the "Emblems and Modes of Use" due to a vision Roy had while having sex. A.C. said Roy was in danger unless he did it properly with these papers, hence the order to Max to carry out his instructions.
  Jack Parsons — got it from Smith
  Helen Parsons — got it from Smith

Dr. Montenegro—got it from Leffingwell—at least part of it, I don't know how official it was as Smith was under interdict and A.C. dead. But Monty also visited Karl many times at West Point and no doubt picked up anything he may have been short on. I do know that he was ordered to pick up the paper "Emblems and Modes" from me when I was late in mailing it back to Karl. This order would not have been given unless Monty was a true IX°, due to Karl being a stickler for form and secrecy.

Joe Miller—got it from Jane who actually taught him some techniques with physical sex. This is why he boasted that he was a priest of Thelema when you and I first contacted him in 1969.

Georgia Schneider—got it from Max and corresponded with A.C. about it. A.C. had some ideas about how a woman might work it. Georgia got into very hot water with the help of Joe Crombie on her workings and almost landed in jail for murder.

Ray and Mildred Burlingame—it was Mildred's boast that Ray worked this all the time.

Louis Culling, either from Russell or from Smith, he discussed it with the latter often. Wrote a book and alluded to it in other writings—on sex magick. Partly wrong and partly right.

As to "Emblems and Modes of Use," A.C. states over and over that anyone could read this, but it would do them no good as the practices held within them their own safeguards. Many modern day folks have ferreted out from A.C.'s writings and from Grant and a host of other authors, true methods of working the IX° O.T.O. They work it, too, as has come to my attention from time to time. But if they aren't self-disciplined in body, mind and emotions, they run a grave risk and indeed I have seen this risk taken by one of my friends who nearly ruined his life with the wrong sort of discipline for working the true IX°, that is very little discipline, and using the powers for selfish ends.

But the results of the workings look so natural, that often these persons cannot trace the boomerang results of their workings. They think they are plagued by bad luck or any other force, even astrology, other than their inept handling of finer forces which are really beyond their comprehension. It is no good for a mere tyro to attempt to work the IX°, even if intellectually, he has some idea how to do it.

A.C. said there was no reason for secrecy as regards "Emblems and Modes," even a typist could type it up, with no use to her in the end, as it might not even be understood. I am sure I saw it in print in some book but my research to date has not uncovered the source.

Now, if you will look carefully at the Constitution of the O.T.O., you will discover that the IX° is not really a political body. They seem to act more as guides for the younger members, and it is stated that they move quietly and unknown among the least of us, and work their magick in silence and with love for humanity. I really think it a mistake to have produced such a body of political IX° who know nothing of the secret workings and couldn't work it without harm, even if they did know, as they are greatly undisciplined.

However, I accept the fact that this was an emergency situation for the voting privileges that you have vested in the IX° and it seemed the best way to do it at the time. But I would suggest strongly that these voting privileges be transferred to the Senate, even if, to begin, all IX° become part of this Senate as well as those of V° and over. And I would suggest that since we are starting, pioneering, and need a transition period to the full implementation of the Constitution, that the Senate serve for a shorter term than 11 years, which frightens many off as then they think the next Grade would not be easily available to them. Unfortunately we have these social or Grade climbers who love to be at the top and think they can lord it over others, and mostly some of them cannot even pass some of the tests instituted for Man of Earth, I° through III° or even IV°. (Not sure where the boundary line exists).

In due time, we may give to the IX° their original meaning as stated by A.C. in the Constitution and elsewhere, especially in *Liber Aleph*. Also in the *Commentaries on Liber AL*.

Now as to this Brou-ha-ha about [X] holding the IX°. The idea goes that I gave it to him. I do not give this Grade to anyone. I do not repeat what you are doing. If it is a political IX°, then you are the only one who can give this Grade as a political Grade. This I adhere to strictly. After you, the next Caliph may do this. But I would like to suggest that any new IX° be passed on by his peers in a session of IX° which is not open to the public in any form. I think we might sometimes have a Caliph, as is now the case, who is interested in making political IX°. When I saw the operation of this Grade last March, I rather think they might wish to get rid of this idea of political IX°.

Any <u>real</u> or Magickal IX° makes himself into this Grade, or attains it, by his knowledge, his self-discipline of body, mind and emotions and by his successful practices of the Theurgy of the Grade and of the secrets contained therein. They are only secret because the bulk of humanity may not attain to such perfection as they don't really wish to work hard at such a thing.

What I did was to acknowledge that [X] could be self-disciplined, that he knew about this working far beyond the normal grasp of the normal scholar, that he could work the magick without harm, and that he was willing to sign the Oath and work the theurgy only for the benefit of the Order and of Humanity. No selfish motives, you see, no grasp for power or status were pushing him. He kept his true position secret for 3 years but I considered that it was necessary that he also have voting privileges as he is a true ornament for the Order and will bring great credit to it in due time. He could have remained a secret IX° for a much longer time if the present events had warranted it. But when I see inferior people voting on issues which affect us all and this genius must be on the sidelines, I thought that the time had arrived in which to act.

Let me digress and establish, against [Y]'s ideas, that working the IX° is a magickal act and not necessarily a mystical act. He has confusion in his mind about the distinction between these two terms. The O.T.O. is a magickal body more than a Mystical one. Magick works on the outside world and the Mystic is working on his inside world. The O.T.O. is first and foremost supposed to be interested in establishing Thelema throughout the world, A.C.'s direct injunctions to us.

So then, I merely acknowledged a true Magickal IX° that had come to my attention. I did not make a IX°; any such person attains his own Grade by his progress in understanding and the working of true magick. It seems that those at the top in the O.T.O. wish, to date, to ignore the Oath. Well, it is to your own peril, those who are real Magickal IX° are eager to sign it!

To date, I have been approached by 2 persons ignorant of the real meaning of the Grade to make them into a IX°. I didn't laugh in their faces, I laugh privately. I would never do so as they were undisciplined and knew very little about the workings of the Grade or even about its dangers. I referred each to you to make them political IX°, if that was what they wanted.

As I made clear on March 19, some of our so-called IX° are only political and could not work the magick of this Grade for the life of them, much less work it without harm! I would like to suggest that in due time this sort of person be phased out. The safeguards can be in the Oath, who is willing to sign it, and in the exam, which could be even more difficult than the present version. Maybe we could also, all together, dream up other safeguards?

After all, is this going to be an O.T.O. which is constructed as A.C. would have it, or is it going to be the product of lesser minds who push and scramble for the next Grade up without doing any work for it, much less service to their fellow Thelemites or even to humanity at large? There is too much of gossip and political backbiting and other ills rife in the Order at present. One remedy would be to give Grades only to those who have really worked hard for them and deserve them because of outstanding service. I think political favoritism was never intended by A.C. and to my mind has never worked too well in the history of nations.

I would like to suggest that, first, any future IX° would have demonstrated to some other IX° whether they have the self-discipline and can work the theurgy of the Grade with good effect and no harm to themselves or anyone else. Second, also, that this future IX° will have done a great deal for the O.T.O., showing a true spirit of service and concern for the rest of us in the Order. And that, third, the person selected be able to get on in a general fashion with the body of voting IX°. (I know, for instance, a person who can work the Grade secrets but who would be disruptive in the Order and in any gathering and who has not done any significant work for the Order. This person would never get any help from me on IX° teaching, training, secrets, or whatever else.) Points 1 through 3 perhaps ought to be considered as there are plenty of young people who can now work the secrets to a certain extent and we wouldn't want them among those of us who are oriented to the TRUE O.T.O.

Now then, be assured that my standards for a Grade of IX° are those of A.C. and outstrip yours considerably. I would never make a political IX° as I think this a harmful practice for the welfare of the O.T.O., but if you think you need them then this is up to you. But the consequences are also _for_ you.

Be assured that I never hope to impinge upon your power; I have deliberately kept my distance for some years now so that you would not have any worries on this score. I have enough to do with my present work and find myself enjoying it very much. I certainly would not like to be in your position and have your worries!

But I am very much interested that the O.T.O. be conducted just as A.C. wrote. If it goes in a different direction, then who knows? Would it be truly Thelemic? To my mind, A.C. had the ideas of a far greater genius than any of us can hope to be in many incarnations. His O.T.O. ought to have a chance and if any of his ideas won't work, time to change later when all have had a chance to grow into well-informed and balanced Thelemites. Now we are very young and not skilled in practicing Thelema. We make many mistakes; we need more wisdom and balance. But for goodness' sakes, let us try A.C.'s experiment in Thelemic organization and living!

To date we have 11 or 12 IX° and thus, 11 or 12 profess houses. This means that the Constitution ought to go into effect, you know. We may not yet have 1,000 members, but the profess houses may make it necessary that we implement the Constitution.

I hope I have covered all the salient points. Let me add that the O.T.O. ought to be governed, in time, by true aristocrats, as A.C. intended. The cream of this large body of people of the present O.T.O. <u>will</u> rise to the top and is now doing so. Anyone who becomes reactionary and resents or blocks this "cream" or aristocratic person is probably due for some rude awakenings and plenty of personal trouble. Plenty of this in Cap. II of *Liber AL* and I am sure I do not have to repeat this to you.

I wrote all of this down as it can now become a matter of record and you may show it to anyone whom you think may profit from it or who would like to see it. It is not enough to tell you these things on the 'phone as my past experience with you is certain on one point, that you are likely to forget. I write this as a more permanent working and have repeated most of what I said to you via the phone.

I hope all is well with you; [X] and [Y] and I are planning a trip to Berkeley and would certainly like to meet with you as per your invitation of this morning. Also, you are welcome to visit 418 Lodge at some future date; please just let me know in advance.

Love is the law, love under will,

Fraternally,
Phyllis

Letters between Seckler and Gerald Yorke

In the years following Karl Germer's death, much of Crowley's legacy was in disarray, and Seckler was desperate to ascertain the survival of Crowley's writings and other archival materials. This correspondence with Gerald Yorke conveys a flavor of this pivotal moment in Thelema's history, as these two competent and devoted individuals collaborated to ensure the future of Crowley's body of work.

7674 Jasmine Ct. Feb. 23, 1969
Dublin, Calif. 94566

Mr. Gerald Yorke
Forthampton Ct.
Gloucester, England.

Dear Mr. Yorke,

Mrs. Sascha Germer and Miss Jane Wolfe both stated in different ways and places that you had made three copies of everything Aleister Crowley had written and had sent one copy to Karl Germer, one to the British Museum and one to be sequestered elsewhere for posterity.
 Since all the manuscripts and books were stolen from Mrs. Germer a year and a half ago, I have been terribly worried about their fate and have been trying to make discreet enquiries as to just who was responsible. Jane Wolfe left to me the bulk of her letters and I came across the bit of information in the first paragraph, above. If this is true, it would relieve me of a great deal of worry, expense and trouble — and maybe even of danger.
 I tried to work with Mrs. Germer when Karl died but she had ideas of her own on that score and became so difficult that I could be no more use. You see, I have been in Thelemic work on the west coast here for years and Jane was my guru.
 So now I ask you kindly to verify the above information and would be deeply grateful if you could assure me that all of Aleister Crowley's works were safe. Could you also let me know

who owns the copyrights? Would we be out of order if we should reproduce some of Crowley's writings? I worked on typewritten copies of some of the things under Karl Germer's direction and so have only a little here that maybe could be published. Would you kindly give me any idea you may have on this score?

Very sincerely yours,

Phyllis Wade

Forthampton Court. Gloucester. England.   2 March 69

Dear Mrs. Wade,

Your 23 Feb. What happened was this. Germer and I sent each other a copy of what the other had not got and made a 2nd carbon, and all that had survived only in Ms was copied with 2 carbons. Thus there was one complete archive in the States and 2 in England. But my collection of the printed works was the most complete one. One set of the English copies and all the books will go to the Warburg Institute which is part of London University, where it will be properly looked after. It would have been neglected and lost in the British Museum. Most of the books are already at the Warburg together with the original colored drawings for *The Book of Thoth*. Germer sent all the more important O.T.O. MSS to England for safe keeping before he died.

When Germer died I sent Sascha the money to ship her archive to England for safe keeping, being certain that she was not a competent custodian and probably would be glad to be relieved of it. But apparently she could not bear to part with it, so that some or much of it has been stolen. I asked her who by, she gave me two Christian names, but when I asked for surnames I got no reply. I think from her letter they were mainly interested in O.T.O. material and charters and such stocks of unsold books as had survived. They did not get the O.T.O. MSS.

If, as you get older, (I am 67), or now if you feel like it, you would like to send me to ensure their safety and their addition to the main archive, to which they should belong, the letters and papers left you by Jane Wolfe, please do so. We have parts of her Cefalu diaries, copies of A.C's letters to her which she made herself, and of Cameron Parsons to her. We also have copies of the contents of Jack Parsons' black box made before Cameron destroyed them and odds and ends of recent American material. It will help to complete the material if we have what she left you. I would reimburse you for the cost of sending them.

Thus Crowley's work is safe and very extensive, for I took a magical oath to preserve it in 1928 when I was one of his disciples, at the same time that Regardie was there. I left him as my teacher after 3 years as I never accepted the whole of *The Book of the Law*, but we remained friends until his death. I left the occult Thelemic path for Hinduism and then Buddhism.

Now for the copyright position. The copyrights belong to the O.T.O., or rather to A.C.'s branch of the O.T.O., as not all the old national branches accepted him on Reuss' death. Unfortunately Karl did not appoint any successor in his will. He chartered one person for England, whose lodge functioned for a year or two and then closed down. I do not know whom he chartered in the States, nor how many lodges operate or operated. Is there a temple or lodge functioning anywhere with you as in the old days of 1003? If no-one can produce a valid charter made out to them by Karl they cannot claim the copyrights in law, and so would not get royalties etc. from any reprint.

The only functioning lodge that I know of is the Swiss one. It was chartered properly by Karl. They celebrate the Gnostic Mass properly but decently on Sundays and advertise it as a Sunday service in the Zurich newspapers. Every Equinox for some 6 or 7 years they have brought out an equinoctial publication varying from a book like *Book 4* part one, and then part two, or several of the numbered official publications from the Equinox etc. like *Liber LXV* etc. etc. in a German translation. They use the Reuss translation for the Gnostic Mass. There are some 15 of them I think. I regard them as the real heirs. But they are not interested in claiming the copyrights, being self-supporting and rightly not wanting to be bothered by quarrels about the succession. I do not know if the Rio de Janeiro lodge was chartered by or merely affiliated itself to Karl. I suspect the latter. The Mexican lodges were chartered by Reuss and not by A.C., though the latter was in touch with them when Dr. Krumm-Heller was the head. But there is no O.H.O. today.

The literary executor appointed in A.C.'s will is John Symonds in London. In law he has the right to authorize or forbid quotations and republications or fresh publications of A.C's work. But this does not apply in the States, except possibly for *The Book of Thoth* if Karl deposited, as he was instructed to do, two copies with the Library of Congress. So in fact you can publish almost anything by A.C. in the States. But if you try to get an English publisher for it, John Symonds would invoke the law, with what result is somewhat uncertain. But Regardie has done an <u>excellent</u> anthology on A.C.'s work up to 1913, which Llewellyn are publishing in the States this autumn. The Aquarian Press was going to bring it out but over here, but John Symonds has sent them a lawyer's letter to restrain them from doing so. He is under contract with Jonathan Cape to edit A.C.'s works for them; a 900 page edited and shortened version of *The Confessions*, which covers all the unpublished typescripts of it—only the first 2 volumes came out, being published by the Mandrake Press of which I was a director. If *The Confessions* sell the next volume will be edited from the unpublished diaries.

Afraid I am not prepared myself to copy material for you, as I have not the time.

If you can find out for me whether any lodge of the O.T.O. is in fact working in the States at the moment, I shall be grateful and particularly if you can find out who stole the stuff, as it should be recorded for historical purposes.

Yours sincerely,
Gerald Yorke

A copy of Germer's diaries is in the main archive over here, but has not been copied. Nor has the modern American material.

Llewellyn have just published in the States *Roll Away The Stone* by Regardie which reprints with an admirable article A.C.'s main articles on Hashish etc. in the *Equinox*.[210]

Please forgive typing.

---

210. Regardie, Israel, *Roll Away the Stone: An Introduction to Aleister Crowley's Essays on the Psychology of Hashish* (St. Paul, MN: Llewellyn Publications, 1968).

7674 Jasmine Ct. March 16, 1969
Dublin, Calif. 94566

Dear Mr. Yorke,

Thank you for your letter of March 2, '69 and its very comprehensive replies to my letter. Also, please excuse me that this must be handwritten as I broke my left arm on March 1, and it will be several weeks before I can type again.

When Karl's books and manuscripts were stolen from Sascha, she immediately sent me a night letter in which she accused [X] of being among the gang of thieves. It just so happens that [X] has absolutely no interest in Thelemic materials and she was also elsewhere on that fateful day and we have eye witness proof to that. I sent a night letter back to Sascha informing her she was wrong. Then I wrote a long letter explaining how she was wrong. The letter was returned unopened. The night letter she had to listen to as that is like a telegram and they phone it in to the recipient. So you see, I would be very grateful if you could let me know the 2 Christian names that Sascha wrote to you when informing you of the event. A week later, she sent a long letter which went on with her accusations and in it she remarked that one of the young men had said he was a member of the O.T.O. So with that clue, I begin to think there may be a group going in So. Calif., but as I say, my enquiries must remain discreet for the time being as I should hate to have a similar thing happen to me. Sascha's letter stated they had gotten her to open the door to them through "false pretenses." Well, if some of my former friends had that type of action in mind, I would be a "sitting duck," as I live alone.

Several years before Karl died he had reason to break with the group in So. Calif. and I also had strong reasons. So when I had completed my college training I came to the San Francisco region to do my art teaching and have now been teaching in Livermore for 14 years. I am now 51 and am the Phyllis Seckler Jane mentions in some of her correspondence. I am now divorced from Mr. Wade.

Thank you for your offer to take Jane's files and add them to those in the Warburg Institute. As it happens, I promised Jane I would write a book about her and so I need these letters and diaries to fulfill my promise. One does not break a promise—I learned that early in my occult work. When I have written the book—that is another thing. But there are still 3 years before I may retire from teaching and then I hope to plunge into the teaching of Thelema in this area upon my retirement. So it may be several years before I could consider sending these things to the Warburg Institute. In case you are not alive then, could you let me have their address? Understand please, that I am not making any definite promise for if I did so, I might seriously hamper the efforts of young students here who could profit from these files and especially from the things that Karl Germer wrote. Karl had a great deal to do with my own development when I had taken a different route than Jane was equipped to teach. I think you can see how valuable his letters still are to me. I would offer to make copies of Karl's and Jane's correspondence if I could see my way clear at the moment, but I can't, and since I do not promise anything if there is a chance the promise would be broken—well, I guess you will understand. However, I would like to do this for you if I could.

Several of us here have regretted for years that there was no Tarot pack to accompany *The Book of Thoth*. Are Frieda Harris' designs for the Tarot available at all? My understanding of years ago was that she wanted a large sum of money for the original designs and no one had that sum, and so the Tarot was never printed into a pack of cards. Is this correct or false? What chance is there today that a pack could be made up from her designs?

I ask all this before we are forced out of desperation to make photo copies of things, enlarge them, color them (I am an artist) and then reproduce them as a pack of cards. Would we be sued if we did this?

I read a copy of Crowley's will which was in Jane's files. In it Frieda Harris, Louis Wilkinson and John Symonds are named as literary executors. Are the first two dead?

Excuse me for being out of touch but Karl was so suspicious and Sascha even more so, of everyone, that I held my peace on many subjects out of respect for them both. I didn't want either one to get suspicious of me, rightly or wrongly, and maybe I have been too quiet. But much of that has ended and I now feel the time has come to ask.

As you can see, I know nothing of the group in So. Calif. except what Karl chose to tell me before he died and I didn't pry, either, for the above reasons. I knew all of them; I was for 2 years at 1946 Winona and stayed twice at 1003 Orange Grove. I drew my own conclusions and decided quiet work was better. I am not sorry but I also am now rather cut off. However, now is the time to remedy the situation—up to a point.

I would like to ask you some questions point-blank.

If Israel Regardie was in possession of Karl's books and MSS, or Dr. Montenegro, would either of them tip their hand to you or Symonds? Perhaps by asking about copyrights? Are you in contact with Symonds?

I don't know what we would do here if we wanted to start an O.T.O. lodge as no charters that I know of were given out. Perhaps the group in Switzerland could charter us when we were ready? Would you let me know their address please? You see, while planning for the future, I am trying to build on firm foundations, and not on the shaky foundations that existed heretofore in Calif. I feel we must make a new start and proceed without any stumbling blocks out of the past. So your last letter was invaluable for its information and I hope you can help us a little further. Could you let me have Symonds' address, also?

Again, thank you for your very courteous and informative reply.

Sincerely yours,
Phyllis Wade

P.S. I do hope you will be discreet about whom you inform that I have Jane's MSS. and letters. Louis Culling advertised some time ago for information leading to their whereabouts. He is a slippery character and no one has ever been able to trust him. I think you can see my position?

Forthampton Court Gloucester   20 March 69

Dear Mrs. Wade,

Your 16 March 69. I am afraid that Sascha wrote that [X] was the girl who threw acid in her eyes. But it is quite clear that poor Sascha's mind is no longer clear and that she easily gets mixed up. So, please, on no account let her know that I have told you. Your letter saying that it could not be [X] who was responsible will remain in the file to clear her name. It does however look as if 3 men and one woman at sometime or other connected with 1003 were responsible. She (Sascha) has not replied to my letter asking for full names.

Poor Regardie had nothing to do with it and three weeks ago lost all his Crowley books and Golden Dawn materials when his house was burgled expressly for all this material. I will not tell anyone that you have the Jane Wolfe material, or you might well be next on the list.

If I ever get reliable information as to who was responsible I will let you know so that you can be warned against the people responsible. But suspect old members of 1003.

John Symonds is still alive and I am in touch with him. He has nothing to do with the copyright in Frieda Harris Tarot card designs. She left them to me in her will, and I have deposited them with the Warburg Institute. If you want coloured photographs of the originals you get in touch with them and argue the copyright position with them. They will I expect make some charge if you are going to reproduce them. I expect they can quote you for the cost of having coloured transparences made. I have no objection to your making such use of them as you want.

    Herr Metzger's address is:
    Gasthof Rose
    CH-9063 Stein AR
    Zurich. Switzerland.

As Karl left no successor in the O.T.O. I doubt whether any further legal charters can be issued in the States. Certainly any charter stolen from Sascha is automatically invalid. Metzger therefore is the only person of whom I know who has a valid charter from Karl and so entitled to give a valid one to someone else. Karl before his death revoked the charter that he gave to someone in London.

The address of the Warburg Institute is Woburn Square London W.C.1 and the librarian is J. B. Trapp. If you write him mention that you got the address from me.

Yours sincerely
Gerald Yorke

As long as the Jane Wolfe papers and letters are in your safe hands, I am content and hope that your book about her is successful. Do please make an extra carbon of it for me to place in the archive.

P.S. I have never heard of Dr. Montenegro. Regardie and I in our youth were disciples together of A.C. and left him as our teacher at approximately the same time. He is an honorable friend of mine and would have had nothing to do with Sascha's loss. He has never been interested in the O.T.O. side of A.C., being a Rosicrucian Qabalist.

7674 Jasmine Ct. April 5, 1969
Dublin, Calif. 94566

Dear Mr. Yorke,

Thank you for your letter of March 20. Since that time that I last wrote you, several things have happened.

I got in touch with Mildred Burlingame and last weekend she spent 2½ days with me and we went thoroughly over the matter of stolen A.C. books and Mss.

In fact, your letter of March 20 forced this move on my part as it hit me like a ton of bricks when I read of Regardie's loss. I hope you will understand that I have never met Mr. Regardie and so, not knowing him or of him, I made the mistake of thinking he might know about Sascha's loss of library, etc. Please excuse my blunder but I must needs mention everyone I know of in order to eliminate the true from false.

Mildred, meanwhile, told me she knows Israel Regardie and clued me in on various events. Some of Mildred's O.T.O. rituals and books were taken by a Jean [B], Mildred is quite sure, as only those books Jean B. did not have were taken. Jean B. was a student of Ray Burlingame's for about 10 years. She was in England in Winter of 1965 and one month after her return in Jan. 1966, Mildred's rituals were taken by a person who would have to have a key to her place. Jean B. was the only other person with a key. In Oct. of same year, after M. had had all locks changed, a nailed down window was forced open and M's books were taken.

Mildred has contacted Regardie about this event and the latter reports a <u>very</u> <u>secret</u> group working in L.A.

If this is so, I do not know of them and I hope they do not know of me as I broke off all So. Calif. contacts years ago in order to be able to say to Karl and Sascha honestly that I had not contacted any of them. Also, I had inner warnings about it all. It seems my intuition was correct.

Yes, Sascha also wrote to me immediately after the theft (a night letter first) that my [X] had been one of the thieves. I was in hopes that you had a different name. Of course [X] was not there, as I explained before; also her husband was with her on that day and a friend saw them near home. I have asked [X] to get a notarized statement to this fact.

Curiously enough, Sascha had every reason to know what [X] looked like as we had spent 2 days with Sascha and Karl in West Point. Sascha practically admits that the face of the woman working with the thieves did not look like [X]'s face. But she says it was [X] because of the hands! Would you like for me to send you a copy of the letters she sent to me?

Thank you so much for the information of the cards of the Tarot. Has there ever been an estimate of how much it would cost to print them? If so, how much? I can't promise great things right now but things are stirring here and if we are lucky we may be able to tackle certain publishing chores. It is now 65 years since *Liber AL* was written and I am sure things are about to happen. Meanwhile, I am doing everything I can to push matters along.

Yes, I shall do all in my power to care for the Jane Wolfe materials and will certainly send you a carbon of the typescript on my book when it is well enough along to do this.

Dr. Montenegro was a student here of Roy Leffingwell but Mildred's talk with me has taken him out of my mind entirely in regards to the thievery that has been going on.

I am pinning my hopes on Mr. Regardie being able to unmask the bunch responsible.

Thank you again for your kind cooperation.

Very sincerely yours,
Phyllis Wade

Forthampton Court Gloucester   11 Apr 69

Dear Mrs. Wade,

Your 5 April. No need to send me a copy of Sascha's letters to you or to get a notarized statement from [X]. Poor Sascha's mind is evidently disturbed at times and your letter will go into the pile and keep things straight.

Frieda Harris had estimates for reproducing the pack in color and the cost was £4000, but this was doing the thing perfectly. This is not my line of [illegible] and I have no idea of the cost.

Let me have a copy of anything that you and your friends publish, so that the Warburg collection is complete.

As long as Jane Wolfe's papers are safe, I am content.

Yours
Gerald Yorke

7674 Jasmine Ct.   June 28, 1969
Dublin, Calif. 94566

Dear Mr. Yorke,

You will be pleased to know that we have the name and location of the women involved in the theft of Sascha's library.

Many things have been happening since I last wrote to you. We were planning to start a College of Thelema and have started the ground work for this project. Grady McMurtry was appointed by Aleister Crowley as his personal representative in the United States and to take charge of the work of the Order in California and to reform it. This was in 1946. At that time these instructions were subject to the approval of Karl Germer and there was nothing to be done due to Karl's particular set-up and thinking.

Now an emergency exists as is clearly evidenced by the theft of Karl's library. Also, the time has come to carry out A.C.'s instructions. On reflection, this lapse of time was needed, for it has helped to weed out some of the wilder elements from the group workings.

We would like to also set up a bona fide O.T.O. organization but must proceed with care and caution. Grady is writing to Mr. Metzger in Switzerland about this.

The thief who stole Sascha's library is named Jean [B], but we are not absolutely sure of the three men who accompanied her. We think her husband, [D], may have been among the group and we also guess that a [B] may have been among the group. We have an eye witness report that A.C.'s robes were pulled out of a box one evening, that the copy of the Stele which Karl had in his home was displayed prominently and that there was a room full of diaries, letters and books. Jean B. was heard to say that they deserved all this. She is running a "fake" O.T.O. in Los Angeles and is trying to swear all her members to deep secrecy. However, some have suspected something wrong and we may be getting a little help, we hope, in the recovery of Karl's library.

However, Sascha did not let me read Karl's will and I understand you have a copy. Sascha is very difficult to work with and though we expect to see her soon, we do not expect much cooperation, if any. How could we recover this library if it does not belong to the O.T.O. and makes Sascha his executrix? But I know this will is replaced by a later one. Would it be out of line to ask you what the last will contains? There would be no use restoring this library to Sascha only to have it stolen again from her lonely and unprotected house.

I have expressed the thought to Grady that perhaps the whole collection of manuscripts and letters should go back to you since you paid Sascha to send them. I do not care to have it all around as it is far too bulky and I am thinking there are inimical forces about some of it anyhow.

My only interest in that library is in rare manuscripts of

Crowley's which might need publishing. We are planning some publication activities and may have something out by next month or two at the most. We find there is a great deal of interest in A.C.'s works here on the west coast and *Liber AL* has been published by Mr. Jerry Kay in Los Angeles and *777* has been put out by an outfit in Chico. Also, the Tarot cards from *The Book of Thoth* have been reproduced by a photographic process by the Sangreal Foundation, P.O. Box 2580, Dallas, Texas. I am sending for some of these. They are not in color, of course.

Mildred Burlingame is working with us and in the process of our investigation we had the great good luck to meet Dr. Regardie and I must say that I found him to be a charming gentleman. He helped us a great deal to find the thieves. We are not quite sure whether the same people stole his things as well.

Apart from all this, Grady and I have been married, so you see, we can combine our joint efforts on the above mentioned projects. We are very much in love with each other and very happy.

We would appreciate it very much if we could be informed of any publications of Crowley's works, including Symonds' publication of *The Confessions*. Naturally we wish to build up a fairly complete collection for our future students. Do you think Symonds' publishers might put us on their mailing list?

Thank you again for all your assistance.

Phyllis McMurtry
formerly Phyllis Wade

P.S. We have not decided yet whether publicity is the proper procedure against Jean B. so we would very much appreciate it if you would keep her name quiet for a while longer.

Forthampton Court Gloucester   2 July 69

Dear Mrs. McMurtry,

I enclose this in a normal envelope as I typed over a section which would have been stuck down.

Your 28 June. The photostat that I have of Karl's will sent me by Sascha runs as follows:

★★★

This is my last will and testament:

In the event of my death or accident I leave the whole of my property and possessions to my beloved wife Sascha Ernestine Andre-Germer as sole heir. This refers to my personal property, of which she is the sole executive. As regards the property of the Ordo Templi Orientis, of which I am the Head, I direct that this is passed to the Heads of the Order, but that my wife, Mrs. Sascha E. Andre-Germer, has to be the executor of this part of my will, together with Frederic Mellinger IX° of the O.T.O. I direct that my body be cremated.

New York, N.Y. December 4, 1951. Signed Karl Johannes Germer.

Witnessed by Henry J (name illegible). Frederic Mellinger.

★★★

As you see this leaves everything up in the air, for who are the 'Heads of the Order?' A.C committed the same idiocy by leaving all his copyrights, typescripts Mss etc. to the O.T.O. as such. Whoever establishes a title to this will be able to claim royalties, I think, for all A.C.'s work now being published in the States. I suggest that you get in touch with Mellinger, as Sascha is not always clear headed in her old age.

Meanwhile, many congratulations on your marriage. A.C. always wrote well of your husband.

Whoever stole the archive, and it looks as if the [B]'s may have been responsible, should be prosecuted.

I know nothing of any later will, and do not now remember whether Karl sent me the photostat at the time it was made or whether I got it from Sascha after his death.

The most important thing to find is the original MSS of *The Book of the Law*, although it does exist in published photographic form. My collection, part of which is already at the Warburg

Institute, and a further section will be sent when I have got down to bringing the catalogue up to date should really be the recipient of the bulk which you do not want to hold. As I think you know Karl sent me the O.T.O. Ms for safekeeping years ago.

I am delighted that you are both in touch with Regardie; he is sane and honorable and knows more about the magical side of A.C. than anyone else in the States. But he is not interested in the IX° and the O.T.O. side.

I have a copy of Jerry Kaye's edition of *Liber AL*. Please let me have the name of the publishers of the Chicago *777* so that I can get it.

Write mentioning my name to

Carr P. Collins, Jr.
Sangreal Foundation Inc.
P.O. Box 2580
Dallas, Texas 75221

He visited me here last week with copies of his edition of the *8 Lectures on Yoga* and *Book 4* parts 1 and 2 in one volume each with a foreword by Regardie. He has a third title in the press. I gave him permission to reproduce the Tarot pack in color and sent him up to the Warburg Institute, with whom I have deposited the originals, to arrange for proper color photographs. I suggested various unpublished items which he could tackle in the future. The Helios bookshop can arrange for any MSS or typescript that I hold to be photostated over here, so that I do not have to send irreplaceable material to the States. So get in touch with him in order not to duplicate anything which he is bringing out. He has the money to produce the books properly and is in touch with Regardie.

Jonathan Cape are publishing a 900 page volume consisting of the bulk of the published and unpublished *Confessions* edited by John Symonds with the technical assistance of Kenneth Grant, who is a properly attested IX°, had a charter from Karl which the latter revoked when he and Kenneth disagreed over something. I advised Karl not to do so. You can order the book from a bookseller. I expect it to be out this autumn as the page proofs have been corrected. If it sells they will bring out a volume of the magickal diaries again edited by John Symonds. I have refused to collaborate in this as I do not consider Symonds a suitable person for the job, even though Kenneth Grant will be advising him. Grant has a carbon copy of all the magickal diaries: I used him for typing them from the originals and when I typed copies of what Germer had not got, I made a carbon for Grant. Remind me in a year's time to let you know whether the project is still on.

If Grady has not got a charter from Karl to open a lodge, I suggest that he applies to Metzger for one, for Metzger is the only person to my knowledge to have been chartered by Karl, apart from Grant. He puts on the Gnostic Mass as a public service so advertised in the Zurich press on Sundays.

I suggest that you also get in touch with Frater Theophilus, who I believe is IX° and who has visited Metzger. He is Dr. Gabriel Montenegro Vargas, P.O. Box 76, Daly City, California 94016. But do not mention my name as I do not know him and he does not know that I have his address. I looked at a letter concerning someone else by mistake. Regardie may know of him. From a copy of a letter from him in my possession, he seems to be a confirmed Thelemite and a sensible man, refusing O.T.O. material to someone whom I also turned down partially.

I am delighted that you are in touch with Mildred Burlingame whose letters to me show her to be sane and balanced. Or am I mixing her up with someone else?

Will keep quiet about the B's until I hear from you to the contrary.

Yours sincerely,
Gerald Yorke

7674 Jasmine Court August 8, 1969
Dublin, Calif. 94566

Dear Mr. Yorke,

Thank you for your letter of July 2. There are many things to comment about here. First, some years ago, while in Hampton, New Jersey, Karl had occasion to quarrel with Frederick Mellinger. He tells about this quarrel in one of his letters to Jane and I would quote from it now except that there isn't much time to look it up. The upshot of the quarrel was that all relations between the two were broken for good. I never heard of Karl mention Frederick when he was out here. I knew Frederick myself, having had my first astrology lessons under him and was at Orange Grove house when he was. We do not know if he is alive or dead, at the present.

When I was trying to help Sascha right after Karl's death, she mentioned that there was another, later will, than the one that mentions Mellinger. She was quite mysterious about the later will and thought that it mentioned Marcello Motta of Brazil but Sascha later hinted that it did not. Now, what I would like to ask, did Sascha send you the photostat of Karl's will at the time of his death or shortly after, in 1962?

We now have the O.T.O. started and a Headquarters Lodge established at the above address. All three of us hold the IX° in the O.T.O.—that is, Grady, Mildred Burlingame and myself. It may be that when we have the organization legally incorporated under the laws of the State of Calif. that we may be able to do something to recover the archives. Meanwhile, much needs to be done, and it keeps up constantly busy. Grady is so busy that I must write this letter in order to dispel some of the misconceptions you may possibly have formed from too little information.

We met Jerry Kay on our last trip in June to Los Angeles where we also met Regardie. Jerry Kay is anxious to put out a color copy of the Harris designs of the Tarot deck. He has the capital, the printing facilities and the enthusiasm for this project. Lee Heflin has offered to fly back to England to make the necessary color photographs or slides of the Harris paintings. I believe you talked to Mr. Heflin on the 'phone when he was over there in July. He reports that he visited the Warburg Institute and he seems to think that the Sangreal Foundation did not make the necessary pictures of the paintings. Today we are leaving for Los Angeles to confer with Mr. Regardie and with Mr. Heflin, who will travel with us, and with Mr. Kay. We shall probably learn the true picture about the Tarot deck from Mr. Regardie, I hope. I myself have written to the Sangreal Foundation about whether they are going to print the colored version of the Tarot deck, but do not as yet have a reply. If they have no firm commitment to this project, then Grady and the others are certain that we could do it. The Sangreal people did not print all of the Holy Books in their book by that name. They left out *Liber AL, Liber Trigrammaton* and *Liber LXI vel Causae*. We must ask Regardie about this and the reasons for it, maybe he knows.

777 was put out in Chico by Larry Brock. I enclose his card with his address. He printed this at the insistence of another friend. We have now gathered some of these people into our organization. Many of them got acquainted with Crowley's works through other means than through us.

Grady has written to Metzger. We have not yet had a reply. Grady spoke with Dr. Gabriel Montenegro about the latter's visit to Switzerland and his meeting of Metzger. A week later Dr. Montenegro was dead. We all had known him for a long time and Mildred had been in touch with him almost constantly. His death was quite upsetting as we had hoped to include him in our plans.

We are going to send you a *777* that was put out in Chico, so don't take the trouble to send for it. One of the bookstores objected to the binding but since this was put out before Mr. Brock knew us, we had nothing to do with it.

Thank you again for all your trouble for us and your interest. We truly appreciate it, and you shall certainly have a copy of whatever we are able to publish.

Yours very sincerely,
Phyllis McMurtry

Letters to Marcelo Motta

The following letters were written in the immediate aftermath of Karl Germer's death. Here Seckler discusses the fate of the Germer estate, as well as providing instruction on a number of magical principles. The final document—an "open letter" from 2000 e.v.—concisely conveys Seckler's stance on the status of A∴A∴ and the threats to its integrity, many years after the death of Motta. We present this document here, published for the first time, in service to Seckler's commitment to protect the sanctity of that Holy Order.

November 20, 1962

Dear Marcello,

Do what thou wilt shall be the whole of the Law.

Thank you for your letter of the 7th of November, which informed Sascha and myself of your present position and also gave such good advice.

I am afraid I must explain my attitude on some matters but I hope you will understand I seek to leave you with your own—since in Thelema one must also let the other person accomplish his own will. But I also feel that a little of the light of common sense may alleviate a situation, so I sometimes break loose and express it.

First, I feel it is a mistake to write to me instead of Sascha, especially when you have so much information and instruction for her. This caused me an extra trip as I felt she should have your letter as soon as possible after I had received it, since it concerned her so closely. It is very foolish of you to think mail is monitored, which I assure you it is not here in America. Further, what you had to say could have been read by any idiot with no harm to either of the three of us.

Because the letter was addressed to me I naturally opened it and read it, and allowed my family to see it too. […][211] However, since the letter was opened and was handed to Sascha in that form the next day after I received it, she demanded to know to whom I had shown it. This was after I had waited for her to read

---

211. Discussion of Seckler family members has been redacted to protect the privacy of living persons. – Eds.

it. Then she intimated in a suspicious manner that I had shown it to some enemy of hers and of Karl. I couldn't imagine what she had in mind, nor to whom I might show such a letter. I was momentarily hurt to think that she could entertain such suspicions of me. I went away that day in great inquietude of mind and have sought the Angelic guidance all this week whenever the matter was brought into my memory again. Finally, tonight the answer came, and I now write this letter to you and will show the copy of it to Sascha.

I want you both to understand fully my approach to this matter of "attacks."[212] My extreme conviction is that they cannot occur when one obeys the Angel. Therefore, for me, they don't exist. I quote *Liber AL*, I, 46 and 47: "Dost thou fail? Art thou sorry? Is fear in thine heart? Where I am these are not."[213] I am forever astonished that Thelemites refuse to be strong as *AL* enjoins. And I am also convinced that lack of strength occurs because Angelic guidance is far off or not heard, or turned away from. On this matter my first advice to anyone suffering from "attacks" or suspicion of same is to consult the Angel immediately.

I am also well aware that I am treading on thin ice, for Karl himself explained to me at great length the manner in which he was "attacked" by the F.B.I. and various other inimical forces. His convictions on this point served to keep me from visiting his home more often than I did.

I'll explain further. Jane once confronted him with the fact that he was "neurotic" on this matter and he admitted it was true. She later told me about it. Then when I met Karl and heard his long stories about "attacks" I realized that part of it was true and part probably manufactured. He managed to torture himself quite considerably while brooding over this matter. I always felt sorry for him, but said very little about it to him, for he loved his way of thinking so greatly that he became enraged if anyone opposed him by a little common sense. This is always true of clinical cases of such neuroses. The patient himself must see for himself how he hurts himself needlessly, and no outsider can do this for him. I am no psychiatrist and so did not meddle.

---

212. Motta had written to Seckler expressing concern that he was the target of "magical attacks." The Germers had occasionally conveyed similar suspicions, and Seckler felt she needed to respond with instruction and advice on the matter. – Eds.
213. Crowley, *Liber AL vel Legis*, 46.

However, from my own experiences in the spiritual realms I am just as convinced that life is JOY and that attacks do not exist when one is close to the Angelic voice and guidance. *Liber AL* helps to strengthen this conviction. So speak to me no longer of "attacks." But I wish to leave you with your own point of view—if you enjoy them, who am I to say they don't exist for you? At least in your own imagination?

I advise a further knowledge of *Liber AL*—Cap. I, verses 31, 32, 58, 61, and Cap. II, verses 9, 17, 18, 20, 21, and so on ad infinitum.

I like your attitude very well about death. You are right, Karl does not die, he lives, and in a better form and probably having shed his neuroses. May all the Gods help this magnificent star on his journey through the unseen realms. But that is badly put—for each of us is a God in his own right. Some more so, some less, and Karl fundamentally is a great one, but wore a veil of sorrow on earth. For why, I do not know.

As for Schlag—that too is silly. I met him once, sat very close to him for a full day in a car on a trip to San Francisco from L.A. I also routed him in argument. I have not seen him since. I sensed how dangerous he was immediately but he was also fool enough to give me the particulars of his birth date and hour. He is stupid besides. I gave him no such information about myself nor about Thelema. How can you go on so about which Abramelin demon he is possessed by? Do you have an acquaintance with the demons yourself? Or are you making up a good science fiction story—the kind that will possess your own mind and finally eat it away in a neuroses (or worse) of your own?

Sascha is reading old letters at the present and does not seem inclined to pack away precious manuscripts and put them in a safe place such as a safe deposit box. She is of the opinion that boxes are suspect along with everything else. As of last Sunday she has not yet found the Will left by Karl. I do not feel like interfering with these goings on as she has already leveled a suspicion at me. However, I say this boldly and fearlessly, I can no longer be of any assistance if I am going to be suspected. This frame of mind I am unable to work with for it too well ties my powers in knots. I have the ability to correct and collate manuscripts, to write to publishers, to file, sort and put in order and to know exactly where I have put things. Karl himself recognized these abilities and remarked on one occasion that I had executive powers. This is true. I could copy the manuscripts you request—and as you say—a little at a time since I spend a full day teaching and run a house-hold besides, and also owe a duty to my artistic side. But Thelema and A.C.'s manuscripts hold such a fascination for me that I would gladly copy them one by one—starting with the most important, of course.

Now I have offered my services on this point. Since you are probably the heir to the library from what Sascha says, since she witnessed the will, and since she is the executor, I can do nothing without either of you asking me to so do.[214] And I can do nothing if I am not trusted.

Sascha lives 165 miles from me and there is much to do to settle this estate. I am only too glad to help her since I thought of Karl so highly on spiritual planes and since I feel Thelema in every last pore of my body and every last cell.

Let me fill you in on Sascha's situation. She is 5 miles from any store and relies only on the kindness of neighbors for her mail and for occasional trips to the store for food, since she does not drive. She is all alone, but protected by 3 dogs who make quite something of the approach of strangers. She lives in wild country which spews forth an occasional coyote or wild animal of the cat family. There is also much cattle in the neighborhood. She would really like to be near a store, and in more civilized surroundings, and near a doctor, and near a bus line. But the property is paid for, I understand, and so she does not have to pay rent. Her monthly payments on social security are only enough for food. That is the present situation.

The door to the library has a lock and key, and so do the file cases, but Sascha is convinced "they" also possess a key. I say no more.

It is also my opinion that A.C.'s literary remains are guarded by a powerful spirit, as I felt this one evening when I was staying overnight.

Now, as to Thelemites in California. That is a long story which I really ought to write down some day. A.C. had to destroy Agape Lodge for they couldn't follow the simplest command in *The Book of the Law*—that which appears at the beginning of this letter. They further interpreted every passage about love to mean

---

214. This later proved not to be the case, but Seckler was offering her assistance in good faith, believing it to be so. – Eds.

Sex. They were the lunatic fringe that you see around every occult manifestation and lots else on earth besides. Unfortunately, one or two of them were let in on certain IXth degree secrets and so have become dangerous since. One of these is Dr. Montenegro, whom please avoid if you meet—or no, maybe not avoid, but take precautions as the Angel might advise. The rest are foolish at the least, not much else. I advised Sascha not to let these persons in on Karl's death until the manuscripts were safely put someplace else. She may choose not to follow this advice; I don't know. I shall not press the point but felt strongly about it myself and counted it as coming from Above. I think there is protection in the magickal realms, but perhaps not much on the physical side. While Karl lived he was the best protection possible. The job ahead can probably only be accomplished by someone so strong as he—or maybe stronger.

Love is the law, love under will.

Fraternally,
276 — Phyllis

18862 Casa Blanca Lane January 6, 1963
Saratoga, California

Dear Marcello,

Do what thou wilt shall be the whole of the Law.

By now the Xmas fever in the mails must be abated and you have probably received my last two letters of Nov. 20 and Dec. 9, 1962. Please let me know on which date you received these. Also, I sent the copy of the facsimile writing of *Liber AL* and this was registered and properly sealed and stamped. But this was not sent airmail, and the post office man said it should take a month or two from the date sent—Dec. 9. So also allow 2 weeks over that for the delays in the Xmas mail and you should receive it by March 1, I should think.

I am surprised that you would dare to print *AL*, but that is your lookout!

Now, in case those letters I sent you were intercepted???? I shall answer your doubts.

Yes, Karl did die on Oct. 25, 1962. It is no trick. Further, Karl could not play an "A.C. trick," since he was Karl and not A.C. WHY must some people still be enamored of the personal side of A.C.? The side A.C. himself liked to term "the demon Crowley?" Karl knew better than that, I assure you.

Further, I had to laugh when you thought I might have gone insane. Nothing could be funnier or farther from my modus operandi. If anything, I have too much common sense and intelligence, and my feet have always been firmly anchored to the ground.

Now then, in the upset over Karl's death, Sascha said many things to me which led me to believe you were named in the will, as my first two letters to you stated. Then after that she found the will and I tried to straighten out my statements to you in my 3rd letter of Dec. 9. After this, I shall not try to quote her as she is a thorough artist, and was not built with a concise and accurate memory on some matters. This I discovered through the long conversations I had with her. I have not seen her letters to you, although she states she has written before Dec. 9 or at least thereabouts. Nor do I know any more about Karl's will, since Sascha has been highly incensed at me since the letter of Nov. 20 when I mentioned neuroses. She also, as did Karl, misplaces letters or other documents and then is quite bitter about what "they" have taken this time. And all the time the object in question is perhaps in a different place in the files. Karl supposedly lost a letter written to me on March 17, 1962, and wrote it down carefully that it was lost. What actually happened was that the carbon was reversed and so made an impression on the <u>back</u> of the letter which he sent to me, and therefore he had no copy. So you see, here is a part explanation about some of his "attacks." Oh, Marcello, do be careful to explore every sensible explanation before you dream up a magickal attack! How you could hurt Thelema by carelessness in such matters!

But enough, it has been a busy day.

Love is the law, love under will.

Fraternally,
Phyllis

Do what thou wilt shall be the whole of the Law.

I am writing this as a separate note about matters pertaining to the leadership of the Order of Thelemites. Because these matters address specific individuals, I do not want to include mention of names in my more official statement.

The original form of the Constitutions of the Order of Thelemites, written by Aleister Crowley, states that the successorship to the Head of the Order shall be as follows: "In the event of Our death or disability, a General Council of the Order shall be summoned within a year and a day of that event, by S.H. Fra ∴ O.I.V.V.I.O. 8°=3▫, S.H. Sor ∴ Alostræl 8°=3▫, 156, M.H. Fra ∴ Semper Paratus 6°=5▫, or such other persons as We may by subsequent appointment designate. This Council General shall discuss the existing conditions of the Order freely for 11 days; after hearing the same, the member of the A∴A∴ highest in rank (and then in seniority) shall assume Our present functions, and govern the Order in Our place." By the end of his life, he had crossed off all of these names, and written in one to replace them: Frater Saturnus (Karl Germer).

Some people, in discussing this document, read the above to mean that an election was to be held. But it doesn't say that. It says only that "the member of the A∴A∴ highest in rank (and then in seniority) shall assume Our present functions, and govern the Order in Our place." This, of course, was Karl.

To the best of my knowledge, upon Karl's death, I was "the member of the A∴A∴ highest in rank (and then in seniority)". The office fell to me.

I very much dislike claiming things, and I dislike people who go around claiming this and that high title. All they do is make themselves look ridiculous to anyone who really has eyes to see.

I wouldn't come out and lay claim to this title or office at all except to protect the A∴A∴ from those who would try to own it as their private property, using the Order of Thelemites as one of their weapons. Recently, one group has tried to do this, building on a claim that Marcelo Motta was the Head of the Order of Thelemites after Germer's death, and that they have somehow inherited it from him.

Let me speak plainly: I was admitted into the A∴A∴ as a Probationer by Jane Wolfe on June 3, 1940. I have a paper signed by Jane to document this fact, and she had one signed by Aleister Crowley to document her admission. On June 24, 1952, Karl Germer, who was an $8°=3°$ of A∴A∴, wrote to Jane, "I'm sure she [Phyllis] has gone through $5°=6°$ some time ago." On July 7, 1952, he wrote to me, "you have risen to or above Tiphereth where the voice of the Secret Guide is gradually taking over and begins to speak to your soul."

In contrast, 10 years later, on Jun 9, 1962 (<u>after</u> *Liber Aleph* had come out, with Motta's claim to be a $6°=5°$ and Imperator of the A∴A∴), Karl Germer wrote to Marcelo Motta, "you are at best a Neophyte!" That is, a $1°=10°$ of A∴A∴ "at best." On July 5, 1962, Motta wrote back to Germer acknowledging that he did not even claim the $2°=9°$ grade of Zelator, and had "abandoned any claims to anything whatsoever."[215]

Karl died less than four months later. It is clear that he didn't think Motta was any kind of an Adept at all. When I had contact with Motta years later, he still wasn't.

I am writing this letter for the files of the College of Thelema and the Jane Wolfe branch of the A∴A∴, in case my statement is needed. I don't like making any claims at all, and write this only to set the record straight.

Love is the law, love under will.

Soror Meral (Phyllis Seckler)
June 26, 2000

---

215. Motta later identified himself as a $2°=9°$ of A∴A∴ in a letter to Sascha Germer in January 1963, several months after Karl Germer's death. – Eds.

REINCARNATION[216]

As a phoenix arises from fire and ashes
So the end of life burns up in consuming flames
Until all that is left are the flashes
Of memory's accumulations laying claims

To all that went before in soul's growth.
Memories which can never be shaken
Out of the whole fabric of soul's cloth:
Memories until the soul demands to slaken

Thirst for life, for love at the fount of light.
So from life to life we end in heaven's fire
Doomed to struggle onward as best we might;
Our feet are not prisoned ever in earth's mire.

But respite comes upon us, though we forget
The rest and sweetness of death while on earth.
It is no use for ignorance to fret
About a new life, death means rebirth.

Ah, those we love, again we meet
Beyond the grave and in new lives too.
What use to mourn when in time we greet
Each other and live our lives anew.

But beware to hate, for heaven's law
Decrees that karmic debts be paid.
And if a soul succumbs to such a flaw
Then many lives may pass before the error fades.

So now my loves, I depart upon my ways
And as the phoenix I will arise again
Out of the ashes of my numerous days
And we will dance to karmic strains.

---

216. This poem was read on the occasion of Soror Meral's memorial celebration in Sacramento, California, as she had requested in instructions prior to her death. – Eds.

We will learn to aspire always to the highest
Of aristocratic life, of refinement and love.
We will create again as does the artist
Whether of poesy, of painting, of music, until above:

We see our stars gleaming in heaven's dance:
We who are single sparks of fire in heaven's space.
Oh, set your sights on high, attain more than a glance
Of starlight bliss, of soul's greatest grace.[217]

1996

---

217. Originally published in: Phyllis Seckler, *In the Continuum*, 5.10 (1996): 6.

A Note on Copyrights

In October 1996, the Board of Directors of the College of Thelema ("C.O.T."), then under the Executive Directorship of Phyllis Seckler (Soror Meral), passed Resolutions confirming the publication policy of the C.O.T. The resolutions affirmed that the policy of the C.O.T.'s journal, *In the Continuum* ("*I.T.C.*"), had always been that the author of material submitted to *I.T.C.* would retain the rights to their work. The C.O.T. would retain the right to continue to publish the author's material in *I.T.C.* in perpetuity. The Board further affirmed that this policy applied to the material written by Phyllis Seckler, just as any other contributor. Accordingly, she retained the copyrights to her own material throughout her life, and held them at the time of her death in 2004.

Phyllis Seckler's Last Will stipulated that any property not specifically bequeathed would pass to the Phyllis Seckler Living Trust, in the person of its Trustee. Since Ms. Seckler's copyrights were not specifically bequeathed to any individual or corporate entity, they passed to the Trust. In August 2008, the Trustee formally transferred the copyrights to the writings of Phyllis Seckler to the Temple of the Silver Star ("T.O.T.S.S.", under a prior corporate name.) The Trust acknowledged the Temple of the Silver Star as the sole legal custodian of Seckler's literary estate, diaries, library, and archives.

T.O.T.S.S.'s rights extend to the material written by Ms. Seckler and originally published in *In the Continuum* and its successor journal, *Black Pearl* (which operated under the same publication policy as *I.T.C.*) pursuant to the C.O.T. publication policy discussed above.

T.O.T.S.S. supports the right of the College of Thelema to publish Ms. Seckler's work in its original form within *In the Continuum* and *Black Pearl*, in perpetuity.

Board of Directors
Temple of the Silver Star

About the Editors

Dr. David Shoemaker is a clinical psychologist in private practice in Chapel Hill, North Carolina, specializing in Jungian, transpersonal and cognitive-behavioral psychotherapy. David is the Chancellor and Prolocutor of the Temple of the Silver Star. He has been a member of Ordo Templi Orientis and A∴A∴ since 1993, and he has more than twenty-five years of experience supervising initiates of these traditions.

David is the Past Master of 418 Lodge of O.T.O. in Sacramento, having succeeded Soror Meral (Phyllis Seckler), his friend and teacher. He also serves as a Sovereign Grand Inspector General of O.T.O. and Bishop of Ecclesia Gnostica Catholica. David was the founding President of the O.T.O. Psychology Guild, and is a frequent speaker at regional and national O.T.O. gatherings.

David was a co-editor of the journals *Neshamah* (Psychology Guild), and *Cheth* (418 Lodge). In addition to his essays in these publications, his writings have been published in the journals *Mezlim* and *Black Pearl*, and his chapter on Kabbalistic Psychology was included in the Instructor's Manual of Fadiman and Frager's *Personality and Personal Growth*, an undergraduate psychology textbook. In addition to the present volume, he was the editor or co-editor of the TOTSS publications, *Jane Wolfe: The Cefalu Diaries 1920-1923*, *Phyllis Seckler (Soror Meral): The Thoth Tarot, Astrology, & Other Selected Writings*, *Phyllis Seckler (Soror Meral): Collected Poems 1946-1996*, and *Karl Germer: Selected Letters 1928-1962*. His Living Thelema podcast has been presented regularly since 2010, and the popular book of the same name was published in 2013. *The Winds of Wisdom*, a collection of David's visionary experiences with the thirty Enochian Aethyrs, was released in 2016, and *Llewellyn's Complete Book of Ceremonial Magick* (co-edited with Lon Milo DuQuette) followed in 2020.

In addition to his work in magick and psychology, David is a composer and musician. He can be reached via his website at livingthelema.com.

Gregory H. Peters has been a student and teacher of Eastern and Western systems of attainment for nearly 30 years, having worked with several organizations and traditions in various capacities over this time. He became a Probationer in the A∴A∴ under Phyllis Seckler in 1992, and has been deeply involved with the work of the A∴A∴ ever since.

In addition to A∴A∴ and Western orders, Gregory has received initiation and worked deeply with several Hindu and Buddhist tantrik lineages. He has written many scholarly papers on Tantra, Thelema, Freemasonry and other aspects of both eastern and western esoteric systems. He is the author of *Stellar Tantra: The Gnosis of the Self*, and *The Magickal Union of East & West: The Spiritual Path to New Aeon Tantra*. As a fruit of his work with A∴A∴, he founded the Order Sunyata Vajra, an international mystical magical society that follows the Thelemic current deep into its non-dual roots.

Gregory lives and works in the San Francisco Bay Area, and enjoys traveling the world, exploring ancient ruins and sacred sites, trekking, stargazing, deep forests and high mountains.

Rorac R. Johnson was the founding Vice-Chancellor and Grand Præmonstrator of the Temple of the Silver Star. He has been a student of A∴A∴ since 1999.

Rorac is a musician, artist, martial artist, writer, editor and healer. He has written articles and poetry for the journal *Cheth* (418 Lodge, O.T.O.), and he also co-edited the new edition of *The Compleat Rite of Memphis*. He lives in Sacramento with his wife and beloved daughters.

Organizational Contacts

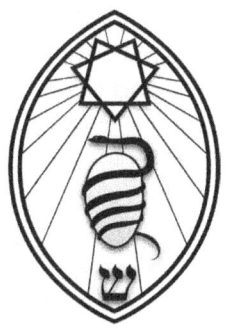

Temple of the Silver Star
Academic Track

The Temple of the Silver Star is a non-profit religious and educational corporation, based on the principles of Thelema. It was founded in service to the A∴A∴, under warrant from Soror Meral (Phyllis Seckler), to provide preparatory training in magick, mysticism, Qabalah, Tarot, astrology, and much more. In its Academic Track, each student is assigned an individual teacher, who provides one-to-one instruction and group classes. Online classes and other distance-learning options are available.

The criteria for admission to the Temple's academic track are explained on the application itself, which may be submitted online via the T.O.T.S.S. website. The Temple has campuses and study groups across the U.S. and around the world. Public classes are offered regularly; schedules are available on our website.

Temple of the Silver Star
Initiatory Track

The Temple of the Silver Star's initiatory track offers ceremonial initiation, personalized instruction, and a complete system of training in the Thelemic Mysteries. Our degree system is based on the Qabalistic Tree of Life and the cipher formulæ of the Golden Dawn, of which we are a lineal descendant.

Our entire curriculum is constructed to be in conformity with the Law of Thelema, and our central aim is to guide each aspirant toward the realization of their purpose in life, or True Will. In order to empower our members to discover and carry out their True Will, we teach Qabalah, Tarot, ceremonial magick, meditation, astrology, and much more. Our initiates meet privately for group ceremonial and healing work, classes, and other instruction. We occasionally offer public classes and rituals.

Active participation in a local Temple or Pronaos is the best way to maximize the benefits of our system. However, we do offer At-Large memberships for those living at some distance from one of our local bodies.

If you are interested in learning more about our work, we invite you to download an application from our website and submit it to your nearest local body, or to contact us with any questions.

Dr. David Shoemaker
Chancellor and Prolocutor

totss.org

Do what thou wilt shall be the whole of the Law.

The A∴A∴ is the system of spiritual attainment established by Aleister Crowley and George Cecil Jones in the early 1900s, as a modern expression of the Inner School of wisdom that has existed for millennia. Its central aim is simply to lead each aspirant toward their own individual attainment, for the betterment of all humanity. The course of study includes a diversity of training methods, such as Qabalah, raja yoga, ceremonial magick, and many other traditions. A∴A∴ is not organized into outer social organizations, fraternities or schools; rather, it is based on the time-tested power of individual teacher-student relationships, under the guidance of the masters of the Inner School. All training and testing is done strictly in accordance with *Liber 185* and other foundational documents.

Those interested in pursuing admission into A∴A∴ are invited to initiate contact via the following addresses:

A∴A∴
PO Box 215483
Sacramento, CA 95821

onestarinsight.org

The Student phase of preparation for work in A∴A∴ begins by acquiring a specific set of reference texts, notifying A∴A∴ of the same, and studying the texts for at least three months. The Student may then request Examination. More information about this process is available via the Cancellarius at the addresses given above. Please use only these contact addresses when initiating correspondence. NOTE: While our primary contact address is in California, supervising Neophytes are available in many countries around the world.

If you are called to begin this journey, we earnestly invite you to contact us. Regardless of your choice in this matter, we wish you the best as you pursue your own Great Work. May you attain your True Will!

Love is the law, love under will.

INDEX

A∴A∴, ix, 3, 4, 7, 50, 51, 93-95, 105, 130, 135, 141, 153, 179, 182, 195, 208, 226, 230, 233, 235, 236, 239, 241, 270, 276, 277, 280-282, 283, 285
Abelard, Peter, 27
Abramelin, 139, 221, 272
Achad, Frater (*see* Jones, C.S.)
Adonai, 1, 119, 199, 200-201, 209
Æon of the Child, 97
Æon of Horus, 87, 107, 229
Æon of Thelema (*see* New Æon of Thelema)
Agape Lodge, 56, 59, 61, 245, 273
Ahathoor, 92
Air (element), 14, 19, 20, 21, 89, 91, 92, 102, 113-114, 116, 118, 119, 180
Airola, Mr., 64, 73-75
Aiwass, 112, 169
Ajna, 198
Albertus, Frater
  Alchemist's Handbook, 124
Alchemy, 47, 85, 99, 101, 124, 143, 144-145, 151, 165
Alostrael (*see* Hirsig, Leah)
Antony, Mark, 27
Aquarian Press, 255
d'Arc, Jeanne, 230
Arthur, King, 225
asana, 135, 167, 170
Assiah, 34, 123
Astrology, xii, 6, 13-22, 46-47, 48, 73, 82, 89-92, 101, 114-116, 118, 124, 126, 127, 131, 135, 151, 152, 154-155, 161, 162-164, 165, 167-168, 169, 199-200, 203, 209, 222, 236, 237, 239, 242, 244, 246, 268, 281
  Aquarius, 14, 20, 46, 82, 89, 90, 92, 116
  Aries, 14, 20, 46, 82, 114
  Cancer, 14, 20, 46, 114
  Capricorn, 14, 20, 46, 115
  Gemini, 14, 15, 20, 46, 114, 209
  Leo, 14, 15, 20, 46, 89, 90, 92
  Libra, 14, 20, 46, 48, 114
  Pisces, 14, 20, 46
  Sagittarius, 14, 15, 20, 46, 115, 199
  Scorpio, 14, 20, 46, 89, 90, 92, 116, 200
  Taurus, 14, 20, 46, 89, 90, 92
  Virgo, 14, 20, 46, 114
Atziluth, 34
Azar, 221

Babalon, 91, 92, 104, 105, 110
Berkeley (CA), 65, 76, 250, 281
Berkeley Lodge, 233, 239
Beth, 14, 142
Bhagavad-Gita, The, 20, 46-47
Black Pearl, 191-201, 280
Boaz, 34
Briah, 34
Brock, Larry, 269
Brontë sisters, the, 98
Bucke, Richard M.
  Cosmic Consciousness, 27, 169
Buddha, 77
Buddhism, 65, 77, 206, 254, 280
Burlingame, Mildred, 61 n.66, 246, 260, 261, 264, 267, 268
Burlingame, Ray, 246, 261

Cabala/Cabalah (*see* Qabalah/Qabbalah)
Cameron, Marjorie, 253-254
Cape, Jonathan (publisher), 255, 266
Collins, Jr., Carr P., 266
Catherine the Great, 230
Catholic Church, 166, 225
Cefalu, 253, 280
Chicago, 266
China, 140
clairaudience, 170
clairvoyance, 170
Cleopatra, 230
College of Thelema (C.O.T.), 22, 135, 161, 236, 237, 238, 239, 262, 277, 280
Craddock, Ida
  Heavenly Bridegrooms, 208
Crowley, Aleister
  Master Therion, 4, 51, 78-79, 82, 84-86, 88, 91, 111, 114, 127, 130, 131, 138, 144, 145, 146, 150, 151, 152-153, 160, 179
  works:
    Berashith, 112
    Blue Equinox, The, 4, 41, 51, 88
    Book 4 (Part I), 27, 37, 123, 254, 266

287

Crowley, Aleister (*continued*)
works:
Book 4 (*Part II*), 119, 266
Book of Lies, The, 105, 186, 223, 224
Book of the Law, The, ix, 3-8, 10-12, 22-23, 25, 27-29, 36-37, 40-44, 47, 49, 51, 53, 55, 82, 84, 85, 87, 88, 96, 102, 106, 107-112, 114, 116-117, 124, 126, 132-133, 135, 140, 142-149, 152, 161, 169, 172, 176, 191, 193, 196-198, 202-203, 209, 212-213, 219, 227-229, 254, 265, 271, 273
Book of Thoth, The, 22, 47, 60, 242, 253, 255, 257, 264
'Cocaine,' 133
Collected Works, 30 n.41, 112
Collegii Sancti, 130
Commentaries on the Holy Books and Other Papers, 145 n.136
Eleusis, 112
Equinox, The, 4, 41, 85, 94, 112, 119-120, 130, 136 n.126, 150-151, 162, 186, 210, 219 n.194, 221, 235, 254, 255
Gems From The Equinox, 94, 162
Holy Books of Thelema, The, 48 n.57, 58 n.65, 79 n.70, 103, 106 n.94, 118 n.109, 121 n.115, 123, 145 n.136, 182, 183 n.163, 199, 201 n.180, 209 n.184, 213, 215 n.190, 217 n.192, 268-269
'John St. John,' 85, 186, 223
Konx Om Pax, 82, 153
Liber AL vel Legis (see *Book of the Law, The*)
Liber Aleph, 8, 9, 11, 27-29, 38, 43, 88, 186, 210, 223, 233, 240, 247, 277
Liber CD vel Tau, 130
Liber CL, 88
Liber CLXXXV, 130
Liber Jugorum, 27
Liber VII, 79, 95, 103, 118, 135, 140, 182, 194, 209, 215
Liber XV, 136 n.126, 219 n.194
Liber XVI, 27
Liber LXV, 48, 58, 79, 95, 106, 135, 182, 194, 197-200, 254
Liber Pyramidos, 145
Liber Viarum Viae (*DCCCLXVIII*), 130
Magical and Philosophical Commentaries on the Book of the Law, 25, 112, 116 n.107, 146
Magick in Theory and Practice, 53, 87, 93-94, 120, 125
Magick Without Tears, 50-52, 57, 58, 94, 95, 97 n.86, 103, 133, 134, 187 n.165, 221
Qabalah of Aleister Crowley, The, 119
Revival of Magick and Other Essays, The, 45
777, 119 n.111, 170, 264, 266, 269
Soul of the Desert, The, 200
'Temple of Solomon the King (Continued), The,' 119 n.112, n.113
"Thien Tao", 27
Vision and the Voice, The, 57, 121, 123, 140, 150, 182, 210
World's Tragedy, The, 238
crystal-gazing, 170
Culling, Louis, 246, 258

divination, 170
drugs, 22, 25, 118, 133, 136, 143, 171, 176, 236, 245
cocaine, 133
tobacco, 171, 178
DuQuette, Lon, vii-x

eagle, 92, 116, 200
Earth (element), 14, 19, 20, 21, 89, 90, 92, 113, 114, 115, 118, 119, 180, 191-192, 206
Elizabeth I, Queen, 98, 230
Elizabeth II, Queen, 98
Enochian magic, 159, 168, 169
Eye of Horus, The (bookstore), 63

Falcon Press, 25 n.27, 94 n.81, 237, 238
F.B.I., 62, 63, 271
Fire (element), 14, 19-20, 21, 24, 25, 89, 90, 92, 113, 114, 118, 119, 123, 206
Flaming Sword, 35

Fortune, Dion, 37, 99, 227, 230
  Mystical Qabalah, The, 227
fortune-telling, 170
Freud, Sigmund, 101

Gauguin, Paul, 181
Germer, Karl, xiii, 40, 56, 59-63, 66-69, 71, 73, 74, 76, 93, 182, 194, 195, 202, 203, 208-232, 234, 236, 237, 245, 252-253, 255, 257, 263, 265, 267, 270-271, 276-277
Germer, Sascha, 40, 59-61, 63, 66-69, 71, 73, 74, 76, 213, 216-217, 229, 252-253, 263, 265, 270-271
Gnostic Catholic Mass, 85, 104, 106, 125, 181, 196
Gnostic Mass, 254, 267
God, 12, 28, 30, 87, 96, 104, 109, 119, 124, 125, 129, 134-135, 151, 152, 156, 173, 185, 200, 205-206, 222
Golden Dawn, The Hermetic Order of the, 6, 89, 113, 114, 115, 123, 125, 139, 169, 171, 203, 259, 281
Grant, Kenneth, 25 n.27, 246, 266, 267
Gualdoni (coroner), 66-69, 73-75
Gunas, 20, 21, 46-48
  Rajas, 20, 21, 46, 47
  Sattva, 20, 21, 46
  Tamas, 20, 21, 46-48

Hadit, 1, 27, 28, 30, 44, 91, 92, 107, 111, 116, 117, 156, 198, 213, 219, 228, 231
Hampton (NJ), 57, 58, 194 n.171, 211, 216, 221, 267
Harris, Lady Frieda, 257, 259, 262, 268
Hasbrouck, Muriel Bruce
  Tarot and Astrology: The Pursuit of Destiny, 15
Heflin, Leo, 268
Helios Bookshop, 266
Hell, 100, 126, 175
Heru-Ra-Ha, 91, 107, 109
Hinduism, 36, 78, 170, 206, 254, 280
Hirsig, Leah, 230, 276
Hitler, Adolf, 10, 182, 205
Holy Bible, The, 70, 71, 173, 206, 221

Holy Guardian Angel, xii, 6, 8, 12-13, 29, 38, 39, 42, 48, 50, 54, 70, 77, 78, 85-86, 94, 104, 106, 108, 109-111, 125-127, 134, 139, 140-141, 144-145, 147, 148, 153, 155-158, 160, 167, 170-172, 176, 177, 179, 180-190, 194-196, 198, 203, 208-210, 213-215, 221 n.198, 222-223, 225
Hoor-Paar-Kraat, 91, 107-108
Horus, 97, 98, 230
Hymenaeus Alpha (*see* McMurtry, Grady)
Hymenaeus Beta, 4 n.5, 25 n.27, 38 n.42, 45 n.53

Ida, 34, 36, 199
In the Continuum, ix, xii, 3-191, 202, 236, 237, 280
India, 140
International, The, 133
invisibility, 170
Isherwood, Christopher, 46 n.55
Isis, 97
Islam, 23

Jachin, 34
James, William
  Varieties of Religious Experience, The, 26-27
Jesus Christ, 26, 186, 212, 223
Johnson, Rorac, xii-xiii, 280
Jones, Charles Stansfield, 78, 79, 186, 223, 245
Jones, Marc Edmund
  Guide to Horoscope Interpretation, The, 16-17
Jung, Carl, 6, 9, 21, 101, 152, 162, 173, 203, 281
  Secret of the Golden Flower, The, 218

Kabbala/Kabala (*see* Qabalah/Qabbalah)
Kaczynski, Richard, 45 n.53
karma, x, 3, 7, 29, 39-40, 42, 47, 48, 52, 73, 107, 126, 136, 154-155, 161-162, 165, 168, 191-193, 278
Kay, Jerry, 264, 266, 268
Khabs, 152, 153, 191, 193
Khephra, 91, 92

King, Francis
  Secret Rituals of the O.T.O., The, 3
Krishna, Gopi
  Kundalini, 199 n.177
Krumm-Heller, Dr. Arnold, 254
Kundalini, 36, 111, 168, 175, 197-200

Labor Day, 60
Lao-tze, 77
Leffingwell, Roy, 245-246, 261
Lesser Ritual of the Pentagram, 113, 115, 124, 125
Library of Congress, 255
Lilith, 230, 231
Livermore, 202, 227, 256
Livermore High School, 244, 256
Llewellyn Publications, 29 n.37, 113 n.103, 114 n.105, 139 n.129, 255
London University, 253
Los Angeles (CA), 62-63, 208, 244, 261, 263, 264, 268, 272

Mandrake Press, 255
McMurtry, Grady, vii, ix, xiii, 62-65, 67, 73, 74-77, 236, 239, 241-251, 262, 263, 264, 267-269
maya, 153, 154
Mellinger, Frederick, 59, 265, 267-268
mercury, 47
Mercury (god), 104, 142, 198
Metzger, Hermann, 59, 259, 263, 267, 269
Mexico, 254
Mezla, 103, 106
Miller, Joe, 246
Moon (Luna), 14, 22, 79, 104, 106, 121, 123, 124, 162, 163, 199, 200
Motta, Marcelo, xiii, 58, 66, 68-69, 233 n.208, 234-235, 239, 268, 270-275, 277
Mozart, Wolfgang Amadeus, 181
music, 87, 143, 147, 173, 176-177, 178, 203, 279

necromancy, 170
Nephesh, 143, 161, 225
New Æon of Horus, 87, 98, 229
New Æon of Thelema, 4, 102, 112

Nietzsche, Friedrich
  Thus Spake Zarathustra, 11
Niksa, 159
Nile, River, 48
Noah, x
Nuit, 1, 6, 28, 30, 44, 47, 86, 87, 91, 92, 104, 105, 108, 110-111, 113-114, 116-117, 126, 129, 138, 146, 148, 149, 150, 152, 154, 156, 160, 174-175, 180, 193, 194, 196, 197, 198, 201, 227, 228, 231

Osiris, x, 96, 97
Ordo Templis Orientis (O.T.O.), ix, 3-7, 23, 39, 41, 50-52, 56, 60, 61-63, 66-67, 73, 76, 130, 135, 141, 144, 159-160, 179, 208, 233-235, 236-239, 241, 246-250, 253-255, 256, 258-261, 263, 265-268, 281

Parsifal, 229, 231
Parsons, Helen (*see* Smith, Helen Parsons)
Parsons, John Whiteside, 245, 254
Parsons, Marjorie Cameron (*see* Cameron, Marjorie)
Peters, Gregory, xi, xii-xiii, 280
phallic symbolism, 197-201
Philosopher's Stone, 85
Phoenix, 279
Piccadilly Circus, 133
Pingala, x, 34, 36, 199
Planets, 13, 15-22, 48, 101, 104, 121, 123-126, 161-164, 174
  Earth, vii, 25, 44, 55, 69, 81, 85, 99, 162, 163, 165, 172, 175, 189, 195, 203, 204
  Jupiter, 14, 121, 123, 124, 163
  Mars, 14, 121, 123, 124, 153, 163
  Mercury, 14, 121, 123, 124, 163
  Neptune, 163, 164
  Pluto, 164
  Saturn, 14, 36, 48, 121, 123, 124, 163, 169, 216
  Uranus, 163
  Venus, 14, 121, 123, 124, 163
Pope, 50
pornography, 172, 196
Prabhavananda, Swami, 46 n.55
pranayama, x, 167

Qabalah / Qabbalah, 14, 15, 30, 33, 34, 35, 57, 63, 70, 71, 78, 80, 83, 89, 109, 118-120, 130, 132, 143, 152, 167, 194, 199, 221, 227, 237, 244, 260, 280, 281

Ra, 92, 108
Ra-Hoor-Khuit, 6, 44, 91, 108, 109, 110, 126, 148, 160, 228
Regardie, Israel, xiii, 56, 61, 94 n.81, 233-240, 254, 255, 258, 259-262, 264, 266-268
  works:
  Golden Dawn, The, 113, 114 n.105, 139 n.129
  How to Make and Use Talismans, 124
  Middle Pillar, The, 29
  Roll Away the Stone, 255
Rio de Janeiro, 254
Robyn (lawyer), 66-68, 74, 75
Ruach, 35, 103, 104, 123, 134, 139, 152, 225

Sacramento (CA), 241-242, 278 n.216, 280-282
Sacred Magic of Abramelin the Mage, The, 139
salt, 47
Samadhi, 6, 167, 216
San Andreas, 66, 68, 74, 75
San Francisco, 242, 256, 272, 280, 281
Sand, George (Amantine Lucile Aurore Dupin), 98
Sangreal Foundation, The (publisher), 264, 266, 268
Schmolke, Herbert, 214
Schneider, Georgia, 246
Schneider, Jean, 245
Schneider, Max, 245
scorpion, 92, 200
Seasons, 89, 91, 92, 114, 176
  Autumn (Fall), 89, 91, 92, 93, 114, 255, 266
  Spring, 89, 91, 92, 114, 214
  Summer, 57, 61, 62, 89, 91, 92, 93, 114, 194 n.171, 243
  Winter, 89, 91, 92, 115, 261

Seckler, Phyllis (Soror Meral)
  Thoth Tarot, Astrology, & Other Selected Writings, The, xii, 88 n.77, 152 n.149, 281
Semiramis, 230
Sephiroth, 34, 119
serpent, 36, 38, 92, 116 n.106, 139, 184, 197-201, 230
Serpent of Wisdom, 35, 200
sex, 10, 25, 41, 44, 96, 106, 143, 145-149, 171, 172-175, 177, 196, 197-201, 212, 225, 228, 230, 245, 246, 273
sex magick, 5-6, 246
Shakespeare, William
  Midsummer Night's Dream, A, 132
Shiva, Frater
  Inside Solar Lodge: Behind the Veil, 62 n.67
  Inside Solar Lodge: Outside the Law, 62 n.67
Shoemaker, David, xii-xiii, 280, 281-282
Smith, Helen Parsons, 64, 245
Smith, W. T., 221, 245, 246
Solar Lodge, 62
Solvé & Coagula, 151
Sphinx, 25, 88-89, 90, 92, 116, 118
Steiner, Rudolph, 99
Stele of Revealing, 230, 263
sulphur, 47
Summum Bonum, 136, 143
Sun (Sol), 1, 14, 15, 22, 74, 79, 90, 91, 105, 106, 108, 109, 113-115, 120-121, 123, 124, 162-164, 198-200
Sushumna, 34, 35, 36, 199
Svadisthana, 175
Symonds, John, 25 n.27, 254-255, 257, 258, 259, 264, 266-267

Tantrism, 200, 280
Taoism, 77, 203, 206, 219
Tarot, xii, 14, 15, 22, 46, 82, 85, 92, 119, 130, 142, 152-153, 167, 237, 257, 259, 261, 264, 266, 268, 280, 281
  Adjustment, 14
  Aeon, The, 14, 200
  Art, 14, 199
  Chariot, The, 14

Tarot (*continued*)
  Death, 14, 92
  Devil, The, 14
  Empress, The, 14
  Emperor, The, 14, 82
  Fool, The, 14, 104, 119, 200
  Fortune, 14
  Hanged Man, The, x, 14
  Hermit, The, 14
  Hierophant, The, 14, 92
  Lovers, The, 14
  Lust, 14, 92
  Magus, The, 14, 104, 142, 153
  Moon, The, 14, 104
  Priestess, The, 14, 103, 153, 199
  Star, The, 14, 82, 92
  Sun, The, 14, 200
  Tower (War), The, 14, 153
  Universe, The, 14, 199, 200
telepathy, 170
television, 127, 135, 172
Temple of the Silver Star, xi, 280-282, 284
Tetragrammaton, 92
Thelema, xii-xiii, *passim*
Theosophy, 168
transmutation, 170
Tree of Life, The, 30, 33, 34, 36, 37, 38, 78, 79-83, 103, 104, 121-123, 130, 134, 139, 152-153, 194, 197-200, 226, 281
  Binah, 33, 36, 80, 81, 83, 104, 150
  Chesed, 33, 36, 80, 81, 83
  Chokmah, 33, 36, 79, 80, 83
  Geburah, 33, 36, 80, 81, 83
  Hod, 33, 36, 80, 81, 83
  Kether, 33, 79, 80, 83, 104, 105, 108, 119, 199, 226
  Malkuth, 33, 80, 83, 197, 199
  Netzach, 33, 36, 80, 81, 83
  Tiphereth, 33, 38, 79, 80, 81, 83, 91, 104-105, 108, 110, 111, 119, 139-140, 156, 194, 198, 199, 226, 277

  Yesod, 33, 80, 83, 86, 199
Tum, 92
Twain, Mark, 68

undines, 166

Van Gogh, Vincent, 40
van Rijn, Rembrandt Harmenszoon, 181
Vargas, Dr. Gabriel Montenegro, 59, 246, 258, 260, 262, 267, 269, 274
Venus, 104
Vernal Equinox, 90
Victoria, Queen, 98

Wagner, Richard
  Parsifal, 41, 104 n.91
Warburg Institute, 57, 253, 256, 257, 259-260, 262, 265-266, 268
Washington, D.C., 62
Water, (element) 14, 19, 20, 21, 89, 91, 92, 100, 101, 103, 113-114, 116, 118, 119, 127, 159-160, 180
West Point, 58, 61, 64, 66, 242, 246, 261
Wilkinson, Louis, 25 n.27, 257
Wolfe, Jane, 58, 130, 208, 245, 252, 253, 259, 260, 261, 277, 281
Wolfe, Mary K., 218
Wordsworth, William
  Ode: Intimations of Immortality from Recollections of Early Childhood, 190-191

Yetzirah, 1, 34
Yin, 34
Yang, 34
yoga, 6, 27, 48, 53, 64, 109, 132, 135, 160, 185, 200, 204, 209, 239, 266
Yorke, Gerald, xiii, 57, 203, 252-269

Zurich, 254, 259, 267

www.ingramcontent.com/pod-product-compliance
Lightning Source LLC
Chambersburg PA
CBHW071655160426
43195CB00012B/1481